SHOW
GROOMING

SHOW GROOMING

THE LOOK OF A WINNER

Second Edition

---

*Horse Show Grooming, Tack, and Attire
for All Breeds and Sport Types*

---

by

CHARLENE STRICKLAND

with Linda Allen and Jim Baker

*Illustrations by Heather J. Lowe
and Robin Peterson*

Breakthrough Publications

310 N. Highland Avenue, Ossining, New York 10562

For Information address:
Breakthrough Publications
310 North Highland Ave.
Ossining, NY 10562
www.booksonhorses.com

ISBN 0-914327-57-7
Library of Congress Catalog Card Number: 94-74155

Designed by Jacques Chazaud
Manufactured in the United States of America
02 01 00 99 98   9 8 7 6 5 4 3 2

To my long-suffering husband,
Geoffrey,
for tolerating this project.

CONTENTS

ACKNOWLEDGMENTS   *ix*

INTRODUCTION   *xi*

PART I – GENERAL TECHNIQUES

  1. Basic Tools   *3*

  2. Daily Cleaning   *11*

  3. Bathing   *23*

  4. Maintaining Coat and Skin   *33*

  5. Mane Grooming   *41*

  6. Tail Grooming   *52*

  7. Clipping Techniques–Trims   *65*

  8. Clipping Techniques–Body   *78*

  9. Hoof Beauty   *86*

 10. Body Enhancements   *91*

 11. Foal Grooming   *100*

PART II – SPECIALIZED TURNOUT FOR SHOW

 12. Quarter Horses   *105*

 13. Color Breeds   *117*

 14. Hunters   *123*

 15. Jumpers   *145*

 16. Dressage and Sport Horses   *151*

 17. Combined Training   *161*

18. American Saddlebreds   165

19. Tennessee Walking Horses   175

20. Arabians   180

21. National Show Horses   187

22. Morgans   191

23. Andalusians   195

24. Peruvian Pasos   201

25. Paso Finos   205

26. Ponies   209

PART III – ATTIRE

Introduction to Attire   217

27. Western Attire   220

28. Hunt Seat Attire   237

29. Saddle Seat Attire   254

PART IV – SHOW STRATEGY

30. Show Grooming Management   269

31. Show Day   278

APPENDIX   289

GLOSSARY   291

REFERENCES   293

INDEX   295

ACKNOWLEDGMENTS

Many thanks to consultants Linda Allen and Jim Baker, for contributing their insights across the realm of presenting show horses. Both editions of this book compile the knowledge shared by these professionals and firms in the show horse industry:

Suzi Drnec of Hobby Horse Clothing Company—Western and saddle seat attire

Sue Seidel of Show Season—Saddle seat attire

Jim Porcher—Arabians and National Show Horses

Alpha Russell—Appaloosas

Gary and Todd Dearth—Arabians

Megan Dante—Quarter Horses

Bonnie Hill—Arabians

Molly Hartman—Morgans

Peggy Jo Koll, judge of Quarter Horse and Western breeds

Pete Wood, judge of Quarter Horse and Western breeds

Alison Haxton, AHSA Steward

Dr. Roland Ramsauer, Zuchtverband für Deutsche Pferde

Monty Roberts, horse trainer

Alina Lingscheit of Dressed to Win—Western attire

George Davis of Davis Hats—Western hats

Wanda Denton of Silver by Wanda—Western silver trim

Lillian Shively—Saddle seat attire

Janet Squires—Tennessee Walking Horses, hunters, and Arabians

Bobby Beech of National Bridle Shop—Tennessee Walking Horses

Jane Shaw—Hunters

Patty Haser—Hunters and hunt seat riders

Patricia Kinnaman—Dressage

Joanne Madden—Dressage

David DeWispelaere—Dressage

Marja Sandberg—Dressage, hunter/jumper, Pony Club

Stephanie Abronson—Welsh and hunter ponies

Lira Parks—Hunter and hunter ponies
Albert Gesierich—Dressage
Arthur Hawkins, AHSA "R" judge of hunters
and jumpers
Alfonso Castillion—Hunters
Carl Lewis—Hunter/jumper
Ziaa Szymanski—Race horses
Albert "Whitey" Kahn of Le Cheval, Limited—
Saddle seat attire
Gayle Lampe, and student Loretta Gallivan—
Saddlebreds, Arabians, and Morgans
Frank Depolito—Saddlebreds
Debbie Jennings—Saddlebreds
Darrell Brown—Tennessee Walking Horses
Sue and Cynthia Burkman—Arabians,
Andalusians
Karen Wonnell—Arabians
Cesar Nespral—Arabians

Arthur Perry, Jr.—Morgans
Debbie Sullivan—Morgans
Sandy Cloud and Adrian Bruce—Andalusians
Maggi McHugh—Western, trail and stock seat
equitation
Gill Swarbrick—Western
Nan Tyson—Half-Arabian Pintos
Lonny Shirk—Quarter Horses
Dave and Donna Freer—Buckskin, Dun, and
Palomino Quarter Horses
Chuck and Beverly Crandall—Appaloosas
Berleen Pless—Quarter Horses
Andy Moorman—Quarter Horses
Dan Delaney, American Quarter Horse Asso-
ciation
Verne Albright, Peruvian Pasos
Merilyn Patterson—Peruvian Pasos
Joe and Karen Neri—American Paso Finos

CONTRIBUTING RETAILERS AND MANUFACTURERS

The Paddock Shop, Los Angeles, California
Dover Saddlery, Wellesley, Massachusetts
Jimmy's Twentieth Century Saddlery,
Prescott, Arizona
Calabasas Saddlery, Calabasas, California
Broken Horn, Baldwin Park, California
Sergeant's Custom Shop, Galesburg, Illinois
The Horse Blanket, Saugus, California
Get Sharp, North Hollywood, California
Slym-Line Sweats, Danville, California
Saddles by Tartan, Calabasas, Calforina
Foxwood Manufacturing, Inc., Olney,
Illinois
Beautiful Tails, Subaico, Arkansas

Healthy Hair Care, Sellersville,
Pennsylvania
Laube Product Sales, Van Nuys, California
Protecto Horse Equipment, Clawson,
Michigan
The Dehner Company, Omaha, Nebraska
Double K Industries, Inc., Northridge, Cali-
fornia
Reed Hill Ltd., Wappinger Falls, New York
Lexington Safety Products, Lexington, Ken-
tucky
Bowlegs USA, Rocklin, California
Health-Mor, Inc., Cleveland, Ohio
Superhorse International, Denmark

INTRODUCTION

First impressions—in the horse show world, your appearance influences your score. From the moment you pass through the in-gate, you communicate a visual image to the judge. This official begins to place you in a sorting process by observing your horse, and your performance can move you up or down from the first impression.

To tell the judge, "I'm a winner," you must present your horse at its best. You exhibit an animal that looks professional in its turnout. Every detail of the horse, its saddlery, and your attire is neat and polished.

Grooming transforms the animal from its natural state and enhances its innate beauty. That championship look results from efficient management and old-fashioned elbow grease. Before the day of the show, you will spend months of effort bringing your horse to its peak of show ring condition, with no letup. Competition is intense, and there are no short cuts.

Why take the time to prepare yourself and your horse for showing? A horse show is a performance, a sport that entertains spectators. Showmanship is an important element of any winning performance, and an homage to the centuries of equestrian traditions.

Those traditions demand a certain level of elegance and dictate how horse and rider appear. These "rules" may not appear in the rulebooks, but seasoned competitors and show officials continue to observe these guidelines.

Besides the unwritten rules, association rules specify details of show grooming. In many shows, the judge has the right to dismiss you from the ring if you don't meet the regulations. You can be disqualified if your horse is not groomed correctly, your clothes are of the wrong type, or your turnout lacks a piece of tack.

Your appearance proves how seriously you have prepared for the show. When you first attract the judge's attention, you demonstrate that you care enough to prepare your horse properly. The judge and spectators rate you on what you've taken the time to do—not what you meant to do.

Grooming is a challenge. You and your horse appear on stage, whether you perform before one person or a stadium of thousands. The sharpest exhibitors know the art of presenting themselves with charisma, yet they are able to stand out in a subtle manner from the rest of the competition.

There is a fine line between appearing too sedate and being too flashy. You must conform with the rules and prevailing fashions, but you don't want to get lost in the crowd. You want to advertise yourself. At every show, you'll see a competitor initiate a new trend by experimenting with a subtle, yet tasteful, difference. The rider who uses a new type of saddle pad, a unique browband, or an eye-catching accessory can influence show-ring fashion–at the next show, someone else might copy the change!

As you play to the judge in your turnout, remember that you're trying to please him. You can't try anything totally out of the ordinary, or you may find yourself examined by show officials. When you enter the ring, you subject yourself to the judge's opinion. A judge could disqualify you if he feels your grooming or tack seem to give your horse an unfair advantage over your competition.

Grooming does benefit the show horse. The attention you give your horse during grooming makes the animal happier and more comfortable. Show horses

A well-groomed show horse enjoys regular handling. "Primoroso IV," Andalusian stallion owned by Rainbow Farms.

thrive on the regular handling they receive from their grooms. When a horse looks good, it feels good. A contented horse will perform better.

Grooming also brings up the question of equestrian ethics. Some procedures may appear unnatural, but this book focuses on humane methods. You'll also find some advice that instructs on ways to improve a horse's appearance, which might be called cheating. Actually, attempts to camouflage a less-than-perfect animal rarely succeed. You can't fool judges, because these expert horsemen already know all the tricks!

Emphasize the positive and exhibit a perfectly presented horse. If you are a dedicated horseperson, riding or handling a beautifully groomed animal will complete your enjoyment of the art of horsemanship.

ABOUT THIS BOOK

This second edition offers additional guidance to help you prepare your horse for the show ring, either in hand or under saddle. It compiles grooming procedures and show turnout recommended by the experts. The horsemen and women interviewed for this book have contributed their own unique opinions, which represent all major breeds and riding styles, both East and West, British and European. The knowledge and experience of these professionals—grooms, trainers, breeders, show officials, retailers, and equipment manufacturers—will help you to produce championship results.

To obtain the result of a clean, polished horse, the professionals follow different approaches. The techniques here list *Alternate Methods* for the same result. Some involve commercial products, while others suggest homemade mixtures.

Besides style techniques, advice also includes guidelines for correct tack and attire, as regulated by show associations. Association rules do change, along with fashions. For current show regulations, you should read the current rulebooks that apply to your breed or discipline. You can keep up with the latest styles by being an active member of your association, studying photos in magazines, and attending major events.

The book is organized into three parts. Part I, General Techniques, describes procedures that apply to all show horses. Because grooms offer different opinions about producing the same results, you'll find alternate methods. You can select the technique that works out best with your horse.

Part II, Specialized Turnout for Show, compiles official requirements, show ring traditions, and classic and current fashions for grooming and tack of the most popular breeds and types of horses. Chapters also describe correct attire for riders and handlers in the three major disciplines.

Though the information in these chapters features specific types of horses, grooms often borrow from other disciplines. You may discover procedures that can improve your horse's appearance, despite its breed.

In Part III, Show Strategy, experts offer tips on efficient pre-show planning and show day preparation.

The emphasis in this book is the style, or how the horse and rider appear in the show ring. Style is only the frosting on the cake, because any show horse must be in top condition. Proper feeding, medical care, and exercise are vital in order to prepare the animal. Though grooming can contribute to a horse's health, it must be a part of a complete fitness program.

A book won't make you a professional groom, so watch the experts in person. You'll discover that every experienced horseman has opinions. Suggested tools and techniques may or may not succeed in producing the desired results on your horse. You will need to experiment and sort out the best approaches for your horse—or even develop your own methods!

PART I

GENERAL
TECHNIQUES

1. BASIC TOOLS

Professional grooms agree that the best tool is your hand. With your palm and fingers, you can massage the horse's skin, stroke its coat, and separate hairs of mane and tail. Your hand is more sensitive and warm than any grooming tool, which makes the contact more pleasurable for your horse.

However, you also use a variety of tools for specific purposes. To perform the procedures outlined in this guidebook, you'll need a complete grooming kit.

First on the list are products that are designed to assist in cleaning of the horse's body. This chapter describes the tools you should have; Chapter 2, "Daily Cleaning," explains how to use them.

CURRYCOMBS

Currycombs, used for loosening dirt, come in a variety of styles. The most popular models are the hard rubber curry and the plastic curry. The hard rubber curry consists of a stiff backing with firm teeth. The plastic curry has a more flexible construction that allows you to bend the tool to massage the contours of the horse's body. The teeth bend as you push the tool against bone and muscle.

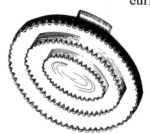

Hard rubber
curry comb

You can choose either model with or without a handstrap, and either pointed or rounded teeth. In most cases, the rounded teeth are gentler than pointed ones on the horse's skin. The tips can massage and stimulate the horse's skin and muscles, without irritation.

Match the feel of the teeth with the sensitivity of your horse's skin. The curry's shape also needs to fit your hand so you can press the tool firmly against the horse's skin.

In a flexible curry, check the number of teeth and the quality of the material. Used every day, the teeth of inexpensive curries wear down or snap off in cold weather. Models of polyurethane have proven flexible yet more durable.

Grooms usually consider metal curries too harsh for the fine skin of show horses. The metal prongs can pull out hairs as well as dirt. These are best used as cleaning tools, to scrub loose dirt and hair from your brushes.

Small round
plastic curry

The small round curry and the curry mitt are formed from soft rubber or plastic, so you can rub the contours of the horse. They are useful for scrubbing off mud.

Two other tools used for rubbing are the cactus cloth and the burlap rag. The cactus cloth is a piece of fabric loosely woven from fibers of the maguey plant. When rubbed against the coat, it massages the skin, cleans and shines the hairs, and absorbs sweat. The burlap rag, another favorite material for rubbing, is usually fashioned from an empty grain sack.

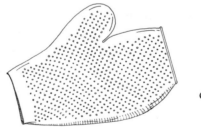

Rubber
curry mitt

BRUSHES

Expert grooms maintain a variety of body brushes, using up to seven or eight different styles in every grooming session. The bristles can be either natural (vegetable or animal hair) or synthetic (plastic or nylon) fibers. Some horsekeepers contend the natural bristles produce a better shine, though the vegetable bristles are not as durable as manmade ones.

Ranging from heavy to fine bristles, brushes fall into three general categories:

1. *Dandy.* Stiff bristles, two inches long, are mounted onto a wood back, with the best quality wire-drawn. A traditional favorite is the rice-root brush. This may be wire-drawn, with an open back so water can drain through the brush. The toughest dandy brush, the mud brush, has thick, rough fibers to brush off dried mud.

2. *Body or All-Purpose.* These medium-weight brushes feature bristles mounted on a wood or leather back. Fibers are usually of a shorter length (about three-quarters to one inch), and the brush usually includes a hand strap for better control.

3. *Finishing.* Made of softer fibers, this brush is gentler on the coat. A shoe buffing brush is an alternative to the standard style.

A new type of brush combines the rubber teeth of a curry with the finishing action of a brush. Use the rubber brush to dislodge dirt and flaky skin, either for daily cleaning or during shampooing.

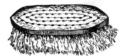

Wire-drawn
rice-root brush

Finishing brush

Body brush

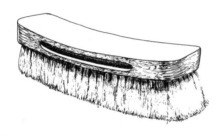

Shoe buffing brush
with soft bristles

RUBBERS

To rub the horse's coat after brushing, you can use a Turkish or terry cloth towel, or the traditional linen or silk stable rubber. Some grooms feel a cloth surface is superior to the bristles of a brush for getting a finishing gleam on a horse's coat.

SPONGES

Small, hand-sized sponges are useful for cleaning a horse's face and body. Keep them separate by purchasing different shapes, colors, or textures, and designate specific ones for either face or body. The natural sponges may be more comfortable for the horse and easier to use, since they do not become stiff when dry.

You can substitute soft rags in place of sponges. Rags can be disinfected in boiling water, while you can't thoroughly clean or treat sponges.

WISPS   A standard tool in Europe for massaging horses, wisps are not as popular in the United States. You can form a wisp by twisting lengths of grass hay, or buy a manufactured one—a pad shaped of hard rubber or leather, that may have a hand strap.

To make a wisp, twist hay or rope into a three-foot-long section. Form it into a figure eight, then tuck in the ends to make a hard block.

You can adapt a pommel pad to make another wisp, which is easier to use than that made of hay. Stuff the cloth pad with a firm material, such as a rolled piece of leather, and fold it to measure about ten by three inches. You can sew on a strap for easier handling.

Steps in forming a wisp from grass hay

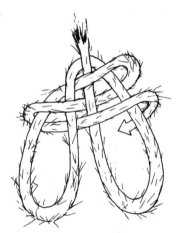

VACUUM   The livestock vacuum can save a great deal of time in a large stable. For the groom with only one or two horses, however, purchasing this tool may not be cost-effective.

A proven portable vacuum is the large, heavy-duty canister model as illustrated. Although it is expensive, it quickly removes dirt.

A recent innovation is a wall-mounted vacuum, equipped with a metal brush and a range of attachments. The machine's hose can be suspended over the grooming area for convenient use.

You can substitute a shop vacuum, or a portable, hand-held model. The latter is best used for a quick cleaning or touch-ups at the show.

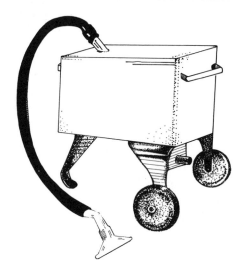

Livestock vacuum cleaner

A wall-mounted electric vacuum provides the ultimate in luxury. Attachments connect to this unit for rapid currying and brushing of a barnful of show horses.

OTHER GROOMING TOOLS

Additional tools used regularly while cleaning the horse include the hoof pick, sweat scraper, bot egg knife, fly spray mitt, buckets, hairbrush (natural or plastic/nylon bristles), and pump sprayer.

For special treatments that you perform occasionally, add the following tools to your grooming kit.

Aluminum sweat scaper

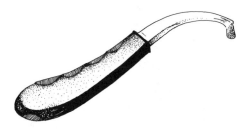

Bot-egg knife

BODY SPONGES AND SCRUB BRUSHES

Use oversized sponges for soaping and rinsing the horse's body. To clean the walls of the hooves, you can scrub with a vegetable brush or the rubber brush.

PULLING COMBS AND THINNING SHEARS

These implements help you to remove or trim excess hairs from mane and tail. Choose a pulling comb with metal teeth; the teeth of the plastic combs can snap off under pressure.

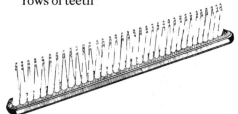

Plastic pulling comb made with three rows of teeth

Thinning shears

ELECTRIC CLIPPERS

To shorten hairs on the horse's face and body, electric clippers provide quick, even results. This appliance is available in three sizes: small, medium, and large.

1. *Small.* Use these only for trimming facial whiskers and hair inside the ears. With a small motor, they are quiet and less likely to irritate most horses. Blades on small clippers won't cut a very large area at a time, and the motor lacks the power to cut coarse or thick hair.

2. *Medium.* These are the most popular clippers. By using the wide variety of interchangeable blades, you can trim every part of the horse's body.

Blades for this machine are numbered, with the smaller numbered blades coarser than the larger ones. By comparing the #8½ blade to the #40, you will see how the teeth are spaced farther apart on the coarser #8½ blade. This results in a longer cut. When you use the #40, you clip surgically close.

You can use medium clippers for body clipping, when fitted with a wide #8½ or #10 blade. Lighter than the large clippers, these are easier to hold and do not tickle the horse as much. They are more likely to overheat, however.

A new brand of medium clipper offers two speeds, with the high speed of 3600 revolutions per minute (rpm) noticeably faster than existing models. The clipper can be converted to a cordless type with an optional battery pack. Its sealed DC motor doesn't blow hair and debris, either.

Another newer clipper is the belt-mounted type, where the motor attaches to your belt or the wall of

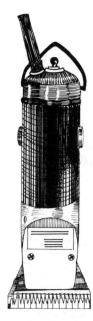

Medium clippers fitted with wide blades

the grooming stall. Operating at 3500 rpm, this machine keeps the clippers cool by separating the motor from the handpiece.

3. *Large.* This appliance is also called the body clipper, because it is mainly used for a body clip. The blades are wider and the motor more powerful than most medium clippers for the fastest results on large areas. The size of the machine and its blades make it less suited for use on the contours of lower legs and the head. (Use the medium clippers on these bony areas.)

Large clippers are the noisiest and most likely to upset the horse. Some models provide a variable speed control, so you can clip at a slower, quieter speed.

When clipping, you can wear a bandanna or painter's mask over your nose and mouth so you will not breathe in loose hairs.

As a substitute for electric clippers, you can use scissors with curved blades. At the show, do the last-minute touch-ups with a women's safety razor with a disposable blade.

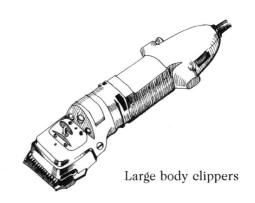
Large body clippers

MISCELLANEOUS TOOLS

Every groom adds extra items to his or her grooming kit. The following products will be handy during some maintenance procedures: scissors, leather punch, bridle cleaning hook, saddle rack, and, for the short groom, a step stool or picnic bench.

MAINTENANCE OF GROOMING TOOLS

Keep the items in your grooming kit clean and in good repair. The tools you use to clean the horse will not function properly if they are dirty.

Clean brushes by dipping the bristles into a solution of warm water mixed with one of the following: ammonia, one teaspoon salt, Ivory soap, or one-half cup shampoo. Or, you can rub the brush with a soaped, damp towel. Rub a cotton swab in between the bristles to remove dirt and hair.

Rinse the brush thoroughly by dipping in clear water. Shake out excess water and dry the brush by wiping bristles onto a dry towel, or allow it to air dry with the hairs pointing down, so water will drain off the brush. Water soaking into the wood can damage the back of the brush. Treat a leather-backed brush with saddle soap.

Grooming tools can spread skin disease, such as girth itch. If this is a problem in your barn, keep the affected horse's tools separate. Disinfect them often to avoid contamination of other animals. You can dip the teeth of curries and bristles of brushes in Clorox bleach to disinfect them, or use a livestock disinfectant.

Replace grooming tools when necessary. Using a curry with broken teeth or a body brush with a broken hand strap reduces your efficiency. These items aren't costly, and you get maximum benefits from minimal investment.

Keep your grooming appliances in good repair. Avoid electrical hazards by repairing cords that pull loose or begin to fray. If an appliance starts to short out, have it fixed promptly.

When you store your clippers, avoid stressing the cord when you wrap it around the machine. Allow a twelve-inch loop to hang free, then wrap the remaining cord around the body of the clippers.

Clippers need special attention. Twice a year, have a professional clean and grease the machine, checking the gears and clearing out the short hairs that collect inside. If you are mechanically inclined, you can learn how to take apart, clean, and reassemble the medium clippers.

When using your clippers, avoid overheating the motor. Oil the head and teeth of the large clippers before and during the job. If the machine feels hot, turn it off to cool before continuing. Air-cooled clippers will not heat up as fast.

Prolong the life of clipper blades by keeping them clean. Always clean the horse thoroughly before clipping, and dip the blades into a clipper cleaning solution while working. (See Chapter 7 for various solutions to use.)

Have the blades sharpened when they start laboring as they cut. Dull blades force the machine to run harder and cause the motor to overheat. Sharpen the blades of body clippers after three clips. If you use your medium clippers daily, expect to sharpen the blades monthly. If you use them only once a month, expect blades to last for several years before requiring sharpening.

You can sharpen clipper blades many times, and you'll need to replace them only when they cannot be sharpened any more. You can buy your own kit for sharpening blades, but most grooms send blades to a reputable professional sharpener. This expert knows exactly how much metal to grind off the blades. Some sharpeners remove too much, and blades will not last as long.

2. DAILY CLEANING

For that show ring glow, the experts agree that there is no substitute for regular grooming, called "strapping" in England. No product can replace the sheen of healthy skin and hair of a well-conditioned horse whose coat has been rubbed daily. This task takes a lot of elbow grease—you should expect to spend thirty to sixty minutes each day for your cleaning routine.

Prepare for grooming by outfitting the horse in either a stable or grooming halter. It should stand tied in a well-lighted area.

Suggested tools include:

- Currycomb
- Dandy brush
- Body brush
- Finishing brush
- Towels, stable rubbers, or burlap sacks
- Two small sponges.

SAFETY PRECAUTIONS

Establish a regular routine of always grooming your horse in a safe area. Always tie the animal securely, either to a tie rail or in crossties. No matter how gentle the horse, avoid accidents by observing safe procedures with every animal.

The safest location is a separate indoor grooming stall. This removes the horse from traffic in the barn, and you can have access to grooming supplies stored permanently in or near the stall, on shelves or in cabinets. If you share a barn with other equestrians, avoid tying a horse in the barn aisle and blocking the passage.

Some grooms restrain the horse in a grooming chute. The size of a trailer stall, this pipe stall confines the horse in a small area, where you can groom it without tying its head.

If your horse accepts the restraint of hobbles, you can

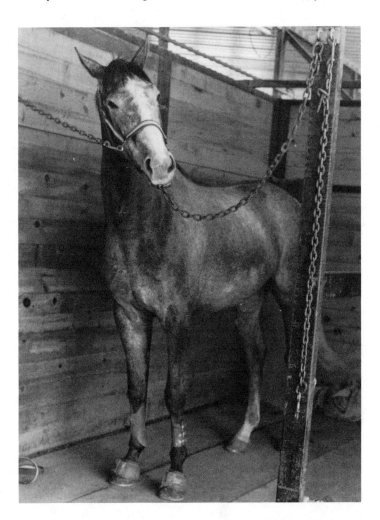

A hunter stands ready for grooming in a grooming stall inside a modular barn.

"tie" it with this tool. Hobbling removes any barriers of ropes or chute, giving you unrestricted access to the horse's body.

Whatever site you choose, verify there are no hazards that will endanger you or your horse or interfere with your handling. Look for level, dry footing. There should be no low ceiling or overhangs, and walls or fences should allow sufficient working space on all sides of the horse.

For best results, the grooming area should be free of drafts. Overhead lights should illuminate the horse with few shadows. In northern Europe, many barns have installed a solarium—a framework of infrared lamps that emit heat rays. The lights duplicate the heat of the summer sun and warm the horse after exercise, so it dries quickly.

You will appreciate other conveniences such as nearby electrical outlets, which prevent the need for long extension cords. Grooming will be much easier if your barn has hot and cold running water, with faucets located near the grooming area.

When handling the horse, keep your movements slow and deliberate to avoid startling the animal. To maintain a smooth flow of procedures, check for a complete kit of all grooming tools before you start. If you must carry tools to the horse, stow your supplies in a portable tote basket, grooming box, or grooming apron.

When working with any horse, stay alert to its reactions. Protect yourself by not standing or squatting in a potentially hazardous zone. Test any unfamiliar procedure, even with a sensible horse. When you first try hosing the horse or clipping its body, start on the animal's near shoulder. This seems to be the most non-threatening spot on most horses.

First, rub the horse's coat to loosen body dirt. If the horse is dusty, first rub the hairs with a cotton rag, burlap sack, or a towel, against the grain of the coat. This will start to loosen the dust on the surface and stimulate the circulation.

Next lift dirt to the surface by rubbing with a rubber currycomb. Many people have learned to curry by holding the tool in the left hand. For best results, you might want to switch the curry from hand to hand, which will allow maximum pressure on the angles of the horse's

As exhibited at Germany's Equitana fair, the solarium adds light and warmth to the grooming stall.

LOOSENING DIRT FROM THE BODY AND FACE

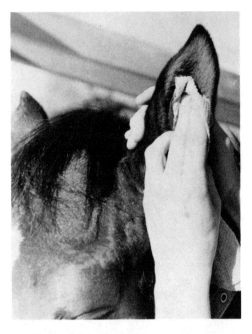

Use a soft rag or towel to clean the ears.

body. If you want, try using two curries at once, one in each hand.

Beginning at the neck, behind the ears, press the currycomb against the skin and rub it. You can use either a circular, back-and-forth, or downward motion. To loosen dirt most effectively, you have to apply "elbow grease." Push the curry through the coat and into the skin, with your wrist bent and stiffened during each stroke.

Stick with a regular routine so you clean all sections. Work your way along both sides of the horse's body by currying neck, chest, shoulder, back, barrel, flank, and croup. Lift up the mane to curry underneath, up to the crest. Reach up to scrub the top of the croup, where dirt tends to collect. Then bend down or squat to curry the underside: from girth along the belly.

Don't forget to curry the legs—besides cleaning the hair on the legs, currying improves the circulation. Use the tool either in a circular or sideways motion, to knees and hocks, both inside and outside.

Some geldings and stallions may develop "stud crud" on the insides of their hind legs. You should prevent this accumulation of dirt by both regular currying of the coat and cleaning of the sheath. (See Chapter 3.)

If you are careful, your horse might tolerate the curry on the lower legs. With a horse that objects to the stiff curry, try substituting the curry mitt or rubber brush on the knees, hocks, cannons, and pasterns.

Most horses enjoy the massage of the curry, and they will lean into the pressure you create. Others resent this grooming. You can adjust the action to the horse's preference by varying the model of curry, or lighten the pressure on more sensitive areas, like back and belly.

Your curry will accumulate dust, dirt, and dead hair as you work your way along the horse's body. Clean the tool by tapping it on the heel of your boot, a wall, or a tie rail. "Horsemaster" students in England's famous riding schools are judged on their currying by the number of currycomb marks on the wall—twenty such marks are expected each day! Another evaluation of a thorough grooming as practiced in some European stables is the amount of dust left on the clean stable floor after a groom curried a horse.

Alternate Method: Some people prefer to use a stiff brush to lift the dirt. A stalled horse may not become dirty enough to require currying.

Push the bristles through the hair to the skin. Use sharp strokes to snap dirt off the skin and onto the tips of the hairs.

Gray, white, roan, and Palomino coats often become stained. If manure stains remain after you have curried the coat, you can spot-clean the area. Here are several approaches:

1. Make a paste by adding water to a small amount of cornstarch or baby powder. Rub onto the spot and allow to dry. Or, pack cornstarch into the hairs, spritz the hairs with water, and allow to dry. Brush the coat clean.
2. Rub a little Bon Ami cleanser into the hair. Remove the cleanser with a damp sponge.
3. Scrub the stain with a small dab of dishwashing detergent. Rinse well.
4. Rub baby powder into the coat, going against the grain with a soft brush. Remove excess by brushing briskly.
5. A bleaching method used at the Spanish Riding School is to make a paste from water and a smashed piece of charcoal, then rub the paste into the horse's coat. Allow it to dry, then brush thoroughly to remove. On the Lipizzaners, this procedure first turns the hairs black, but returns them to their natural white as the groom brushes out the solution.
6. Rub the stain with a rag saturated in rubbing alcohol.

After loosening dirt from the body, clean the face. Some horses will allow you to use the rubber or plastic curry-comb behind the ears and on the jaw. With others, try the curry mitt or rubber brush.

Or, use a damp sponge to wipe off the face, and around the eyes, nose, and ears. This will remove dirt that is encrusted in the hair. A sponge with corners, either of a square or rectangular shape, is a good tool for wiping out the nostrils and the corners of the eyes.

BRUSHING DIRT FROM THE BODY AND FACE

After currying, most grooms prefer a dandy brush to brush off loosened dirt. This can be either a stiff or a soft dandy.

A brush with stiff, short bristles will clean the coat better than one with longer fibers, but it may irritate the

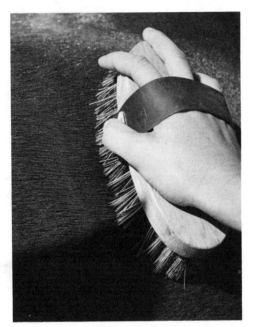

The stiff fibers of the body brush lift dirt from the coat.

skin. Longer bristles tend to flex more against the skin. Be especially careful when using a stiff brush on a thin-skinned horse. For better dust removal, dampen the bristles of the body brush.

Start on the neck, behind the ears. Lift up the mane, if necessary, to start at the top of the neck. Hold the brush lightly on the coat, with the bristles into the hair, and press it downward with the direction of the hair growth.

For best results, push with your body weight into the brush and use short, sharp strokes. Bend your wrist at the end of each stroke so you lift the brush off the coat—this will flip the dirt toward the ground, not on another portion of the horse. Aim to brush from three to six strokes on each section of the coat.

Clean the brush frequently so you don't end up just moving dirt from one part to the next. A good method is to rub the bristles across the teeth of a metal or rubber currycomb to shake loose the dirt and hair. You can hold the currycomb in your other hand as you brush, and clean the brush after every three to five strokes.

On the legs, use a body brush vertically along the tendons and horizontally behind the pasterns. Be sure to brush off any mud from behind the pasterns, to prevent sores from developing.

Brush dirt from the face with a body brush, in the direction of the hairs. Use a light touch, and brush slowly and deliberately around the eyes and ears. If your horse resents the feel of the bristles, use only the soft brush. (See "Polishing the Coat" in this chapter.)

For a thorough grooming, curry and brush the horse a second time. This will remove scurf and loose hair that you may have missed in the first grooming. Or, switch to a body brush with hard bristles, and stroke first against and then with the lay of the hair.

If the horse is extremely dusty, you can spray it with a homemade solution that will allow you to brush out the dust. Mix one quart alcohol with one quart water, and add squirts of Hawaiian Tropic tanning oil. Spray this mixture onto the horse and brush. The lanolin in the oil will help remove the dust embedded in the coat.

VACUUMING DIRT FROM THE BODY

Some grooms with a barnful of horses substitute the livestock vacuum for brushing. Though this effectively removes loosened dirt, it is a shortcut that does not ben-

A dandy brush can wipe dirt from behind the pasterns.

efit the coat by massaging the skin and distributing the oils. If you press hard to massage with the vacuum's grooming tool, the suction may disturb the horse. A compromise is to use the vacuum not more than every other day, or use it only before currying and brushing to save time grooming a particularly dirty horse.

You can vacuum dirt from the horse's barrel, neck, shoulders, and quarters. Do not use it on face, legs, mane, or tail.

Observing how the horse tolerates the pressure, press the tool well down into the coat so the suction removes all loose dirt. Work first against the grain of the hair, and keep the tool moving in a circular motion so you do not irritate the horse. Complete the task by running the vacuum with the hair.

The vacuum is most effective when fitted with a curry attachment. Without this attachment, you can increase suction over a wider area by wrapping your hand around the end of the hose, then hold your hand against the horse's coat.

If there is static in the air, the vacuum will just move the dust from one area to another. You can pick up this dirt with a barely damp rag, or rub the coat with an anti-static sheet as used in the dryer. Another method is to rub a small squirt of hair dressing on your hands, then rub a rag across to pick up just a smear of the dressing. Wipe the horse's coat with the rag, turning the cloth as it collects dust. You can use a product intended for humans like Brylcreem or Alberto VO-5 dressings, or Peach Show

Dressing, formulated for show cattle. All will add a sheen and train the coat to lie flat, in addition to removing dust.

After vacuuming, brush the coat lightly to lay the hair down.

POLISHING THE COAT

When you've removed dirt from the coat, you're ready to rub to polish the hairs. You can choose a soft body brush, towel, or burlap for the horse's neck, shoulders, back, croup, barrel, and legs. This adds a final polish by removing any dirt left on the surface and distributing skin oils along the shafts of the hairs.

Rub the brush or cloth with the direction of the hairs, again putting enough pressure into the tool to rub down to the skin. Long strokes will sweep the dirt and lay down the hair.

Alternate Method: Hold one finishing brush in each hand while brushing. Rub the bristles of the brushes together to clean any dirt they collect.

On the face, use a soft brush carefully, angling it so the bristles brush with the changing directions of hair growth. Move the forelock to the side so you can brush with the hairs above and around the eyes. You can protect the horse's eye by cupping your hand over it when you clean that area. This also works to quiet most animals.

In place of the soft brush, you might prefer to use the soft rag, towel, or damp sponge a second time on the horse's face.

A soft brush picks up oil and dirt from the horse, so clean it with the currycomb every two to five strokes. Avoid smearing dirt to another area by continuing to use a dirty brush.

Finally, use a clean, folded stable rubber, kitchen towel, or burlap to smooth over the horse's body. The textured surface of this cloth will pick up any dirt that you may have missed. Avoid smearing dirt by refolding the towel as you work, which will provide a clean fabric surface for each section of the body.

Check that your horse's coat is clean by running your hand over its entire body. Especially feel the underside of the belly and the top of the croup, which are difficult

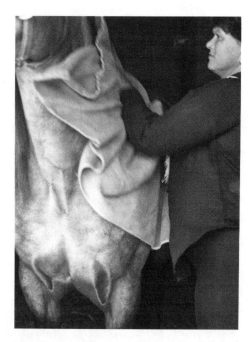
Rubbing with a towel brings out the gleam of the hairs.

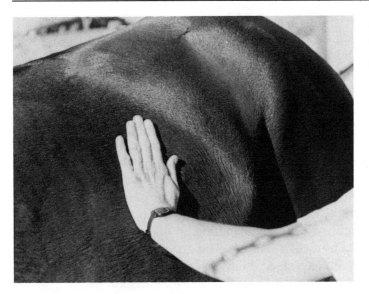

Your hand is your best grooming tool because you can stroke the coat and feel anything unusual.

to clean. With your hand, you can also feel any unusual swellings or scrapes you might have missed while currying and brushing. By feeling your horse every day, you will be familiar with its normal condition.

With a small, dampened body sponge—not one that you use on the horse's face—wipe dirt from the hairless skin under the tail and between the hind legs. Standing to the side, lift up the tail and sponge the dock and anal/vulval area. Be gentle, since the skin is delicate and easily irritated. Wipe off all areas of the udder or sheath.

When you groom your horse in the summer or fall, you may notice yellow bot eggs on the hairs of the horse's legs, barrel, or chest. Remove these immediately with a safety razor or bot-egg knife. Trim eggs from the tips of the hairs by running the blade in the direction of the hair. You'll find it easier to scrape eggs from bony areas than the softer muscled ones.

Clean eggs from the blade and discard them into the trash, not on the ground. By removing them from the grooming area, you assure that parasites will not be picked up by the horse.

As part of your daily routine, separate the strands of the horse's mane and forelock. With most horses, you will use your fingers to untangle any knots, beginning at the ends of the strands. You can brush the mane and forelock if desired. (For more details on mane care, see Chapter 5.)

CLEANING OTHER AREAS

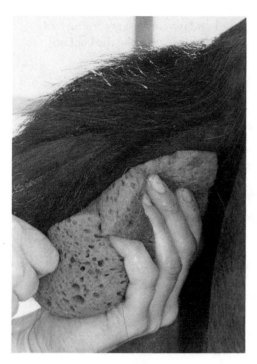

Sponge under the tail to remove dirt.

If you are cultivating a long, full tail, you will probably handle the hairs as gently as possible to avoid breakage. Unknot any tangles by hand, and brush the tail with care. Many grooms keep the tail braided and wrapped to protect the hairs, undoing the wrap once a week to pick or brush the tail. (See complete details in Chapter 6.)

Your last daily chore is to clean the horse's feet. With a stiff brush or rubber brush, knock off any dirt on the walls of the hooves. Use a hoof pick to remove any embedded debris on the sole and around the frog. You can apply hoof paint as a finishing touch. (Chapter 9 includes more detailed information on hoof beauty.)

You will need to repeat grooming after the horse has been exercised. First, however, remove any sweat from the coat, as it damages the skin and hair.

If the horse is hot and sweaty, cover it with a sweat sheet or wool cooler and walk till cool. Depending on the horse, you'll either hand walk or use the hot walker. After the horse has stopped steaming or has walked an hour, remove the cover. (If the horse needs bathing or rinsing after work, follow procedures outlined in Chapter 3.)

When the horse is cool but still wet, speed up the drying process by rubbing the coat with a towel or cactus cloth. Do not brush the coat while it is sweaty. You can apply a coating of talcum powder to dry the sweat, which you can brush off later.

DAILY CLEANING STEP-BY-STEP:

1. Rub horse with towel to loosen dirt.
2. Scrub coat with curry to lift dirt to surface.
3. Spot clean any stains that remain on the body.
4. Curry or sponge the face.
5. Brush or vacuum loosened dirt from body.
6. Rub coat with soft brush or cloth.
7. Rub coat with your hand.
8. Untangle any knots and pick debris from the mane and tail.
9. Brush dirt from hoof walls and pick feet.

TRAINING THE HORSE TO ACCEPT PROCEDURES

Show horses need regular grooming in preparation for the show ring. This handling should be positive and pleasurable for both you and your horse. Most horses learn to enjoy the attention they receive.

Your horse must stand still for grooming. You can school your horse to stand in place by reducing stress. Establish a regular routine for the various procedures, and avoid pressuring your horse by not rushing any actions. A gentle, quiet manner will encourage most horses to relax. Talk to the horse, pet it, and offer bits of carrot during handling.

One way to calm a horse is to blow gently into its nose while talking quietly. This soothes and distracts the horse from any unusual handling.

Ideally, your horse trusts and respects you, but you may need to discipline it in order to reinforce obedience. The extent of discipline varies according to the horse and the situation, but you must decide what behavior you will tolerate.

For instance, you may choose to ignore the minor bad habits of a high-strung horse. Constant punishment could upset this animal. A calmer horse often accepts discipline without overreacting, but you should remember to apply any punishment with the proper timing and severity.

Know your horse's reactions when you plan to introduce an unfamiliar action. You may need to desensitize it and accustom the animal gradually. By spending a few extra minutes now to train the horse, you will put your horse at ease and save time in the future.

Train your horse to accept grooming all over its body, with you working on either side. On sensitive areas, you can teach your horse to allow handling by gentle repetition. Maybe your horse will tolerate only one light stroke of your finger inside its ear—try for two strokes next time. Handled with sensitivity, most horses will accept any handling.

Many grooms feel that taking the time to establish the horse's trust eliminates the need for forcible restraints, such as the twitch. They feel that by training the horse to trust them, they will not have to resort to force.

Restraints may be necessary in some procedures, as a safety precaution to insure that the horse remains still. However, remember that when you resort to force, you may be setting a pattern. Next time you attempt that procedure, you could encounter the same fight. Restraints may actually cause the horse to resist.

With a foal, you need extra patience to school the youngster to enjoy grooming. A foal has a short attention span, and you may need to break a session into intervals throughout a day. Quit on a positive note without pushing the foal too far.

To avoid upsetting a young horse, be sensitive to its body language. The animal may start swishing its tail excessively, try to move away from you, or cock a fetlock. When you observe these signs, recognize if you pressure the horse too much, or cause it to be fearful. With a frightened horse, regain its trust by reintroducing the new procedure.

Besides getting your horse to respect you, you also respect the horse. Some animals resent too much fussing. Pay attention to the animal's expression, and don't overdo your handling. If the horse expresses boredom or frustration, quit.

To remove dried sweat, rub the coat in a circular motion with a cactus cloth, dampened loofa, or burlap. Or, in cooler weather, sponge with warm water, then rub dry with a towel. Continue with regular currying and brushing, and re-blanket.

After the coat is dried, you can add an extra sheen by rubbing hairs with a section of a satin sheet.

Rub the coat with a folded cactus cloth to remove sweat.

3. BATHING

Bathing show horses is a controversial subject. At some barns, grooms bathe horses weekly or more often. At others, horses are rinsed to remove sweat but rarely receive a soap bath.

Soaping the skin removes the sebum (oils produced by the sebaceous glands), which protects the skin against chafing and insects. Frequent soaping may also cause skin problems.

Some trainers especially condemn the practice of bathing horses at the show. This practice can remove the coat's oil secretions, causing the coat to look dull and stand up away from the body. They recommend washing the horse at home several days before the show, to allow time for the oils to come to the surface.

Manufacturers of equine shampoos claim that today's products condition the coat without depleting the skin's natural oils. Choose a mild, non-alkaline shampoo, either a brand formulated for horses, or an inexpensive baby shampoo. Look for a product that rinses out easily.

If you choose to bathe your horse more than once a week, watch the condition of skin and coat for any problems. Choose hypoallergenic brands with proper pH balance to avoid irritating sensitive skin.

RINSING AFTER WORK

Rinsing sweat after exercise is common practice. When you use no soap, rinsing will not remove the natural oils.

Stand the horse, fitted with a water-resistant halter, on a firm, non-slip surface. A wash rack or wash stall is ideal, but you can use a stable aisle or tie rail. Be sure there is no danger of accidental electrocution from exposed wiring or nearby outlets or appliances. Wear rubber-soled boots to protect your feet from becoming soaked, and so you won't slip on the wet footing.

Never let the horse stand in a cold draft while you're washing it. If possible, use warm water. This is more comfortable for the animal, which will then more likely stand quietly while you work.

You can get warm water directly from a hot water heater through its spigot. Attach a heavy-duty hose to the spigot with a coupler, or run the hot water into a bucket. Dilute it with cold water before using.

You will need:
- A hose (if your horse is accustomed to its use)
- A trigger nozzle sprayer, wash curry, or fan garden sprayer
- Large sponge
- Sweat scraper
- Loofa, rubber or plastic curry, or rubber brush

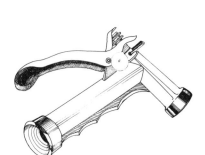

The metal trigger-nozzle sprayer attaches to the hose. Metal threads are more durable than plastic.

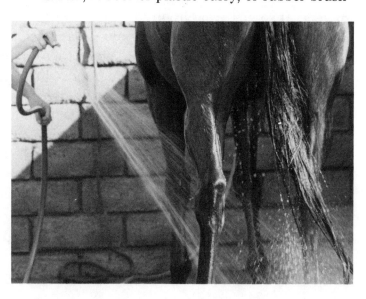

Without an attachment on the hose end, crimp the hose to adjust water pressure during the rinse.

If you use the nozzle, wash curry, or fan garden sprayer, attach the tool to the end of the hose. Starting on the near side at the legs and feet, begin to hose off the horse. Control the water pressure by adjusting the nozzle to increase or decrease the strength of the stream on certain areas. You can crimp the hose to adjust pressure if you prefer not to use a nozzle. Depending on the horse, you may wish a lighter pressure on the back, barrel, and flanks, and a heavier stream against chest, neck, and legs to loosen sweat and dirt.

Using a strong water pressure with the nozzle acts as a massage, similar to a shower at full blast. With some horses, this pressure feels good on tired muscles and avoids stiffness.

With the fan garden sprayer attachment, you can hold it directly against the skin to whisk dirt away. Water pressure can be about one-half strength.

The wash curry serves as a scrubber. Or, you can scrub with a regular curry or wet loofa in one hand, while holding the hose in the other.

Use caution when aiming water toward the horse's head. Ease the pressure and avoid getting too close to the ears. If the horse objects to your hosing its face, turn off the hose and use a sponge or cloth to wash the head.

A plastic wash-curry allows you to scrub with running water.

Alternate Method: Instead of rinsing with water from a hose, sponge water from a bucket. This allows you to add other body washes, which stimulate and tone the skin as refreshers or braces. Vetrolin liniment is formulated for this purpose, or use a homemade body wash of two parts liniment to one part alcohol. Both will cool and relax the horse after work.

Sponging a hot horse with warm water and vinegar can cool the horse while removing sweat.

After rinsing, use the sweat scraper to squeeze off excess water from the body and upper legs. Slide the scraper along the grain of the hair with a slight pressure. Then hand rub to lay the hair down, using your hands or a clean towel. If possible, tie the horse to dry in a sunny, sheltered location.

If the weather is cool, you can sponge only the sweaty areas with warm water, rub dry with towels, and put a cooler on the horse while it dries.

This model of sweat scraper is designed
for one-handed use.

BATHING PROCEDURE

You will need the same items as for rinsing, with the
addition of a shampoo and bucket.

If the horse isn't wet from sweat, brush its coat to
loosen dirt. Rinse the coat.

Mix the shampoo into a bucket of warm water, diluting it according to manufacturer's instruction. Don't add
more than suggested—too much lather can be detrimental to the coat, and it does not necessarily clean the horse
better.

Dip the large sponge into the soapy water and begin
to cover both sides of the body with the shampoo, starting at the neck. (Depending on your horse, you might
wish to soap the mane and tail first, or even start with
the head.) To make sure the shampoo gets down to the
skin, you can use a rubber currycomb or curry mitt to
scrub along with the sponge.

White markings may require extra scrubbing. Some
grooms squirt shampoo, straight from the bottle, onto
white socks. Use the rubber brush to scrub the hooves.

You may wish to soap the face with a smaller sponge.
Be sure no shampoo gets into the eyes or nostrils. Protect the eyes by cupping each with your hand as you
sponge above and behind.

Standing to the side, never directly behind, soap the
tail by rubbing undiluted shampoo into the hairs. Be sure
you remove all scurf by scrubbing through the hairs
to the skin of the dock, and also wash underneath the

tail. (Be prepared for your horse to clamp its tail down when you attempt this cleaning.)

When you soap the mane, also scrub down to the skin to remove all dandruff and dead skin. Rub the mane with your hands to clean the strands thoroughly.

With warm water from the hose or bucket, rinse thoroughly. Do not leave any traces of soap to dry in the coat, because this will dull the hairs and cause flaky skin. The teeth of the wash curry help you scrub out the soap. If you rinse with a sponge, use a clean one, and change the rinse water in the bucket to keep it free of soap. Keep rinsing until the water runs clear, with no trace of bubbles from the shampoo.

Sponge the head with a clean sponge and warm water. Again, protect eyes and ears. Rinse the head several times to be sure you have removed all traces of soap.

Rinse the tail thoroughly. If you use a bucket for rinsing, dip the tail into the water. Rub the hairs with your hands, or you may wish to use the curry on the top of the tail.

Alternate Method: You can soap and rinse one side of the horse's body, and then move to the other side to soap and rinse.

Optional: After the first rinse, apply a second vinegar rinse to remove any soap residue. Mix one-half cup vinegar into a jug or bucket of warm water, and pour or

Rub the soapy sponge against the hair to wash white markings.

You can pour a rinse directly from jug or bucket.

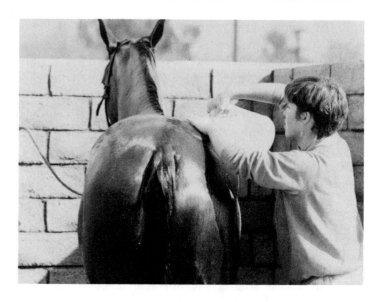

sponge it onto the coat. Then rinse with warm water from hose or bucket.

To replace the natural oils, add some olive oil to a bucket of water, and rinse it onto the coat. Allow this to set for ten minutes—then rinse with plain water.

When rinsing is complete, help the horse to dry faster by scraping off as much water you can. After using the sweat scraper, rub the coat, mane, and tail briskly with stable rubbers or towels.

Cover the horse with an antisweat sheet or a cooler, depending on the temperature. Walk the horse till it dries, or leave it tied in a grooming area or its stall. If you turn a freshly bathed equine into a paddock or pasture, it's sure to find a convenient dusty spot for a roll!

To add shine and help keep the horse clean, you can apply a coating of Laser Sheen or Absorbine Show Sheen while the animal is still damp, or before scraping with the sweat scraper. Spray one of these silicone hair polishes on the coat lightly, and use your hands to spread it with the grain of the hair. Rub each section until the coat is completely dry, then go on to the next wet area.

Clean white stockings or body patches with a color-enhancing shampoo like Quic Silver. You can mix one part Quic Silver to four parts water and spray onto the specific areas, or even the whole horse, in place of shampoo. If the horse is very dirty, add a squirt of Palmolive dishwashing liquid to this mixture.

A product like Quic Silver contains some bluing, and you'll notice a purplish tinge to the lather. Be sure to rinse thoroughly so you don't stain white hairs purple.

If your horse's coat shows manure stains, you can apply any undiluted soap, straight from the bottle, onto the stained hairs. Liquid Wisk laundry detergent or Ivory bar soap will whiten yellowed hairs. (Rinse the coat thoroughly after applying these products.) Scrub with a scrub brush, with nylon bristles. When you've restored white areas to a true white, prevent stains by spraying the hairs with Show Sheen.

To scrub stains from the back legs, use the horse's soapy tail.

Holding the tail in your free hand while rinsing, so you can fan the hairs for a thorough job.

CLEANING THE SHEATH

Clean the inside of the sheath of a gelding or stallion, for both health and appearance. If you ignore this procedure, dirt and smegma can collect on the insides of the hind legs. You may need to wash your horse's sheath as regularly as once a month, depending on how much dirt it collects. You should also wash a mare's udder routinely, either separately or during a bath.

Know your horse's reactions to this procedure before starting to clean. Gently slide your fingers inside the sheath while observing the horse's reaction. The horse may spook or threaten to kick, so discipline it accordingly.

You will need:
- Liquid Ivory soap or Excalibur Sheath Cleaner
- Small sponge
- Two buckets of warm water
- Rubber or plastic gloves

Wear the gloves so your hands don't absorb the odor (and your nails don't irritate the horse). Moisten the sponge with warm water and insert it into the sheath to loosen any hardened smegma. (You can loosen the layered gunk in advance by applying a coating of baby or mineral oil to the inside of the sheath.)

Rub soap onto the sponge, and insert the sponge into the sheath to clean all areas so the lining feels smooth. You can wash more thoroughly if you are able to encourage the horse to drop his penis.

Alternate Method: Squeeze soap into the palm of your gloved hand, then insert your hand into the sheath to wash.

Rinse with warm water, squeezing it from the sponge.

Repeat the wash and rinse, being sure to remove all traces of soap.

BATHING A HORSE IN COLD WEATHER

Use caution if you have to bathe a horse during cold, wet weather. Never let a warm or wet horse stand in a cold draft, which can chill the animal and lead to illness.

Safeguard your horse's health by planning ahead. Plan the bath from three to seven days before the show, during the warmest time of the day. Even if the sun is shining, guard against breezes. A cloudy overcast day with no wind is safer than a sunny, windy one.

The horse should have a short coat so it will dry quickly. Gather a crew of two or three grooms for a rapid job, especially if you must bathe outdoors.

In addition to the usual items, gather two or three coolers, ten to fifteen towels, and an animal blow-dryer or two or three human blow-dryers.

Be sure the towels were laundered without fabric softener. This product limits the absorbency of cloth and will slow down the drying process.

If you must use an outside location, bathe the horse's body and neck with warm water as quickly as possible. One person can bathe each side at once while a third handles equipment.

In cold or windy weather, bring the horse inside the barn to complete bathing of legs, mane, tail, and face. You can wash the feet at this time. Or, if they need to be wet for a while before they come clean, wash them first and rinse them last.

After you've rinsed the horse, immediately throw a cooler on its body to start absorbing water. If you see the animal shivering, walk it for a few minutes to warm up. In a drafty barn, put the horse into a stall and close the door to eliminate drafts around its feet. Provide some hay so the horse can eat while grooms work at drying.

Get the water off the horse's legs first. If its legs are cold, its body will feel chilled, too. (Because more bone is exposed on the legs, they are more easily chilled.) Use towels to rub briskly to increase circulation and dry the legs, working the fabric into all the creases of tendons. As soon as a towel becomes soaked, discard it for a dry one. Work on legs until the towels will not soak any more moisture and the legs feel warm.

While two grooms dry the legs, a third can begin to scrape water off the horse's neck and body. Turn back one section of the cooler, to work on that area while the rest is still protected. This is called "quartering." When you've scraped one part, cover it and move to the next.

After a few minutes, the first cooler will be soaked. Replace it with a dry one and continue to scrape. Then begin to hand rub the hair with towels, using each till it becomes wet, then replacing it with a dry one. You may need to move to a third cooler if the second becomes dripping wet.

After the horse is towel-dried so that towels will not absorb any more moisture, you can use a blow-dryer to dry the hair. Best is the heavy-duty animal blow-dryer, which may be a function of an animal vacuum. If you are using several smaller appliances, each groom can use one to concentrate on an area, working on both sides of the horse.

When operating any blow-dryer, you and the horse must stand on dry ground. Be sure your electrical system will handle the power needs for up to three blow-dryers. Keep the appliance in motion to avoid burning the horse's skin—the air can become very hot.

If you must bathe a horse with a long coat, try the hot toweling method. Dunk a towel in hot water and wring it out so it is as dry as possible. Curry the horse briskly with the towel. As the towel absorbs the dirt, rinse it in the hot water, wring it, then curry again. The warm damp towel acts to pull most dirt from the skin and hair.

You can also resort to a dry shampoo in cold weather. Spray on a mousse, or brush on the powdered product. Rub and brush thoroughly.

BATHING STEP-BY-STEP

1. Rinse the coat with warm water.
2. Scrape excess water from the coat, if you don't plan to bathe the horse with shampoo.
3. Mix shampoo and apply to horse's coat, mane, and tail.
4. Rinse thoroughly.
5. Scrape and dry.

---

4. MAINTAINING COAT AND SKIN

A coat in show condition gleams, and the hairs lie smoothly in a single plane. When you study a horse with a good coat, you will need to stand closer than four feet to be able to discern the pattern of individual hairs that make up the coat.

The coat should be a rich, full color. That of a chestnut or bay horse will shimmer as it reflects light. Compare this to the animal with a rough coat—the ends of the hairs look dull and reddish, and they stand up. An uneven surface is created by a buildup of dead skin, dirt, and loose hairs.

The coat of a gray, roan, or dun may not gleam like a mirror, as will the chestnut, bay, black, or Palomino. But with rubbing these coats will also look attractive.

For that show bloom, the horse's skin must be healthy. Besides proper feeding and regular exercise, vigorous grooming from the outside maintains a fine, short coat. With clean skin and a short coat, perspiration will evaporate more freely and the skin will be kept cool.

The procedures that will produce a glowing coat fall into three areas: stimulating the skin and distributing the oils, applying external preparations to the coat, and protecting the coat from the environment.

STIMULATING THE SKIN

Friction against the skin brings the horse's natural oils to the surface. When you massage the skin, you stimulate oil glands close by the hair follicles. The oil softens the skin as it is distributed by friction.

Daily rubbing creates friction. Another procedure, wisping, stimulates the skin and hardens the muscles. Widely practiced in Europe, grooms usually wisp after the horse has been exercised.

Soft Wisp

First you will use a soft wisp, which can be a stable rubber, towel, or burlap sack. After completing the regular daily cleaning, briskly rub the cloth backward and forward into the coat to create a steady friction against the skin. For a gleaming coat, you will rub up to thirty minutes daily.

Grooms trained in the British tradition may prefer a wisp of twisted, soft rope for this rubbing. Whatever tool you use, work the material with and against the hair to add a natural shine to the coat. And rubbing the horse three times a day can also help keep it warm in a cold barn.

Use your hands, on body and legs, to promote circulation. Rub with your palms flat to stimulate the oils in the coat. Five minutes can bring a glisten to the hairs, either with or without first spraying with a coat conditioner.

With firm pressure, rub downward below knees and hocks, and upward above. If you dampen your palms, you'll pick up loose hairs and help keep the coat short. With a horse that is naturally fine-skinned, keep your hands dry, since you could loosen too much hair and cause bald patches.

Hard Wisp

You may choose to follow another British tradition of using the hard wisp—of hay, rope, rubber, or leather—to harden muscles. This produces the most benefit on a horse that is already fit, not one that is out of condition. Wisping benefits the underlying muscles and promotes circulation. You will "bang" the hard and flat muscles of neck, quarters, and thighs, with the grain of the coat.

This well-groomed Morgan displays a beautiful coat, even at a January show.

Start with the neck, untying the horse so you can hold the lead rope. Stand back and with your whole arm, swing the tool downward firmly on the neck muscles. You will see your horse tense its muscles. Wait till it relaxes before you apply the next stroke. Work with a vigorous, steady rhythm, being careful to avoid bony areas or any tender spots. After wisping both sides of the neck, tie the horse and wisp the muscles of the quarters and thighs.

Your horse needs to become accustomed gradually to this muscle toning. If you are just beginning to wisp, start with five strokes on each muscle area the first day. Expert grooms work up to one hundred strokes for each muscle group, twenty to thirty minutes total, on a horse in hard condition. This can be repeated twice a day for best results.

For wisping, you can substitute a cactus cloth or stable rubber. Dampen and roll up the cactus cloth, and apply with a slapping motion. With a rubber, fold the fabric until it is slightly larger than your hand. Apply to the skin with a thumping motion, leaning into the stroke so the rubber slides along the coat.

These procedures help make the horse feel better, and the animal will then look better. External treatments, aimed to remedy bone and muscle soreness, can relieve stress and possibly improve the horse's appearance as well.

For first-class horse care, grooms who prepare highly competitive horses seek an edge over the competition. Alternative therapies become part of grooming.

A trained massage therapist can aid muscle development. Proponents of technologies like ultrasound and electro-magnetic therapy claim these enhance the circulation and improve the coat while reducing swelling.

EXTERNAL COAT APPLICATIONS

Enhance daily cleaning and rubbing with external applications that improve the skin and coat. These help to replace the skin's natural oils and remove sweat, which damages the coat when allowed to dry on the hairs.

Here are some suggestions:

1. After a full bath or warm water rinse, replace the coat's natural oils by adding a suitable product to the rinse water. Be sure the product contains no ingredients that could irritate your horse's skin. Some grooms recommend mixing a few drops of Pine-Sol cleaner disinfectant to a bucket of warm water. The pine oil adds sheen and helps the hair to lie down.

2. In place of a bath or water rinse after exercise, some trainers advocate sponging the body from a bucket of warm water and vinegar. This maintains a glossy coat.

3. To remove sweat after a hard work, pour a little Bigeloil or Vetrolin liniment into warm water and rinse the coat. (You can also add two ounces of mineral oil to enhance the coat's gloss.) If the horse is sweaty only under the saddle and bridle, sponge off the sweat, use a towel to tousle and dry the hairs, and brush the coat well when hairs are dry.

If you leave sweat on the coat and turn the horse out in the sun, the combination of sunlight and salty sweat can bleach the coat. A dark horse may turn orange where the bridle and saddle fit, so be sure to rinse or rub out the sweat after work.

4. Apply a coat dressing or hair polish only on a clean horse. When the coat is still damp, spray lightly with a coat dressing. The silicone-based sprays add a shine

that helps to seal the coat from dirt, although some grooms feel these dressings make the coat too slippery and clog the pores if used heavily.

Try the new product Healthy Hair Moisturizer. Spray or rub this lotion on the coat to condition and lubricate the hairs.

You can also apply the moisturizer by rubbing it into the hair with a terry cloth towel or cotton mitt. Soak the cloth and rub the coat vigorously, with the grain of the hair. Then brush.

5. Grooms agree on the difficulty of adding glow to a gray horse's coat. You can rinse with a bluing solution. Add two squirts of bluing to a bucket of water, or one capful to three gallons. This will make the color shine, with no artificial additives. (On horses with sensitive skin, watch for any negative reaction.) A rose gray probably won't shine, as the coat tends to absorb light rather than reflect it.

6. Another method for that extra gleam is an alcohol grooming, immediately before the show. Mix hot water and rubbing alcohol, half and half. (Alcohol evaporates without removing the coat's natural oils.) With a circular motion, rub this mixture into the coat with a sponge, ending with strokes that wipe in the direction of hair growth. Let the coat dry, then buff to a gloss with a clean, soft cloth.

Most grooms use fly spray on the horse's coat in warm weather. Though this discourages insects, some formulas can cause skin problems.

Some fly sprays are blended with lanolin, aloe vera, and/or sunscreen to help protect the skin. You can also wipe Noxema skin cream around the horse's eyes and ears to protect these sensitive areas from flies. The cream tends to dry out and cake, so you'll need to sponge it off and renew it daily.

Oily fly repellents also attract dirt and make it hard to keep the horse clean. A gentler substitute for commercial fly repellents is apple cider vinegar, best used when flies are not too prevalent. With this product, flies will alight but not bite the skin. You can apply salad vinegar on the horse's legs, again if the fly season is not too heavy.

Feeding nutritional yeast seems to cause the horse's skin to repel flies. They may still land on the animal, but they are less likely to bite.

COAT PROTECTION

To maintain your horse's shiny coat, protect the hairs and skin from the environment. The coat may be clean and healthy, but you still need to guard it against the weather and dirt.

For a coat in top condition, follow the prevailing choice and keep your horse indoors out of the sun. The sun's rays can bleach the hairs of the coat, changing its color and drying the hairs. Staying in a dark stall during the day protects a show coat.

Some grooms, however, contend that sunlight benefits the horse's hair coat, and that it only causes damage to a sweaty coat. They claim sunlight will not dull the coat if you completely remove any sweat before turning the horse out.

If a horse's coat does become faded by the sun, you can try to rejuvenate it. First bathe the horse, then mix equal parts of vinegar and olive oil to sponge all over the coat. Rub the mixture in well, and leave it on for three days before bathing the horse to remove it.

Some horses with sensitive skin seem prone to skin conditions. You may have to treat fungal infection or the lesions of rain rot. Antibacterial shampoos help prevent and correct skin problems. Avoid rain rot by not keeping skin wet (such as under blankets or leg wraps). Don't clip a horse with wet skin. Prevent transmitting the infection through isolating the horse's tack, blankets, and grooming tools.

Blanketing

Proper blankets also help protect the coat by keeping the horse clean. The type of clothing you use on your horse will depend on the climate and your dedication to keeping your horse covered.

A blanket's lining is important, since friction against the skin adds shine to the coat. Most blankets now feature nylon linings. Loose hairs will not stick to nylon, but on a dirty or sweaty coat, this man-made fabric might gall the skin or even cause a rash.

A fleece or flannel lining, of wool or cotton, will also polish the coat. Both do tend to collect loose hairs, which is a problem if the horse is shedding.

Match the blanket's type to your environment. A lightweight sheet will protect your horse in the summer. In the winter, you may need a heavy winter blanket and hood. Check that the horse is warm—slip a hand under the blanket at the shoulder.

You must keep every horse blanket clean. No matter how clean your horse, it can develop skin conditions by wearing a blanket that's dirty inside. Don't expect to use a single winter blanket all season, day and night.

Whatever the season, the blanket must cover the horse adequately. Many ready-made models are not long enough to protect the flanks, and you can find your horse with manure stains on its sides. A correctly fitted blanket should reach to the middle of the gaskin. None of the belly should show below the edges.

Blanket design can decrease the chances of your horse's wriggling free. Leg straps and a bellyband help secure the clothing.

A winter blanket should mold to the horse's contours and fit snugly at neck and hindquarters. Look for a model cut from three or four separate pieces, for a close fit that won't shift. If you notice that the blanket rubs patches of hair from the shoulders, remedy the problem quickly—this hair probably won't grow back till a new season's coat develops. Replace the blanket with one that fits the horse properly, and moisturize the skin. You may wish to line the front of the blanket with cotton, nylon, or satin fabric where it chafes the hair.

Stall Cleaning

Another aid to keeping your horse clean and shiny is a well-prepared stall. Groom smart—you put a lot of effort into grooming your horse, so don't turn it loose in a stall with a thin layer of bedding over a dirt floor.

Stable managers develop their own approaches to bedding a stall. Here is one proven method for a dirt-floored stall.

Prepare the surface of the stall by stripping it down to the hard packed dirt—sweep with a broom until nothing loose is left. Lay one inch of new flooring material, such as decomposed granite. Wet down the material, tamp it by hand, and let it dry. Continue to add layers of decomposed granite, one inch at a time, until the surface is built back up to level.

Leave the stall untouched until the flooring is completely dry, so it binds to the dirt and becomes hard. This allows it to drain and not become loose so it will mix with bedding.

Next add three or four bags of shavings, or most of a bale of straw. Shake straw loose with a pitchfork. Kick about one-third of the bedding up against the walls, so it will keep clean for rebedding as needed. With this deep bedding, the horse will not be walking on the flooring, which should last about a year before it needs to be resurfaced.

Clean manure from the stall as often as possible. At major stables in England, grooms constantly clean stalls—once in the morning, at night, and all day long, "skipping out" (spot-cleaning) the stall if there is a pile of manure.

About once a month, strip all bedding from the stall, allow it to dry out, and add lime as necessary before rebedding.

SHEDDING OUT THE WINTER COAT

The shiny summer coat becomes evident as the winter coat sheds out in the spring. Shedding times vary in length, depending on the environment, your horse's state of health, and your grooming procedures. You can help a coat to shed out through grooming, exercise, and nutrition.

Use heat and friction to encourage the coat to shed. Stable the horse in a warm area, or add heat lamps to the stall. Bathe the horse in warm water. Exercise also helps the coat to shed, by creating the heat of perspiration. Work the horse into a sweat and then rub the coat dry with burlap or a cactus cloth. Rub both with and against the lay of the coat.

Sweating and rubbing are more effective than just brushing or heavy blanketing. A blanket will make the hairs lie down, but it won't necessarily stimulate shedding.

Regular currying will remove dead hairs from the coat. You might want to speed up the process by running a serrated shedding blade down through the hairs. The metal teeth snag the dead hairs and pull them free.

Another tool, an old cowboy method, is the griddlestone. You can purchase this rough-textured, abrasive block from a restaurant supply firm. A new-fangled version, the fiberglass shedding block, duplicates the griddlestone.

5. MANE GROOMING

Almost every type of show horse has a mane that lies on its neck. (Three-gaited Saddlebred horses have their manes roached.) Your horse's mane will be either long and natural, or shortened to a prescribed length. Although the style must conform to breed specifications and current fashion, mane care is basically the same.

Handle the mane carefully. Starting at the ends of the mane hairs, first use your fingers to hand pick the mane. If you brush before separating the strands from each other, you can tear or break the hairs. This is especially important with a full mane, since you want to avoid breaking off more hairs than necessary.

BRUSHING THE MANE

Select a soft hairbrush or horse brush for the mane. These tools cause less breakage and seem to stimulate the hair growth, as compared to a mane comb or dandy brush. On a long mane, you might try a wire pet brush.

Brushing can be overdone—experts advise gentle brushing, and not brushing the mane thoroughly on a daily basis. It's safer to pick strands apart by hand, because you're less likely to break the hairs and cause split ends.

To fluff the mane, hold a section up from the neck with one hand, and with the other brush from underneath, from crest to the ends of the hairs. Remove excess hair from the brush if it collects in the bristles. Avoid fluffing a mane on a horse with a heavy neck, because this could accentuate a conformation fault.

Continue brushing from the top side of the mane to finish separating the strands and to lay the mane down. You might want to dampen the brush and wet the top of the mane, at the roots, as water keeps the hairs from sticking up on the off side. Most grooms believe that moisture stimulates growth of new hair.

Hand pick the forelock as well, separating each strand. Then brush to arrange the hairs into place.

Alternate Method: On a horse with a naturally thick mane, you may need to comb the hairs with a mane comb, maybe even on a daily basis. Continue to hand pick any knots.

Handle twisted hairs of the mane and forelock— tangles, snarls, or knots—with care to avoid hair breakage. It is safest to use your fingers to separate the strands, though some grooms recommend a hoof pick or a wide-toothed comb.

On a stubborn snarl, saturate the hairs with mineral, baby, or neatsfoot oil, or spray with a silicone-based product. Allow the liquid to soak into the hairs, then massage the strands and start to separate them. With some tough snarls or burrs, you may have to wait for an hour or two for the oil to make the hairs slippery enough to untangle. (Oil will pick up dirt, so leave the horse in the stall or tied up.)

After you have removed all tangles, be sure to wash an oil product from the mane before you turn the horse out.

A coat dressing holds hairs in place and adds more sheen. If you plan to braid a mane for a show, avoid using oil or dressing, which makes the hairs too slippery to braid.

To keep a long mane in show shape, some grooms

A fine-textured mane, seen on a Peruvian Paso, is the result of gentle care conditioning.

prevent knots by putting the mane up in thick, loose braids. They braid sections of mane with strips of bed sheets, or wide, heavy ribbon, with the cloth on the outside as much as possible. This protects the mane and adds a wave to the hairs. If you plan to leave braids in place, don't pull them so tight that you irritate the horse and cause it to rub its mane.

Braiding may help you maintain a long, flowing mane, but its success depends on the horse. Watch to see how your horse tolerates a braided mane. On fine hairs, the procedure may pull strands out of the mane.

You may need to remove braids every few days, especially in the summer. When flies irritate the horse, it's more likely to rub its mane.

SHAPING THE MANE

Many breeds are shown with a natural mane, which you cultivate to grow to its longest length. Other types of horses have manes and forelocks shaped into a shorter length and thickness. To sculpt a mane and to train it to lie flat, you must remove the longest hairs.

Thin and shorten a mane by pulling these hairs. There are no nerve endings on each hair root, so this procedure does not cause the horse pain. Pulling these strands from the mane gives more natural looking results than you can achieve by cutting the mane with scissors.

Before pulling, plan what length you desire, according to the breed-specific mane style. Put yourself in the judge's boots and examine your horse. What will best complement its particular conformation?

Many breeds show with short manes, measuring three to six inches all along the neck. With a long mane, the horse might look its best if the longest section falls to the point of the shoulder.

Also observe the mane's texture. If you shorten fine hairs too much, you can end up with a flyaway mane. In this case, aim for a slightly longer mane, maybe one inch more than usual, so the weight of the hair will help hold down the mane. (Chestnut horses usually have finer mane hair than horses with black manes.)

A thick mane pulled too short tends to stick straight up—four inches is usually short enough.

To pull a mane, tie the horse in a well-lighted area. You'll probably need to stand on a step stool, or try training the horse to stand in position by draping a separate halter rope over its poll. The slight pressure usually encourages it to relax and drop its head.

You will need:

- A mane comb
- Pulling comb or hairbrush with stiff bristles
- Gloves (optional, to protect your fingers)

Beginning at either the top of the mane or the withers, spread your fingers apart to grasp a few long hairs with one hand. With your comb or brush in the other hand, backcomb the strands so only the longest ones from underneath are left—not more than ten strands at a time spread out over the section. Ideally the hairs should form a sort of fan shape, not all growing from the same spot on the crest.

Push the mane close against the neck, and pull out the longest hairs by wrapping them around the comb and

Reining, cutting, and working cow horses sport long manes. This leopard Appaloosa displays a luxuriant mane and forelock while he waits for his go-round in the cow horse class.

This dressage horse, a competitor in the 1984 Olympic Games, is groomed with a well-pulled mane.

snapping them up from the roots, away from the direction of hair growth.

You should see gray or white roots at the ends of the hairs you pull. Be sure you jerk the hairs free from the crest without breaking the strands. Hairs that break will first stretch, causing a frizzy effect of the sections that are left. If your horse's mane seems short but thick after you pull it, you're probably breaking hairs instead of removing them.

Alternate Methods: Some grooms prefer pulling a mane by hand. Wear a glove on your pulling hand—the sharp hairs can cut your fingers.

Or, use pliers to do the pulling. Clamp the tips of the pliers onto the longest hairs, and pull them out. You can numb the crest by a couple of firm pulls and then a sharp jerk to remove hairs.

After backcombing the mane hairs, you have a few strands ready to pull.

Even though mane pulling does not cause the horse pain, many animals resent the procedure. Try doing it a little at a time, maybe pulling a few strands every day. If you attempt to pull a long mane into a short one all at once, your horse will probably lose patience with the process.

One approach is to work quickly down the mane, then start again. Your horse may accept this more readily than your concentrating on one area. You'll also avoid having to match lengths in one session, or quitting with the mane unevenly shortened.

Some manes seem to pull easier after the horse has been worked, when the pores are open. Or, you can try numbing the crest somewhat by a few firm pulls of the hairs before you actually jerk them free.

As you pull hairs from the mane, smooth the remaining hairs with your brush or comb so you maintain a consistent length as you work.

Pull the forelock into the proper length and shape for your horse's breed type. Decide if you want the forelock pointed at the end or squared off.

If your horse's mane has very short hairs that stand up, sometimes called "porcupine" hairs, do not pull them. Allow them to grow out. One way to train these to lie flat is to brush them from the off side, using a dampened dandy brush.

When you must shape a very thin mane, with sparse strands, you probably don't want to pull any hairs. In this case, you can try using thinning shears, holding them sideways at a forty-five-degree angle so you can carefully snip the tips of the longest hairs. With this cut, you will taper the ends and avoid cutting all hairs the same length so the mane doesn't look chopped-off.

You can also use a stripping knife, made with serrated teeth, to thin and trim the mane. Run the blade through the hairs to thin, then pull it with sharp strokes to trim.

TRAINING THE MANE

In addition to shaping the mane of the show horse, train it to lie in place. The mane must lie on one side of the neck, which is traditionally the off side. If your horse's mane naturally lies to the right, you may wish to retrain it to the left, depending on the type of shows you attend. In hunter classes, for instance, where it is important to conform, you would feel out of place if yours is the only horse with its mane on the near side. In Quarter Horse shows, it doesn't matter on which side the mane lies.

When a mane is well trained, the hairs lie flat on the neck. They may float from the neck when the horse moves, but when the horse halts, all strands fall into place, with none flipped onto the right side of the neck.

To train the mane, you will need a mane comb and a dampened brush with stiff bristles. With the comb, part a section of mane. Brush it forward, angling the hairs toward the horse's cheek. Part the next section, and repeat. Work your way down the mane, keeping the strands wet so they will dry in place.

With a stubborn mane, you will need to repeat this process at least daily, or even several times a day, before the mane remains in place. Conscientious professional grooms may brush the mane at each grooming, four times daily.

Hairsetting gel will add extra weight to the wet mane. As you brush, add a dollop of gel to the top of the mane and an inch or two down the strands. As the gel dries, its stickiness and weight will hold the mane in position.

Use hairstyling mousse to add body and hold. Distribute the mousse through the hairs with a brush or your fingers.

Dabs of Vaseline petroleum jelly can also train a mane to lie down. Apply to the top of the mane.

Your horse may present you with a mane that refuses to lie in place, due to thick hairs or a cowlick. Here you can try various means to press the hairs flat.

Braid the strands after brushing. You will need ten to fifteen pieces of yarn, cut ten inches long, a sponge, and a seam ripper.

At the top of the mane, part a two-inch section and braid it tightly. When the braid is half done, lay a piece of yarn across it, so you will twine the ends among the hairs of the two outside sections of hair.

You can substitute rubber bands, such as Braidbinders, to tie the braids more quickly than yarn. Many grooms prefer yarn, feelng it will hold the braids more securely and not cut the hairs.

Continue to braid, with the yarn among the strands, to the end of the braid. Tie the yarn twice, once on the top of the braid, then wrap it behind the braid and tie it again. Trim off loose ends.

Repeat this braid down the mane until you've braided

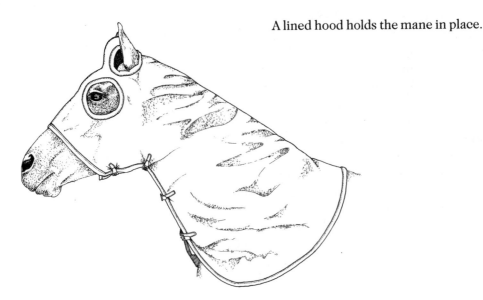

A lined hood holds the mane in place.

and tied all strands. Wet the roots of the mane with a sponge and smooth any loose hairs toward the braided side.

Leave braids in for two or three days, dampening the mane daily. During the time the braids are left in, keep an eye on your horse. If it starts to rub out the braids, remove them. Leaving them in too long can make the hairs pull out. Remove braids by cutting the knots with a seam ripper and carefully separating the strands. Brush the mane flat with a wet brush.

Alternate Method: Braid a stubborn section of the mane with a long strand of surveyor's tape. At the end of each braid, stretch the tape under the horse's neck and up around the other side to the top of the next section you'll braid. The slight stretch of the tape will pull the mane down against the neck. Leave the tape in overnight and then remove.

Braiding should train the mane, but continue regular brushing with a wet brush. A few manes will need another braiding session.

Training a mane is a process that you may need to repeat indefinitely. To keep some manes in show shape, you can expect to brush and braid during the entire season.

This crocheted mane tamer presses
the mane hairs flat against the horse's
neck. Ties hold it in place.

Alternate Method: The hood, neck sweat, and mane
tamer garments can train the mane to lie in place. If you
choose a hood, use one that's clean and softly lined. A
silky, slippery lining across the mane area will help the
hairs to lie smoothly. Most brands of hoods are lined with
nylon.

Usually you use a hood with a blanket. Snap the bottom of the hood to the ring of the blanket, at the withers. Watch that the horse's blanket does not rub the mane
at the withers—a cut-back design will eliminate this problem.

Check the mane daily by removing the hood. When
you replace the hood, feel inside to be sure the mane
lies flat. If it becomes mussed, you're training it to lie
incorrectly.

A neck sweat or mane tamer covers only the mane.
The latter is usually made of a lightweight, loosely woven material.

One method of using the mane tamer is to put it on
the horse every day after exercise. When you rinse the
coat, brush the mane and place a cooler over the body
and the mane tamer over the mane. Tie the horse in the
stall to dry, and remove the clothing later.

CONDITIONING THE MANE

Cultivate a healthy mane with beauty treatments. If you plan to braid a sport horse's mane for show, you probably won't need to use any special treatments other than shampooing, which may be a part of the bath. If dandruff is a problem, eliminate it in the mane or tail with a mixture of Listerine antiseptic and baby oil. Part the hairs and squeeze the liquid onto the skin. Rub it in well with your fingers, and rinse.

For a horse that tends to rub its mane, try soaking the roots with water twice a day. Moisture will also stimulate growth with any mane, short or long. For a fluffy, silky mane, enhance hair growth by preventing breakage.

If you treat your horse's mane twice daily, with either plain water or a conditioner, the hairs will stay flexible. Flexible hairs will not dry out, become brittle, and break. You can choose from a variety of special conditioning agents for equine beauty treatments.

Maintaining a long, luxuriant mane is a continual process. You cannot let up on your care, especially in a dry climate, or the mane hairs can start to break. Even if you quit showing in the fall, continue mane conditioning through the off season.

Apply wet treatments either during a bath or as a separate procedure. First wash the mane with a mild shampoo, and rinse well. To highlight a white mane or tail, use a shampoo formulated for humans' white or gray hair, or one of the color-enhancing products like Ultra's Super White Shampoo.

You can choose among many brands of equine hair conditioners, or rely on a traditional blend. For example, mix a creamy lotion of baby oil, Listerine antiseptic, and

Carefully condition a long mane, handling hairs with care to avoid breakage.

Tuttle's Elexer. Apply to mane or tail and rinse. Other old favorites are creme rinse, baby oil, or a vinegar and water rinse. Straight Arrow's Mane n' Tail is a popular product, and some grooms add baby oil to the lotion.

Whatever conditioner you choose, rub it well into the mane. Brush the damp mane flat to help train it.

According to the product's instructions, remove by rinsing thoroughly. If you added oil to your conditioner, the strands will feel somewhat oily after you rinse and towel dry the mane. If you used too much oil, the mane will collect dust.

You can add style to the mane by shaping it into a pageboy. Fluff a long mane by brushing it from underneath, and then dry with a blow dryer. Point the nozzle upward and blow the hair against its natural growth pattern. With a Western horse that shows with a short mane, use a curling iron to sculpt the hairs so they curl underneath.

A Paint models a sculpted mane, neatly pulled and curled.

MANE GROOMING STEP-BY-STEP

1. Groom by hand-picking the mane and forelock hairs.
2. Brush with a soft brush or hairbrush.
3. Shape the mane by pulling mane hairs.
4. Dampen and brush mane to train it to lie in place.
5. Shampoo and condition mane as necessary.

6. TAIL GROOMING

Like the mane, the tail makes a fashion statement. A well-groomed tail can improve the horse's appearance. A long, flowing tail is usually one of the first things the observer notices about your horse.

HANDLING THE TAIL

Most grooms advise not to handle the tail every day, claiming that vigorous brushing can damage the hairs. Picking hairs by hand is safer. To maintain the tail, you need to keep the strands from tangling or knotting. Remember to work gently to avoid breaking or splitting the hairs. Because it can take three years for one hair to grow back to its natural length, don't use a mane comb on a tail.

Strands separate more easily if the tail is clean, or sprayed with Absorbine Show Sheen or Healthy Hair Moisturizer. Fan the hairs and mist lightly. You can also dab your fingers with baby oil before picking the tail.

With one hand, hold the tail away from the horse's body. With the fingers of your free hand, pick the strands apart. (Some people prefer using a hoof pick.) When you want the tail to look fuller, fan the hairs either while you pick or after all hairs drape freely.

A champion Arabian displays a lush, full tail.

On this coarse tail, the groom has chosen a brush with firm plastic bristles.

Alternate Method: Start at the top and peel hairs through your fingers, or thumb and forefinger, two or three at a time. Spread out the hairs while holding the tail in your hand. Pull them apart, all the way to the ends, and let them fall free as you complete each section. By handling only a few hairs at once, you avoid developing a knot at the bottom of the tail.

Once or twice a week, brush the tail with a plastic tail brush. Brush gently, with a minimum number of strokes. Do not brush straight down the top hairs. Starting at the underside of the dock, sweep the brush lightly, running the bristles down through the hairs. Move your brush outward as you brush.

If electricity in the air affects the tail, you can rub the hairs with an antistatic sheet.

Treat knots and snarls as you do those in the mane. Or, you can wash the tail and pick the hairs when it dries. Another approach is to dip the tail in kerosene to undo tangles.

SHAPING THE TAIL

Like manes, you'll style tails according to the horse's breed. You may wish a full and natural tail, or you can remove excess hairs to shape a switch tail or trim a banged tail.

A thinner, more refined tail makes the hip look more substantial. A tail fluffier near the bottom can sometimes camouflage less-than-perfect hind legs.

Before thinning the hairs, study the tail's natural shape. Hold the hairs near the base of the tailbone and hold it away from the horse so it is parallel with the ground. Check if the hairs at the top are the shortest, with the longest hairs at the end of the tailbone. For a natural look, hairs throughout the tail should appear graduated in length and those at the sides of the dock match in length.

When shaping a tail, pulling hairs by hand gives the best results. (Some grooms find it easier to use pliers to pull the shorter hairs.) Part the hairs at the underside of the dock, at the top of the tail. A few inches down, grasp a few hairs from the underside between your thumb and forefinger. Pluck the hairs in the same way as you pulled the mane. Work your way down one side.

Repeat the procedure along the other side of the tail.

Step back to study the results, then work on the first side to match the second one.

As in pulling the mane, don't try to do too much at once. Reward your horse for standing patiently by pulling only a few hairs in one session. Maintain a nicely shaped tail by pulling it on a regular basis.

Alternate Method: If your horse objects to your pulling hairs, use the trimming knife or the edges of thinning scissors. With these tools, you will clip the ends of the hairs rather than pulling them out by the roots.

BANGING THE TAIL

Banging the tail—squaring off the end of the tail—is a Continental tradition often seen on sport horses—jumpers, dressage, and event horses. Banging removes wispy ends, but leaves the tail full at the bottom. It also encourages the tail to grow thicker.

Aim to trim the tail so it hangs level with the ground when the horse is in motion. Watch the horse move to note how it carries its tail, and direct an assistant to hold the tail up to that level. With scissors, clip off the tips of the hairs, leaving the tail from one-half to one inch longer than you want it to be (fetlock length if a long tail).

A poorly banged tail can ruin the appearance of an equine athlete. When banging, remember that you can always trim off more hair. If you make a mistake and cut off too much, you will have to wait till the hair grows back to adjust the cut.

At a sport horse inspection, this Holsteiner mare displays a nicely banged tail.

Longe the horse at a trot to check that the angle of the trimmed hair is truly level. Then continue to trim until the hairs reach the desired length.

If you must bang a tail without an assistant, be sure you've brushed the tail well, with all strands flowing free. Pull it down tight, flatten it off, and clip slightly upward toward the hocks to compensate for the change in elevation as the horse moves.

To shorten a very long tail, you can use your fingers or a pulling comb to pull a few of the longest hairs.

WASHING THE TAIL

Like the mane, tail hairs benefit from moisture, so treat tail hairs to encourage growth. For a soft, silky tail, keep the hairs flexible by conditioning them. Not all horses can grow a tail that touches the ground, but you can save hairs by eliminating breakage.

For a show horse, shampooing once a week will keep the tail clean. Grooms recommend a variety of agents, listed here.

1. On a white tail, scrub Ivory soap into the hairs. This helps mares that soil their tails when they are in season. Clorox bleach can also clean tail hairs, but use it with care. The solution will sting the skin and may turn the tail yellow. Blend one capful with water in a bucket, and dip the tail into the mixture. Rinse thoroughly.

2. Exhibitor Labs Quic Silver shampoo helps whiten a yellow tail. Apply the liquid and rub it into the hairs. Allow it to soak in for five to ten minutes, scrub again, and rinse. You can follow this treatment with a conditioning rinse.

Also beneficial for a white tail is bluing. Mix a small amount in water and apply to the tail hairs. Leave the solution on the hairs for two minutes, then rinse thoroughly.

3. A mixture of vinegar and rubbing alcohol will also remove manure stains in a light colored tail.

4. After washing and rinsing a white or gray tail, comb in a temporary hair coloring, such as Roux White Minx.

5. If a horse rubs the top of its tail, apply Septaderm lotion. This acts as a conditioner, fungicide, and antiseptic, and it contains alcohol and lanolin. You can also discourage tail rubbing by pressing a handful of Vaseline petroleum jelly onto the top of the dock. You

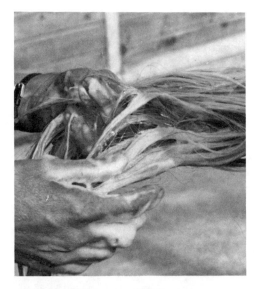

You may need to rub a shampoo into hairs of a white or gray tail to remove yellow stains.

don't need to rub this glob of jelly into the hairs, and you may leave it in place until you need to renew it.

6. Apply a conditioner formulated for manes and tails, and leave the product in the hairs without rinsing. Straight Arrow's Mane 'n Tail is the most popular conditioner of this type.

7. If tail hairs are brittle, rub peanut oil into the hairs by hand two or three times a week.

8. For a coarse, dry tail, apply a solution of almond oil and egg. In a small bowl, pour about one inch of almond oil. Beat in an egg, or two if the horse has a long tail. The egg will keep the oil on the tail hairs while softening them.

Pour the solution onto the tail. Leave it in for half an hour, then rinse with warm water.

Various treatments can make a tail appear fuller and fluffier. If your horse has a straight tail, braid it loosely when wet. You can make one long braid, or several narrower braids. Let the tail dry, and then undo the braiding. You'll add fluff and a slight wave to the hairs.

You can also fluff a tail by brushing the wet hairs. Hold the tail and brush one section at a time, shaking all strands as you brush. Some grooms use the blow-dryer to add more fluff as the hairs dry.

Another procedure, crocheting the tail, can make a thin or limp tail appear fuller and fluffier before the horse enters the show ring.

Separate several strands of tail hairs—a few strands if the hair is extremely fine, more if the hair is thicker. Make a loop by forming a loose overhand knot.

Add a series of two or three more loops to form a chain. When completed, spray the loops with hair spray. Or, instead of setting the loops with spray, you can crochet the tail when it's wet.

Repeat throughout the tail. Spray all loops well, and leave in the tail to dry. You'll enhance the effect the longer you leave the loops in the tail.

Carefully remove the loops, avoiding pulling out any tail hairs. Brush out the tail gently with a hairbrush.

Experiment with this technique to learn its greatest effectiveness. Some grooms find that they can remove the loops after an hour. Others crochet the tail

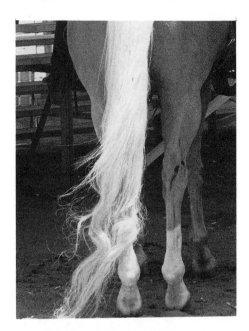

FLUFFING THE TAIL

(Above) a Palomino's perfectly white tail shows the wave that results after knotting. This tail reflects conscientious care, with strands of an even length. While (below) a crocheted tail can make this Arabian's tail appear fuller.

the night before, taking it down immediately before the class. Also, with some horses, this method is overly effective and results in a bushy, too-wide tail.

PROTECTING THE TAIL

A horse that constantly swishes flies will probably not have a lovely flowing tail. Preserve the hairs by controlling flies in the horse's environment, and protect the tail by wrapping it. Besides keeping the tail clean, moisturizing and wrapping also promote growth of the hairs for a fuller tail. The wrap protects tail hairs from sun damage.

Long-Term Wrapping

Some horses, with very long tails, may have tails wrapped all the time. This protects the strands from being pulled out. When a tail is covered with a wrap, the hairs won't snag on a fence. If the tail hangs free, the average horse will naturally pull the longest, finest hairs. With other animals, you may choose to wrap the tail beginning one week before the show.

If you keep a tail wrapped, you can grow it as long as you want. Breeds like Morgans and Arabians typically have tails that brush the ground. A tail can be too long, however—it could look "too long for the horse," or the horse could step on it when backing up.

Grooms braid the tail into a pigtail before wrapping it. This results in a wavy, flowing tail when it is let down.

Choose among these items for wrapping a tail for long-term protection:

- Three long strips of flannel, sheet, or wide ribbon
- Yarn, string, or tape
- Masking tape, gaffer's tape, or Vetrap
- Sock, nylon stocking, or tail bag

With a wet brush, dampen the tail. Moisturize the hairs with baby oil or mineral oil, or saturate them with Healthy Hair Moisturizer. (Baby oil can stain a white tail.)

Separate the strands into three sections. Start the braid about an inch below the tailbone so you don't affect the tail's blood circulation, and loosely braid the first few inches. Continue the braid, tightening the plaits, and tie off the end with yarn, string, or tape. Fold the tail and pull the sock or tail bag over it.

Secure the sock with electrical tape or ties, which you thread through the braid to avoid slippage. (Avoid the black electrical tape on a white tail, because it can discolor the hairs.) With the tail bag, push the closure through the braid and fasten.

Alternate Methods: 1. When braiding the tail, add strips of soft cloth entwined with the hairs. Tie strips at the bottom and wrap tail with masking tape. Then insert the tail into the sock or tail bag.

2. Adding the cloth strips, braid so all the tail strands are covered by the cloth. When you complete the braid, the tail hairs are underneath the strips of fabric. Long strips can add length to your horse's "fly swatter."

3. Braid a pair of nylon stockings into two strands of the tail. Roll up the tail and stuff it into another nylon, and tie it up. Nylon will not cut the hair.

4. Add a track bandage into a section of the tail before you braid. Braid into one pigtail, and loop the end up through the upper part of the tail.

5. Fold the tail over, with the hairs tucked underneath the tailbone, and wrap securely with Vetrap elastic bandage or Guard-Tex Leg and Tail Wrap. You encase all hairs in the wide tape. This method is faster and longer-lasting than putting the tail into a sock. If desired, you can attach strips of sheet, lengths of baling twine, or strands from a mop under the wrap, which will allow the horse to use its tail to swish flies.

6. After braiding, push the bottom of the tail up through one loop at the top. Then wrap only the braided section with Vetrap, starting one or two inches below the tailbone.

7. You may wish to wrap only part of a long, thick tail. Lift and shake the tail, parting the hairs to section off the middle portion: the longest hairs that equal about one-third of the tail. Fold this section by doubling it and wrap it with Vetrap or Guard-Tex.

By wrapping only the middle of the tail, you protect the longest strands while leaving a "flag" of hairs on both sides. The horse still has use of its tail for swishing flies, and the free hairs often cover the wrapped section so the tape isn't visible.

Whatever method you choose, wrap the tail with care. Never tie a wrap tightly so it inhibits circulation, or you can permanently damage the tail. And don't wrap too loosely, so the covering becomes undone. Your horse could injure itself by tripping on a loosened wrap.

Fold the tail by inserting the braided end into itself.

After folding, wrap with a Vetrap elastic bandage.

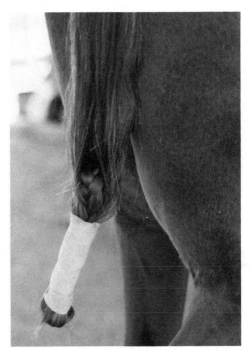

Once a week or at least monthly, let the tail down to brush and wash it, if necessary. Rebraid, using clean materials.

Keep an eye on the braided tail. If it becomes matted or dirty, unbraid and redo it.

Most grooms like the waves added to the tail when braids are removed. The wave catches the light and attracts the eye.

If the hairs look too wavy, use a wet brush or sponge to smooth the kinks. Start at the dock and dampen the top and the hairs underneath. Or, dip the tail into a bucket of warm water. Shake it out and allow it to dry.

You'll also need to protect the tail of a show mare with a foal at side. Foals seem to enjoy chewing their dams' tails. Discourage this activity by soaking the mare's tail hairs in a "taste deterrent" like Bitter Apple or Tabasco sauce. With Tabasco, soak a cloth with the sauce and wipe it on the tail at least every other day. You can also keep the mare's tail wrapped, and apply the sauce to the wrap.

SHORT-TERM WRAPPING

You may need to protect your horse's tail from being rubbed during shipping or before a show. Wrap it in a track bandage if it's not already wrapped or you

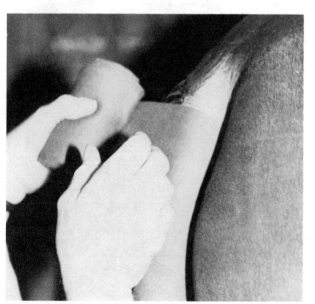

Wrap a tail with care, using a rolled track bandage.

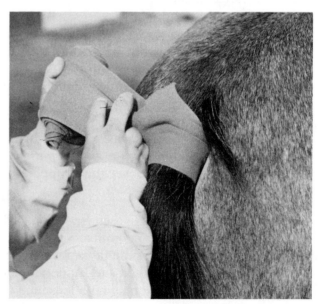

Fold the corner down over the first complete wrap. Smooth out all wrinkles.

want to guard the hairs at the dock. This also helps train the short hairs near the dock to lie in place.

Alternate Method: The easy way is to use a neoprene tail wrap. Simply slip the wrap under the tail, close to the top of the tail, and fasten securely. Realize that the rubber lining will create heat and possibly irritate the horse. If you leave this wrap on for a prolonged period, your horse could start rubbing its tail due to the chafing.

Following tradition, you'll wind a rolled knit bandage around the base of the tail. This requires practice, as the bandage must exert even pressure on the tail so it does not restrict circulation. A tight bandage can permanently damage the tail, whether you tie it with tape or strings.

You'll need:
- A knit bandage, measuring nine feet long by three or four inches wide, that fastens with Velcro or string ties
- Bucket of water
- Sponge or brush

As you spiral down the tail, maintain an even pressure so you do not damage the underside of the tail.

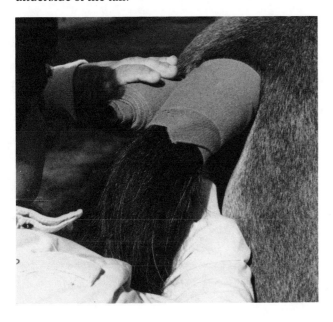

- Masking tape
- Step stool (to stand on if you're short)

Wet the sponge or brush and dampen the tail hairs. Work the bandage underneath the top of the tail, with a few inches on the near side, held in your left hand.

Lift the tail and drape it over your shoulder so you have both hands free. Place the end of the bandage upon the tail hairs, as close to the top of the tail as possible.

Wrap one turn smoothly around the tail. To fasten the bandage, pull up one corner of the end, which you will fold over the beginning of your second turn.

Wrap the next turn over the first, and fold the corner down over the bandage. Then continue down the length of the tail, to the end of the bone, spiraling each turn so it closely overlaps the previous one.

You should produce no wrinkles in the bandage. Aim for it to lie smoothly over the tail without binding. Maintain an even pressure, tugging to keep the wrap snug only when you pass the bandage over the top side of the tail.

A too-tight bandage can easily damage the underside of the tail—be sure you don't exert pressure on the

This tail wrap is fastened with a Velcro closure near the bottom. If less of the skirt is wrapped, your bandage will end up closer to the top. The tail can be bent into a comfortable position.

Here ten tail hairs are bent upward to help secure the bandage.

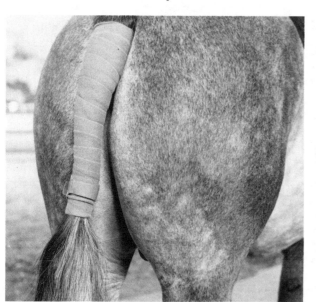

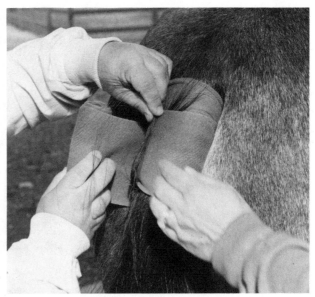

hairless skin as you wrap. Too strong a pull can in-hibit circulation.

When you reach the end of the tailbone, wrap up-ward, back over the turns you have created. End the wrapping near the top, with the end of the bandage on the outside of the tail, not underneath. Shorten it by folding over the end if you need to.

Fasten the bandage with its string ties or Velcro fas-teners. Ensure that this attachment doesn't feel tighter than the rest of the wrap. For extra support, wrap a piece of masking or gaffer's tape over the ties or fasteners.

Tail wraps tend to slide down. If yours won't remain in place, try securing it by leaving a few sections of hair outside one or two wraps as you spiral downward. Sepa-rate a section of about ten strands, adjusting the num-ber depending on the thickness of the tail hairs. Fold them upward, and wrap the bandage over the bulk of the tail hairs. Repeat once or twice more to secure.

Because you leave the wrap in place for only a few hours, these loose hairs should hold the bandage from sliding downward. (They might look kinky when you re-move the wrap, however.)

Instead of wrapping, you can tie the tail into a knot. This quick method offers temporary protection for the skirt of a long tail. You'll find it handy on a rainy day, in a muddy arena, or with a tail that drags the ground. A knot also keeps a tail out of the way while you groom the horse—a wise precaution when you use clippers on the hind legs.

Cut masking tape into one strip four inches long, and three strips eighteen inches long. Starting at the hairs at the end of the tailbone, section strands into three parts. Braid these hairs, and when you reach the end, wrap the short piece of tape around the hairs.

Fold the tail under at the tip of the tailbone. Hold the tail in place and wrap a long strip of tape tightly twice around the hairs, about in the middle of the tail. Affix the tape over a double layer of braid, not sticking to the skin. Don't worry about cutting off the circulation, be-cause the tape will break if you wrap it too tightly.

Secure the other pieces of tape above and below the first one.

A long tail can be knotted so it does not drag on the ground.

Alternate Method: For a quick, temporary tail knot, you can fold and tie the tail. Hold the base of the tail in one hand, and with the other fold the skirt approximately in half, starting about four to six inches below the tailbone. Twine the folded section around the rest of the tail hairs, leaving a loop in the bottom. Stick the end of the wrap through this loop and pull down to secure.

Another temporary wrap is to twist the skirt hairs hard so they twine. Holding the end, wind the hairs around the tailbone. Tuck the end of the tail up into a knot.

TAIL GROOMING STEP-BY-STEP

1. Hand pick the strands.
2. Brush tail with a soft brush.
3. Style the tail by pulling hairs to thin and shorten.
4. Wash and condition the tail.
5. Protect the tail by braiding and/or wrapping.

---

7. CLIPPING TECHNIQUES—TRIM

Grooms trim all breeds of show horses so the animals look neater, though styles vary among the breeds. Clipping excess hair on the head, legs, and bridle path improves the horse's appearance by highlighting its fine bone structure.

Even for the expert, a flawless clipping job poses a difficult challenge. If you're a novice, expect to practice many times at home before you anticipate showing your horse.

Plan your clipping according to your show schedule. Until you've developed skill with the clippers, trim your horse at least one, or even two, weeks ahead. You can always touch up new growth right before the show, but if you make a major mistake, the hair needs time to grow out.

To keep a horse well trimmed, work on a two-week schedule. This will not take much time, and your horse will always look neat.

TRAINING THE HORSE TO ACCEPT CLIPPERS

If you introduce clippers with care and never lose patience while clipping, you should be able to trim any part of the horse without extra restraints. The noise and vibration of the clippers can upset a horse, and some handlers intensify the experience by forcing the horse to submit. Resorting to a twitch or tranquilizer, they create a habit of restraining the animal every time it's clipped.

By following this step-by-step procedure, you can school a horse of any age to tolerate clipping. The process might take weeks, but the results are worth it.

You should already know how your horse accepts handling, and how well it stands tied. If you anticipate it will spook, don't tie it to a tie rail or crossties. Have an assistant hold the horse, standing safely on the off side.

First let the horse become used to the sight and smell of the small or medium clippers. (If you have cordless clippers, use them for this training. The "snaky" cord bothers some nervous horses.)

Stand on the near side just ahead of the horse's shoulder, holding the appliance in your hand. Allow the animal to study the silent machine and its cord. Slowly extend the side of the clippers toward the neck and face, and look for the horse to stretch its neck toward the machine to sniff it. Pat and rub its neck with your free hand.

Move to the opposite side and repeat. Do not point the clippers' blades at the horse until it appears to accept the sight of the machine. This process might take only a minute, if your horse responds calmly.

Next slowly stroke the body of the machine on both sides of the neck and shoulder, speaking in a calm, soothing tone. Rub up and down the legs, on the back, and on the face and ears. As the horse accepts this stroking, you might simulate the noise of the machine, buzzing softly. Watch the horse's expression as you "buzz," as the noise could startle it.

Step back several feet and switch on the clippers, then switch them off. Repeat this until you're sure the horse accepts the noise.

Approach the horse slowly, speaking quietly to the animal. Place your hand on the hard muscle of the neck, and rest the body of the clippers on top of your hand. This allows the horse to become familiar with the vibration and the noise, because your hand will soothe the horse and muffle the vibration.

Starting on a muscled area reduces the reverberation. If you place the clippers against a bony area such as the shoulder or head, the bones will conduct more vibration and possibly increase any anxiety.

Depending on the horse's reaction, remove your hand and place the body of the clippers directly on the neck. If the horse continues to accept the procedure, you might stroke the clippers along the barrel, hip, and shoulder.

With a tense horse, switch off the machine after a moment, and again try stroking the animal with the silent clippers. When the horse relaxes, you might decide to quit for the day.

Some horses require that you repeat the first three steps for a week before you actually begin to clip. By avoiding the need to rush, you will allow your horse to become used to the new tool.

One approach is to play with the horse while training it. Stroke the area and talk to the animal, alternating the clippers with your hand. This can relax the animal so it learns to accept the machine.

Grooms agree the ears are the most difficult to clip. You can train a horse to accept ear clipping without having to restrain it.

Many horses enjoy having their ears stroked. As part of your grooming routine, handle ears daily. Wipe out the ears with a soft rag, and gently rub your fingers all over the outsides as well.

Introduce the clippers slowly, following the steps outlined above. Do not violate the horse's trust by rushing the clipping or trying to clip the entire ear the first time. If the horse still seems upset by the noise, you could stuff cotton inside the ears to muffle the buzzing sound.

Whenever you clip any horse, follow the process of observing the animal's reaction to the machine *before* you start clipping. Don't assume that even a gentle horse won't spook.

Tie the horse in a well-lighted area, on a dry surface close to an electrical outlet. Be sure the horse's hair and skin are clean and dry, to avoid excess wear on the clipper motor and blades. You'll simplify clipping the head by outfitting the horse in a grooming halter. (Be sure this adequately restrains your horse.)

Gather your tools:
• Medium clippers and blades—#10, #15, #30, #40 (optional)
• Small clippers and blades (optional)
• Finishing brush

CLIPPING THE HEAD AND BRIDLE PATH

- Can or jar of cleaning solution (blade wash, kerosene, kerosene and oil, or mixture of sixty percent diesel oil and forty percent motor oil);
- Cleaning rag

Many grooms begin a trimming session with the bridle path. By shortening this section of mane behind the ears, you make the horse more comfortable. The crownpiece of the halter or bridle will lie smoothly, without pressing on loose strands of the mane. Doing the bridle path first is a nonthreatening approach that allows the horse to become accustomed to the way the clippers vibrate and occasionally tug the hair against the skin.

Lengths vary according to the horse's breed type. In general, a longer bridle path looks better on a horse with a long neck. On a short neck, this length can make the neck look divided in half and the head look short.

You can test the length of a bridle path before you cut it. Have an assistant part and hold down the hairs while you step back and study the result. Remember that a too-long bridle path can take at least six months to grow back.

If a horse has a thick or coarse throatlatch, you might trim the bridle path slightly beyond the throatlatch for a trimmer look. In most cases, take the conservative approach and clip a short bridle path. It should not extend beyond the knob on the horse's poll, or down the front of the head. One way to gauge the length is to fold back the horse's ear to touch the beginning of the mane. Start the trim back toward the poll from the point reached by the tip of the ear.

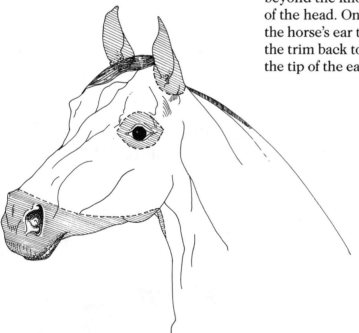

On the head, you will trim the shaded areas: bridle path, ears, eyes, muzzle, jawline, and possibly partway along cheeks and throatlatch.

When you are ready to begin, insert the #15 blade into the clippers, and move the halter crownpiece backward toward the mane. You might wish to tuck the mane under the crownpiece. If you are short, stand on a solid step stool or bench so you can see what you clip.

Press your thumb on the base of the forelock to protect it from accidental clipping. With your other hand, hold the clippers at a vertical angle for better control. Cut downward, toward the center of the bridle path.

Next move the crownpiece closer to the poll, over the section you just clipped. Place the thumb of your free hand to protect the beginning of the mane. Turn the clippers around to clip from the mane to the center of the bridle path.

As you clip, and all during the clipping session, feel the bottom of the blade for heat. A hot blade can burn the skin. If your blades are hot, switch to another set and allow the first blade to cool. Clippers vary—some newer brands heat up much more slowly than older machines.

Periodically cool and clean blades by dipping the running clippers into your jar of cleaning solution, or spray them with a commercial coolant. Allow the blades to drip dry, switch off the motor, and dab the blades with a rag.

Again protecting forelock and mane hairs, run the clippers down the path from forelock to mane, this time holding blades flat for a close cut. You may wish to switch to a finer blade, cleaning up the area by a last pass toward the ears with blades flat.

Some horses may look "scalped" after you have trimmed the bridle path. If you note a sharp difference in the color of neck and trim, blend the bridle path into the horse's neck. On both sides, run the clippers lightly up the neck hairs, starting at the crevice on the crest. When you have completed the trim, brush off loose hairs.

When clippers blades are held flat, you will cut hairs shorter on the first pass.

The skin on the crest may be sensitive, so use a light touch. If you press too deep with hot blades, you can scald the skin and cause heat bumps, which will look unattractive. (You're also punishing the horse, which may resent clipping next time.)

You might wish to use a finer blade, up to #30, for a very clean bridle path. Protect the exposed skin by keeping the horse out of intense light, or apply a strong sunburn block cream. The skin can sunburn and the horse may not allow you to put on its halter for the show!

On some horses, you might undercut the first two

inches of mane hair, so the mane lies flat. You can also undercut the forelock on the near side, planning to pull it over to the right and tuck it under a halter's cheekpiece or bridle's browband.

Before trimming long hairs from the head of the horse, remove the stable halter, if worn. Take it off its head and rebuckle it around the neck. Be sure you untie the lead rope and hold it in your hand. If the horse pulls back with the halter around its neck, it could injure itself.

Start with the #15 blade on medium clippers, or use the small clippers with finer blades. On the muzzle, press clippers against the skin to trim long whiskers. Run the blades against, across, and with the feelers. As you complete each stroke, lift the blades up and away from the horse's skin.

Again, observe your horse's reaction. A sensitive animal might strike out with a front foot when you "tickle" its whiskers. Stand on the horse's side, never directly in front of it.

Use the fingers of your free hand to stretch the skin so you can move the blades over the contours of the muzzle and chin. Angle the clippers outward from the mouth, while holding onto the jaw with your other hand so the horse does not flap its lips or mouth the cord.

It is possible to make the muzzle appear smaller by using a close blade for a surgical clip. Switch to the #40 blade and taper the clip up into the jawline. This also darkens the muzzle by revealing the skin, a desirable effect in breeds like the Arabian.

Alternate Method: Some grooms feel the clipper blades yank the whiskers. You can use blunt scissors, or try a hand-held disposable razor for a very close shave.

The safety razor can blend the hairs of the muzzle into the rest of the face. Try this tool in the winter, when the horse has more hair on its face. Use it with care, only on a calm horse, to avoid cutting the animal's skin.

Grooms following the European tradition may leave feelers on the muzzle or around the eyes unclipped. In the United States, however, unclipped whiskers are considered untidy.

Continue along the jawline, holding the horse's head with your free hand. You might wish to start under the jaw, where any mistakes will not be as obvious.

The small clippers are easier to use on the rounded contours of the muzzle.

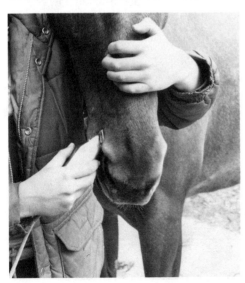

You will have better control of the depth of cut if you hold the clippers upside down, straight out (perpendicular). To avoid gouging the skin, hold your hand steady.

You may feel it's safer to place the blades flush against the skin, since there is less chance of nipping the skin when you maintain a constant light pressure. You will cut close to the skin, however, with less margin for error.

Whichever way you choose to angle the blades, run them with the grain of the hairs, in downward strokes. If you hold the blades flat, don't press down too hard. Pushing on the skin can make the hairs stand up and result in an uneven clip or the unsightly "chop marks." For a longer cut, lightly skim only the tips of the hairs with the blades. You'll need a steady hand for the best effect.

Between the jawbones, you can turn the clippers so they face the horse's neck, clipping with the growth. Near the throatlatch, contour the horse's jowl by cutting the long hairs. Push the horse's head up or pull the skin upward to tighten the loose skin, so you don't nip the wrinkles.

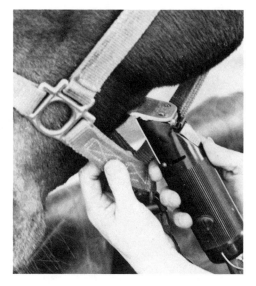

Holding the machine perpendicular controls the depth of the cut along the jawline.

You may use a coarser blade to blend the jawline into the cheek, such as a #10 or #8½. It takes practice to learn the technique of pressing firmly, gradually lifting the blade to shade the clipped hairs into the unclipped ones.

On the cheeks, you can just trim the ends of the guard hairs, or blend the trimmed jawline into the uncut hair on the cheeks. Here you must use a very light touch. Hold the clippers perpendicular, blades facing into the horse's jaw to help you control the depth of the cut.

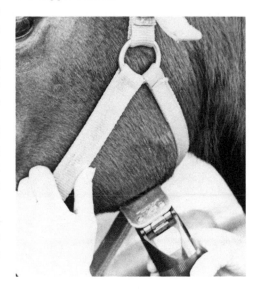

Comb cheek hairs into the jawline with the clipper blades.

You can make a jowl look larger by cutting the hairs with a close blade (#40). Clip the muscle over the bone all the way up to the jaw line.

Work quickly to avoid irritating your horse. Use long strokes and broad sweeps whenever possible. Don't pick away at stray hairs for more than a few minutes, or your horse may become bored or upset.

Next, carefully clip the long "cat" hairs from around the eye. Cup your free hand over the horse's eye, with your thumb protecting the lower lashes. Cut against the grain of these hairs, and keep the clipper blades pointed away from the eye at all times.

These feelers underneath the eye are often difficult to clip, since you can easily nip the tips of the horse's eyelash. If your horse will allow it, carefully lift up its eyelid so the lash is flipped up out of the way.

You may find it easier to switch to the small clippers for this area.

An eye will look larger if you clip the skin around the eye closely, with a #40 blade. Trimming directly against bone is difficult, and you will need to blend carefully to avoid the result of black "raccoon" rings around the horse's eyes. (These are most likely on a gray horse.) Here, you must stand on a stool so you are above the horse's head to direct the clippers.

Trim the hairs on the flat bones of your horse's face, especially if it has a lot of white. You will trim against the grain. Here you can select the #8½ blade for a longer cut (so the pink skin won't show) or the #15 for a cleaner (and pinker) look. Again, your goal is to blend the clipped white hairs into the darker ones.

If your horse has a wide muzzle, you can try to decrease the width visually. Clip the face up to the jowl, so you leave the jowl hair thicker.

Clipping the Ears   With most horses it works best to save the ears for last, after you have trimmed the bridle path and face. By that time, the animal is accustomed to the sound and vibration.

The type of show you attend can influence the cleanness of your clip. For a major event, most grooms want the ear perfectly clipped, with no extra hairs.

Stand on a stool so you can see what you're clipping. With either a #15, #30, or #40 blade, start on the outside edges of the nearside ear. Pointing the blades downward, work from the tip to the base on both sides of each ear. Use long, smooth strokes to avoid gouging the ear, and "scoop" to throw loose hair outside the ear. When you switch sides, be aware that your horse may be more sensitive with the offside ear.

Alternate Method: Gently squeeze the ear closed and place the blades about one inch below the base of the ear. Swoop up the outside edge of the closed ear to the tip. Next start at the top of the ear and go right down the outside edge. This method may be better for a sensitive animal.

Repeat this about three times, clipping both straight and at angles to blend the trim. Ears are difficult to trim, so expect to practice many times before you produce professional results.

If you must remove the hairs from the insides of the ears, brush the fuzz outward with your finger, so it sticks out well. Gently turn the ear inside out and hold your thumb to protect the interior opening from loose hair. Clip the hair close, cutting with the grain of the hair.

Finish by bending the ear to the side, outer edges pointing toward the ground, so you can use the clippers to scoop out any hair you missed. This keeps loose hair out of the ear.

Alternate Methods: 1. You do not need to trim inside of the ear at all. Shows don't require this grooming. Leave the natural protection and compromise by trimming only the fuzz that protrudes from the ear. Hold the ear closed and clip off hair that sticks out.

2. On some horses you can manipulate the ear to clip it without actually inserting the clippers. Fold the ear closed and push the hairs to the outside. This is most successful if you do not plan to remove all traces of hair from inside the ear.

3. For an elegant look, leave matching triangles of unclipped hair on the tip of the ears. Cut a "V" shape down the tip, in a direction that follows the shape of the ear. A sharp point makes ears appear more refined and enhances the tips curving toward each other.

Place a damp cloth or baby towelette over your thumb and wipe out the ears to remove any loose hair. You can wipe out the ears with cotton soaked in alcohol. Or rub baby oil inside the ears for a nice finish, which also moisturizes a dry, scaly ear. A light coating of Vaseline can protect the ears from insects.

To counteract itchy skin after clipping, apply baby oil to the horse's muzzle. Rub down the face with a hot towel. (Soak a towel in water just below the boiling point. Wearing rubber gloves to protect your hands, wring out the towel and rub the horse.) This also removes any loose hairs and flattens hair of the trimmed areas.

For winter "Shaggy Show," a groom chose not to trim the insides of this buckskin's ears.

CLIPPING THE LEGS

With a #10 or #15 blade, clip legs about a week before the show for best results. If you must clip a day or two before, use a coarser blade, such as the #8½. Some people use the large clippers for trimming the legs, especially if the horse has heavy leg hair. With these,

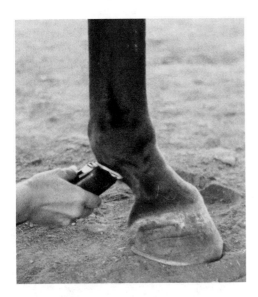

Roll the blades along the back of the leg to end at the heel.

protect the horse's tail from being sucked into the clipper's air-intake vent by tying up or knotting the tail.

For leg clipping, you have two choices: You can trim longer hairs at coronet, fetlock, and the backs of the legs, or you can "boot up" the legs, trimming all surfaces from knee or hock to hoof.

When you trim a leg, watch that the horse doesn't quickly raise its foot. A sensitive animal's reaction could surprise you, especially if you nick the edge of a blade on its pastern or coronet.

To trim, start at the coronet on one front leg. Hold one hand on the coronary band and press into the band with your thumb. This makes the hairs stand up. With the clippers upside down, comb up and out, moving your thumb and the blades around the hoof until the hairs that encircle the hoof are even. You can hold the blades flat or at an angle.

For the back of the fetlock, cut with the grain of the hair. Hold the clippers upside down, pointing the blades toward the horse's heel. Start clipping the long hairs behind the knee or hock. Follow the curve of the fetlock, working under the joint, around the ergot, and down to end at the bulb of the heel.

Work on both front legs from one side, then move to the other side to complete the front legs.

For a closer cut under the pastern and on the bulbs of the heel, turn the clippers with the blades pointing up to trim against the grain of the hair. Clip close, because the fetlock area picks up a lot of dirt, but be careful not to nick the skin.

The ergot on the tip of the fetlock may be so long it hinders clipping. You can make it smaller by peeling layers, rubbing it with pumice, or clipping it short with wire cutters. (Ask your farrier to perform this trimming.)

If your horse is prone to scratches, or sores at the back of the fetlock, leave a line of longer hairs to form a ducktail over the cleft at the back of the pastern. This hair will channel off bath or rain water to help prevent scratches.

Avoid a color line by blending the trimmed hair into the untrimmed areas. You can shade the dividing line by going with the grain, either pointing the clipper blades downward or holding the machine upside down.

Repeat these steps on the hind legs. Clipping is safer and easier if the horse keeps its weight on the leg. Ask an assistant to lean against the horse's opposite hip so the animal does not rest a leg. If you're alone, grab hold of the tail and lean your weight against it to keep the horse's weight on its leg. If the horse starts to move, you'll feel it and can move out of the way.

Instead of clipping all of one leg before moving to the next, you can work your way around the feet by clipping all four coronets, then the fetlocks, etc. By this method, if something prevents you from finishing the session, you won't end up with a horse unevenly clipped. (The clippers might fail, or a power outage could occur.)

If a leg is blemished, you might be able to camouflage the area somewhat by sculpting the hair. Clip closely over the blemish. On the surrounding hair, lift the blades from the leg to leave more hair surrounding the area. This technique requires expert control of the clippers, so you won't get a two-tone look.

Clipping can also touch up hair on the hocks. If the horse rubbed its hocks, new hair may grow in coarsely. The hair affects the appearance of the hocks, so trim it close to the bone.

The time of year can also change the texture of white hair on the legs. Some horses grow thick, coarse hair in the winter. Clip white socks and stockings so the hair lies down.

You may prefer to boot up the horse's legs, clipping all surfaces closely. First plan how far up the leg you will clip, which may depend on the color of the horse's legs. On a chestnut or bay, you may wish to boot up slightly above the ankle joint. With these colors, it's often easier to clip all around the ankle than to try shading the clipped back of the leg with the unclipped front.

With a white-legged horse, you will probably clip below the contour of the knee or hock. Booting up helps whiten the legs by removing badly stained hairs, and the shorter hairs will collect less dirt. When you clip the hairs short, you encourage quicker growth. When hair grows faster, you do need to reclip more often to keep legs looking white.

When booting up, avoid the "poodle" look by finishing your cut at the contour of a joint—ankle, knee, or hock. The natural shadows of knee and hock will help conceal the contrast between clipped and unclipped hairs.

You want an even clip on all four legs, so use a #10 blade (#15 for finer hair) for results that look natural.

BOOTING UP THE LEGS

Angling the blades allows you to cut only as short as desired.

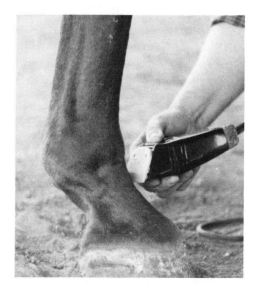

Blending is easier, and the clipped hairs will still have some shine.

With white legs, you might select a finer blade, such as a #30. This will cut the hairs shorter and make blending more difficult. (When cutting hairs closer to the skin, clip two or three weeks before the show to avoid unsightly "pink" legs, in which the skin shows under the just-clipped hairs.)

Start lower on the foreleg than you plan to end, so you can blend into the trim from above. Below hock or knee, stand the clippers on edge to see where the blades will start to cut the hairs. Work down with the hair, because it's difficult to keep the clip even if you work up the leg. For a good blend, let the blades roll down the fetlock and ankle.

Next clip the sides of the leg. On the hairs in the hollows around the tendons, gently roll the skin first to one side, then the other. This will expose the hair to the clipper blades. Clip in long, downward strokes to avoid lines.

On the front of the leg, the hair may be thicker around the knee. Control the depth of the cut by placing your fingers between the leg and the clippers. Stand the blades on edge and slide them down the leg so they roll right over the hair at the coronet.

Trim the hind legs by also starting below where you want the clip to end—usually below the contour of the hock. On the hind leg, this would be about two-thirds of the way up the cannon, where the hair starts to run straight down rather than sideways or on an angle.

For a horse that is hairy at the point of the hock, clip a bit higher. Then aim your clipper blades down the back of the hock to trim only the longest hairs.

Boot up the hind legs using the same steps. Be careful when trimming the inside of the hind leg, around the large vein.

If the horse has long hairs above or behind the knee, or around the hock, knock off the ends so they don't stick out. With a horse that has exceptionally long hair, you will probably choose to body clip anyway (so you wouldn't try to blend the booting up into the unclipped hairs).

TRIMMING STEP-BY-STEP

1. Trim the bridle path with a #15—clean up with a #30.
2. Clip muzzle, jawline, and cheeks with a #15. Blend with the #8½ or #10—clean up with a #40.
3. Clip cat hairs around eye with a #15.
4. Trim ears with a #15, #30, or #40.
5. Trim fetlocks and pasterns with a #8½, #10, or #15.
6. Boot up legs with a #10 or #15.

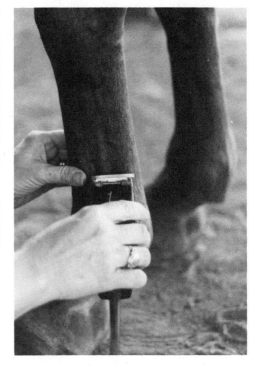

Pull skin to the side so clippers can trim hair along the tendons.

8. CLIPPING TECHNIQUES—BODY

Clipping the horse's entire body shortens the long winter coat. This prevents the horse from sweating excessively and possibly becoming chilled while wet. It also makes the horse look more handsome and simplifies grooming.

This is a tedious chore. Clipping can last up to two hours at a time and might need to be repeated several times a year. Many grooms claim it's detrimental to cut the tips of healthy hairs, and the resulting color loss can be very unattractive. (A Palomino will change from gold to mushy oatmeal!)

ALTERNATIVES TO BODY CLIPPING

Instead of body clipping, you can use artificial means to convince the horse not to grow a long winter coat. It grows more hair according to the change in the hours of daylight in the fall and winter seasons. Shorter days reduce the hours of daylight. Less sunlight being filtered into the horse's eye triggers the body to prepare for shorter, colder days.

If you prefer not to clip, you can prolong hours of light by using artificial barn lights. The horse should experience 16 hours of light, a combination of sunlight and barn lights. A recommended amount is from six to ten foot-candles, or a 200-watt bulb approximately ten feet above the stall. (You can also use a fluorescent light fixture.) Position the lights securely, out of the horse's reach, so they illuminate the stall with no shadows.

Set your stall lights on a timer for extra light in the morning and evening. The sixteen hours tell the horse's system that the days have not changed in length—they provide the same amount of light in December as there was in June.

A draft-free barn and blanketing keep the horse warm during the cold months. The blanket flattens the hair. If the hair stands up, the horse experiences a chilled feeling.

Some grooms add heavy blankets on show horses during the summer months, as soon as the days begin to shorten and the nights to drop into the sixties. Blanketing might begin with a sheet or blanket added just at night, then progress to a blanket worn all the time as temperatures continue to drop into the fifties.

In addition to a blanket, you'll probably outfit the horse in a hood. Some animals will grow longer hair on the neck and head when the body is covered.

A close-fitting "bodysuit" of polar fleece adds warmth without weight. This stretchy material contours to your horse and maximizes the warmth of a blanket.

Avoid exposing the horse to cold, which makes the hair stand on end. Schedule schooling sessions in the warmest part of the day, not early mornings.

Exercise and feed that keeps the horse warm also help sustain a shorter coat. An animal in good condition, under lights and covered with blankets, shouldn't grow long hair. Its coat will still change from a summer to a naturally thicker winter coat.

Stallions usually grow a shorter winter coat. On mares and geldings, however, some will grow a heavy coat no matter what. Clipping is the only alternative for fall and winter showing. And once you body clip a horse, you'll have to continue the practice every year.

TIMING

The experts agree that the timing of the body clip is crucial. You can wait until the winter coat is apparent or fully grown, or choose to clip when the hair is longer than one-quarter inch. Some grooms feel that the longer the coat length when you clip, the greater the effect on the coat color.

Your schedule varies with the weather, the individual animal, and its competition schedule. Some grooms first clip in August. With a horse that is showing on the indoor Eastern circuit, grooms clip sometime in October. If your show season ends in the fall and begins again in February, you might decide to wait till January, a month before the first show. Four weeks will allow the coat to regain shine and color.

The coats of some horses will look show-ready if clipped two weeks before a show. With others, clipping one week ahead yields the desired show coat. The coat usually appears best a few days after the clip, but it's safer to clip a horse too early than too late. Any mistakes have a chance to grow out.

BODY CLIPPING PROCEDURE

Start with a clean horse. You can't expect good results if the clipper blades have to push through dirt or dried sweat. Clean hair allows the clippers to cut smoothly, avoiding clipper lines. Also, the blades will not dull as quickly. Bathe the horse either that day or the day before, and be sure the horse's coat is completely dry. Instead of bathing, you can vacuum thoroughly to remove all traces of dirt, and brush the coat well.

Prepare for clipping by locating at least one assistant. Your handler should hold the horse's lead rope for precise control.

Clip in an area with bright overhead light and as few shadows as possible. The ground should be dry, and the area should be close to an electrical outlet. Ideally the horse will not stand in a draft, which could chill its freshly-clipped skin.

Protect the tail by braiding and wrapping to keep it out of the way. You don't want to clip any tail hairs by mistake.

Gather the following tools:
- Body clippers with new or newly sharpened blades, or two sets of medium clippers with wide blades (having two machines allows one set to cool while you continue with the other)
- Clipper oil
- Blade wash, kerosene, or kerosene and oil solution

Arrows show the direction of clipper strokes along the contours of the horse's body. Always clip against the grain.

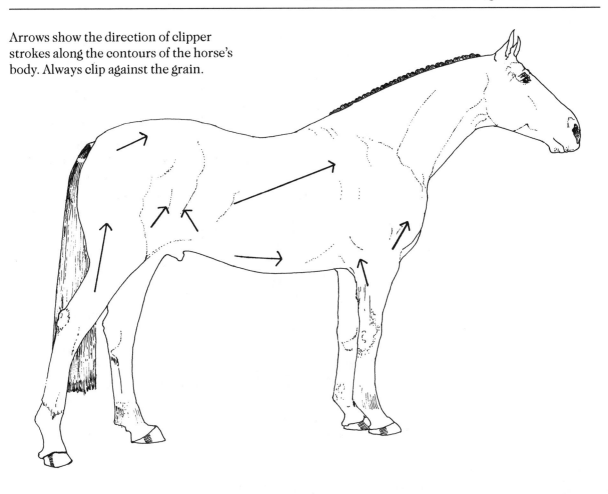

The first stroke sweeps upward along the barrel.

- Cleaning rag
- Towel

If you don't have new blades, reserve the newest, sharpest ones for use on visible, important sections like the shoulder, neck, and hindquarters. Use the older blades for the legs and underneath the belly.

Begin your first clipper stroke on a comparatively insensitive area. Most grooms start on the near side, on the barrel, about where your knee rests while you are in the saddle.

Hold the clippers so they balance in your hand. Clip a long, slow sweep upward against the hair, keeping the blades flat against the skin so the bottom blades can feed hair into the top, cutting blades.

When using the large clippers, you may need to adjust the tension knob for a closer clip. Use sufficient pressure so you don't tickle the horse and it twitches its skin; but try to float the blades as you clip against the flow of hair. Use your body weight with the stroke of the machine. Avoid letting the teeth or blade edge dig into the skin, because this pressure will produce welts.

Your first sweep will be about three inches wide. Follow it with another upward stroke that overlaps the top edge of the first by one-half to three-quarters inch. On all strokes, try to make a continual run with the blades, rather than clipping a short distance several times.

While clipping, try to work as efficiently as possible, without excessive picking at certain spots. The process can be arduous with the large clippers, which become extremely heavy after the first ten minutes. In this respect, you see the advantage of a model with a separate motor and clipper head. Make it easier for both you and your horse by clipping in segments, allowing ten-minute breaks in between.

Always clip against the flow of hair. Clipper tracks, ridges of slightly longer hair, result from not cutting directly against the hair, or the blades becoming dull or misaligned. Prevent tracks by following upward the lay of the hair, and by keeping blades flat against the skin. You can erase them by clipping the area again.

Let the blades float against the skin.

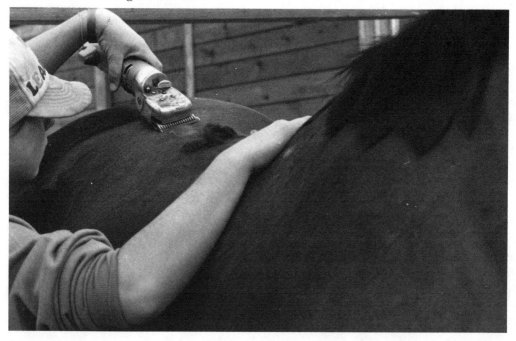

Some ridges may be temporary, caused by pressure of the blades or a reaction to the kerosene solution you use to wash the blades. You might wait until the next day to see if the ridges have disappeared. Picking at them now could make them more difficult to match with the surrounding hairs later.

Continue working toward the neck, making your sweeps broader as you approach the chest.

A difficult area is where the mane grows from the crest, especially if the horse has large fatty deposits on its neck. Clip the area in one long sweep, holding down mane hairs with your free hand (or have your assistant help) and keeping your clipper hand steady. It is safer to leave some body hair adjacent to the mane, rather than nicking any mane hairs.

Alternate Method: Switch to medium clippers. Hold one hand down over the mane, and with the clippers upside down, trim the extra body hair.

Next work on the hip and flank, starting from the hock and moving upward toward the croup.

Use shorter, rounder strokes on the hairs where the hip and flank meet. For smoother clipping, it may help to stretch the skin over the flank.

At the tail, clip to form a point of body hair above the top of the tail hairs. On the near side, hold the clippers right next to the edge of the tail, where it meets the body flesh. Clipping against the hair, make one leg of a triangle. Match this line on the off side. Complete this side of the horse by clipping from forearm to shoulder.

Repeat clipping on the opposite side of the horse.

Clip chest, belly, legs, and head, switching to medium clippers as necessary to touch up certain areas. The smaller blades fit better against the bony prominences.

The hock and the loose skin of elbows and chest challenge even the experts. Have an assistant hold the horse's foreleg outstretched while you use medium clippers on the loose skin of the elbow and the chest between the forelegs.

Brush or vacuum to remove all loose hair.

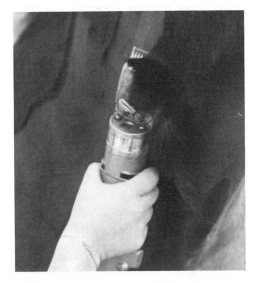

Allow clippers to glide along the neck.

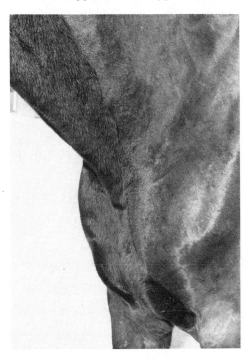

It's best to clip one side first, then the other. Here you can see the difference between clipped and unclipped sides.

CARE AFTER CLIPPING

Avoid a bristly look by continuing to rub the coat daily. Curry and brush the clipped coat regularly to restore its gleam.

After clipping, you need to blanket the horse routinely as protection against the cold. Some grooms feel one heavy blanket is adequate. Others layer coverings, building up to as many as three blankets at night. Some clipped horses will also need to have their legs wrapped for warmth, depending on the drafts within the barn. Check the horse's body to be sure it's not sweating underneath the blanket.

Many horses will need to be reclipped again, as the coat grows out. For instance, a horse clipped in October may need to be redone in December. If you clip too early in the season, you may encourage the coat to grow more quickly. Some horses may need reclipping three or four times, once a month, or before each show.

Avoid clipping in the spring, while the new growth begins to appear. Clipping will damage the new hairs that replace those of the winter coat.

To counteract the harm of clipping and to add a gloss, rinse the coat in an oil rinse. Add one capful of mineral or baby oil to a gallon of water, and rinse the coat. You can also purchase commercial products for after-clipping treatment. Ultra Hot Oil Treatment will restore color after body clipping and moisturize the skin.

Or try an old favorite method to bring back the color, with mayonnaise. On a warm day (or in a warm barn) bathe the horse and massage whole-egg mayonnaise into the coat. Blanket the horse in a sheet you reserve for this treatment, and put it in a stall for four hours. Body heat will "cook" the mayonnaise.

After four hours, shampoo the horse thoroughly to remove all traces of the mayonnaise. Don't leave the mayonnaise on too long, or the treatment can blister the skin.

After you exercise the horse, spray it with a solution of one-third water, one-third vinegar, and one-third baby oil. Rub this into the coat. After five to ten days, your horse should be back to its original coat color.

Alternate Method: You can leave the saddle area unclipped to protect the loins. Clipping the hair so short can cause discomfort, and even soreness. Outline a saddle patch with tape, and clip inside the lines. The unclipped patch won't show when you saddle up.

CLIPPING STYLES

At major shows through the colder months, almost all horses will be clipped over the entire body. You may see eventers, jumpers, or field hunters groomed in any of the following styles at smaller competitions.

1. *Hunter clip.* The horse's body is clipped, but the winter coat remains untouched on the legs and sometimes under the saddle. This style offers the benefits of less sweating and faster cooling out, yet it provides a certain amount of protection from the elements.

You can use masking tape or a felt tip pen to mark the clipping lines. Above the forearms and gaskins, follow the contour of the muscle.

2. *Trace clip.* This style is rarely seen in this country, but it is popular in England, especially on ponies. The body is clipped part way up the sides, along the heat path. Winter hair remains on the back, legs, and head, while lower neck, sides, belly, and around the flank are clipped. The style protects horses in work that live or stand out in the elements for prolonged periods.

3. *Strip clip.* You can trim only certain areas on the horse's underside, feathering up along the sides. Usual areas are the belly and the neck.

BODY CLIPPING STEP-BY-STEP:

1. Start on the barrel.
2. Clip the neck.
3. Clip the hip, flank, and back.
4. Touch up the tail area.
5. Clip chest and belly.
6. Clip legs.
7. Clip head.
8. Brush or vacuum, and blanket.

---

9. HOOF BEAUTY

Any horse should have feet that are well trimmed. In some show divisions, you might even show the horse unshod. Usually, you'll assure that your farrier shoes the horse neatly.

Hire a farrier who knows how to prepare your horse's feet for your show discipline. Learn the current rules that apply to your type of horse, and be sure your farrier shoes your horse to meet specific requirements. If your breed is subject to a specific toe length, schedule the shoeing fairly close to the date of the show.

Your horse's feet should match its conformation in size and shape. Large feet appropriately fit a large animal. On every horse, the front hooves are round and rear hooves oval. The base of each hoof should rest flat on the ground, and the coronary bands should line up parallel to the surface. A shod horse will have six to eight nails on each shoe, three or four nails on each side of the walls of the hoof. Usually the farrier will tack nails in low on the hoof walls, and file the clinches (ends of the nails) almost level with the hoof's surface. If he chooses shoes with toe clips, the clips are flat with the surface of the hoof.

Unless you're showing your horse in hand, the judge probably won't scrutinize its feet closely. In a halter class, he or she will note the signs of a healthy hoof—a solid-looking, dense surface that shows no evidence of chipping or splitting. The surface appears smooth, without obvious ridges or rings. The hoof has a natural luster, created by the periople, a protective layer that preserves the hoof's natural moisture.

Most grooms preserve the hoof's natural appearance by regular applications of hoof dressing, either ointment or oil. In the show ring, they choose hoof oil or hoof polish for cosmetic reasons.

Grooms of different breeds seem to adopt one of two basic approaches to the preparation of the hoof. For many halter classes and the showier breeds, the ideal hoof is polished to a hard gloss. Grooms of less flashy performance horses prefer to use hoof conditioners to dress up the hoof, which add a softer, more natural luster.

Before you apply any cosmetic product to the hoof, clean all four hooves thoroughly. Pick out the soles and around the frogs, and brush the soles clean with the stiff brush. If a piece of the frog has shredded loose, tear or clip it off. Remove dirt from the outside of hooves with the stiff brush. During a bath or rinse, spray hooves clean with a high pressure nozzle or scrub them with a rubber brush.

Check each shoe to confirm that it remains firmly attached to the hoof. You should see no gap between the hoof and the shoe. Feel the clinches on each side of the wall, which hold the shoe in place. Contact your farrier if you find a loose shoe or a clinch that's worked its way loose, so you can wiggle the nail.

APPLYING HOOF DRESSING OR POLISH

When applying a hoof product, stand the horse on a level, clean surface. The hooves should not contact dirt, straw, or shavings, which will adhere to the hoof dressing or polish. You should have clipped hair around the coronary band.

You will need a stiff scrub brush, hoof dressing, and a small paintbrush.

Establish a routine for painting the feet. Start on one side and move in the same pattern, so the horse is prepared for you to work on the next foot.

With the paintbrush, apply a thin coating of hoof dressing or oil. Brush the first line just below the hairs of the coronary band. When applying this preparation for cosmetic purposes, don't allow any to mix into the hairs.

Allow the product to dry before moving the horse out of the grooming area. Some dressings will pick up dirt while the horse exercises, so be prepared to use the stiff brush to knock off any accumulated dirt right before the horse enters the show ring.

You may prefer to apply hoof dressing after scrubbing the hooves during a bath or rinse. Leave the horse tied in the wash rack to allow an oil-type dressing to dry thoroughly.

If you choose to paint the hoof with a polish, the ideal look resembles a freshly manicured fingernail. The hoof must be clean, smooth, and shiny.

Here you will use:
- A medium grade sandpaper, steel wool, or a hoof sanding sponge
- Stiff brush with plastic or wire bristles
- Hoof polish
- Small paintbrush or dauber

Again, clean hooves thoroughly. To smooth the surface, use the stiff brush or steel wool, or sand lightly with sandpaper. Wipe the sandpaper carefully, angling it both vertically and horizontally on the hoof wall. Some grooms sand only the top ring, just below the coronary band. Others aim to level the entire hoof into a smooth surface. For this result, you may need to sand several times.

Sanding can damage the hoof wall and periople, which can affect the hoof's condition. In most cases, the judge will not closely examine the surface of a hoof that sinks into the arena footing.

Instead of sandpaper, try using an electric human nail buffer to smooth the ridges of the hoof. Grooms who recommend this tool feel that it allows better control of the amount of pressure. The result is a less porous hoof, that is not as likely to become dished as may result from sandpaper.

You can also scrub feet with an SOS pad while you bathe or rinse the horse. This cleans the hoof and smooths its surface, with less damaging effects than sandpaper.

Before applying the polish, you can wipe rubbing alcohol on the surface of the hooves. This prevents the polish from drying the hoof excessively.

Choose the proper color of hoof polish to complement your horse's leg coloring. Usually you use black only on a dark hoof. (A light gray horse may have dark feet, and ermine spots on a white-legged horse may indicate dark

Hoof oil is painted on this jumper with a small brush.

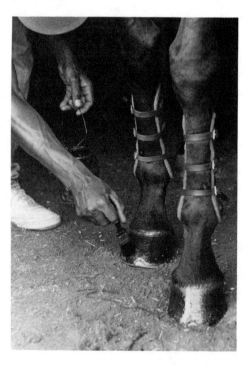

feet.) A white hoof that is polished black appears unnatural, although it's accepted in some breeds.

Clear polish matches any hoof, although brown looks good on a chestnut horse. It adds a leggy look by matching the color of the legs.

Secure the bottle or can of hoof polish into a small box, to prevent it from tipping over during use.

Dip the brush or applicator into the liquid polish, and stroke on a light coating. Start at the top of the hoof to apply polish below the hairs of the coronary band. As any excess drips down the hoof, continue down the front and sides. Circle the polish around the entire hoof so you don't end up with vertical lines, and be sure to cover the heels.

If the hoof is striped, you can either apply a coating of clear polish, or follow the stripes with rows of colored and clear polish. Or, you can define the stripes with colored polish, allow it to dry, then cover the entire hoof with a second coat of clear polish. To paint over the lines of the hoof requires a steady hand and a patient horse.

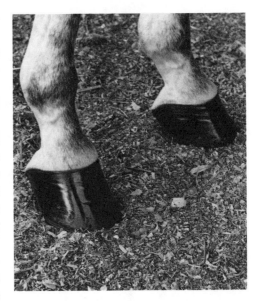

An Arabian models sanded and polished hooves.

Alternate Methods: 1. For a durable shine, wax the hoof with a paste wax polish. Buff the hoof with a towel—then brush on a thin coating of black hoof polish.

2. Spray a light coating of Amway Shoe Spray over the hoof polish for an extra shine.

For a smooth, patent leather look, you can apply a coating of resin material, let it dry, then buff it to a high shine.

You want all four hooves to match, especially on a horse shown in a halter class. On some breeds of performance horses, grooms polish only the front feet.

Remove polish, as it prevents the hoof from "breathing." The hoof is made of fibrous protein, and excess polish can dry it. If shows are close together, you might choose to leave on a layer of clear polish. This will protect the hoof and make more sanding unnecessary.

To remove polish, use Absorbine liniment or Ultra Hoof Polish Remover. Either will avoid damaging the periople. Be sure to treat the hoof daily with a conditioner, to restore any loss of moisture.

SOME FAVORITE HOOF DRESSINGS

1. A light coating of Fiebing's hoof dressing will darken the hoof.
2. Mix Fiebing's with Straight Arrow's The Hoofmaker, which adds lanolin and results in a thicker consistency than plain oil.
3. Add a small amount of pine tar or turpentine to your preferred brand of hoof oil. This mixture will shine as it moisturizes.
4. Dampen a rag with a palmful of baby oil, and rub it into the hoof. Use a clean, dry rag to rub the oil off the hoof—this adds a slight luster.
5. Some English grooms recommend rubbing a cut onion on the hoof to bring out a natural gloss.

10. BODY ENHANCEMENT

Besides body clipping, additional procedures can refine the horse's appearance. You can highlight certain parts of the body by these external applications.

SWEATING

In many breeds of halter and performance horses, the fashionable competitor looks lean yet muscular. Exercise plus sweat wraps reduce fat on neck, throat, shoulders, and body to create this desirable appearance.

When the horse wears a wrap during or after exercise, the garment induces heavy perspiration. This extracts excess water from the cells of the skin. The heat created under the wrap also makes the skin look thinner and finer, so muscles and veins appear closer to the surface. Sweating of the body, especially the shoulders, tends to bring out the oil in the horse's coat.

Don't expect sweating to change a horse's conformation. Sweating temporarily reduces the water content of cells, and they will return to their normal size the following day. Even daily sweating will reduce only a certain amount of fat, and a horse with a heavy neck won't attain the desirable "pencil" neck fashionable in many breeds.

Sweating benefits most stallions, which usually develop heavy crests. It is also standard procedure to "tone and trim" Arabians, Saddlebreds, and Quarter Horse types shown in halter classes. Some grooms use the neck sweat routinely on performance horses as well. Others feel it is necessary only on a horse with a thick throatlatch, which hinders its ability to flex at the poll.

For greatest improvement, select the appropriate garment. You can choose from various styles to fit around the throatlatch, neck, neck and throatlatch, neck and shoulders, or the full body.

Look for synthetic linings that will remain supple, developed specifically for sweating. Standard wrap materials include Neoprene, vinyl, and laminated plastics.

Use the above materials for a short time, as these synthetics create heat and possible irritation. For daily wear, choose throatlatch sweats lined in more comfortable wool, felt, or fleece.

A rubberized lining, commonly used for throat and neck sweats, will wrap securely in place with Velcro closures. To use a horse-sized wrap on younger horses, sew additional sections of Velcro onto the wrap so it can fit snugly on a smaller neck.

Some grooms claim the rubber material is difficult to clean, becomes stiff with use, and is likely to rot and crack from sweat. You can extend the life of the wrap that tears by repairing it with a glue such as Shoe Goo, available from shoe repair shops.

To sweat larger areas, such as the neck and shoulders, shoulders, or full body from ears to tail, you can fit the horse with a vinyl wrap, similar to a tarpaulin material. Use this alone or in combination with a rubberized neck wrap.

Some manufacturers offer laminated wraps, made of layers of different plastics and fabrics. These garments may last longer than the rubberized type because the inner lining is durable and easy to clean.

Under the sweating garment, you may apply a sweating lotion to induce sweating. You can purchase a commercial product made for this purpose, such as Ultra Great Neck II. Or, use one of the traditional liquids, either Listerine antiseptic, glycerin, or a blend of one-half glycerin and one-half rubbing alcohol.

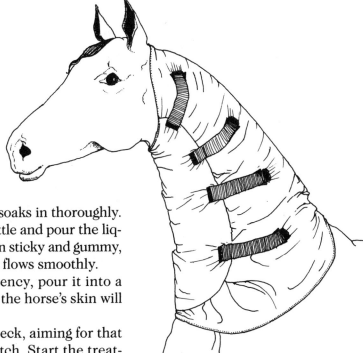

A full neck sweat covers the entire neck.

Work Listerine into the skin so it soaks in thoroughly. If you choose glycerin, shake the bottle and pour the liquid onto the skin. Because this is often sticky and gummy, dilute it with water or Listerine so it flows smoothly.

With any liquid of a thin consistency, pour it into a pump spray bottle. Spraying it onto the horse's skin will keep it off your hands.

Usually you'll sweat the horse's neck, aiming for that long, slim neck with a fine throatlatch. Start the treatment by first grooming the crest, throatlatch, and sides of the neck as you would normally, currying and brushing so the coat is clean.

Next apply the sweating lotion. Avoid putting any product on the face or the jowl—as the horse sweats, it might fling the mixture into its eyes.

Alternate Method: Some grooms prefer not to apply any product underneah the wrap. Certain types of fabric produce good results without any need for a product, and many horses can develop skin irritation from lotions.

Fit the wrap onto the horse. For more heat, you can cover the neck with plastic wrap before fitting the garment. Or, some grooms place two sweat wraps on the horse at once. Depending on the horse, you might fit the heavy, rubberized garment first, then cover it with the lighter, vinyl wrap.

Consider the weather when you select wraps and lotions. In the colder months you might use the heavier wraps next to the skin. The commercial sweating products often have greater effect in cool weather. In summer, switch to lighter wraps, because the horse will sweat more readily.

After wrapping the horse, let it stand for about an hour before you exercise it on the longe or hot walker. (Some trainers pony or ride, but the wrap can inhibit the horse's ability to flex at the poll, thus affecting the horse's training.) With some horses, you will achieve better results by sweating twice a day, with two twenty- or thirty-minute exercise periods. This creates less stress, especially on a halter horse.

After work, remove the wrap when horse has cooled out completely. (Some trainers exercise the horse and then wrap it.) Prevent skin irritation by washing off any remaining sweat before you put the horse back into its stall. Use plain water to remove any product residue, so it doesn't dry into the skin. Also rinse the wraps after use.

Use the full body wrap when the horse is so fat its body appears coarse, or you want to reduce fat in several areas at once. This wrap is more effective in cool weather.

Whenever you leave a stalled horse wrapped, be sure to monitor the animal. A wrap of synthetic or rubber material can cause such extreme loss of moisture that you could make the horse severely dehydrated. If you do leave a wrap in place for a long period of time, check for dehydration by pinching the skin on the shoulder. If the skin remains up two to four seconds, the horse is moderately dehydrated, and you should remove the wrap. Six to ten seconds indicates heavy dehydration, a serious situation.

You may not need to sweat the horse on a regular basis. Too much fat reduction can make a halter horse appear too lean. It should have sufficient muscle tone, with a rounded look to the body. When you see no additional change, you can cease this procedure. You may need to repeat it, however.

LEG APPLICATIONS AND WRAPS

For grooming purposes, you rub or wrap the horse's lower legs to maintain a smooth appearance. Lotions or bandages can prevent or control any swellings.

After exercise, rub liniment into the horse's legs. (Bigeloil and Absorbine are favorite brands.) You may wish to massage the lotion lightly down the backs of the tendons.

Alternate Method: If the horse has been worked hard, try stronger products such as rubbing alcohol, Mineral

Ice leg freeze, or Titen-Zem. (Apply these with care, since some can burn sensitive skin.)

For extra support, wrap legs in standing bandages after rubbing with lotion. Some horsekeepers advise against wrapping legs, claiming that improper bandaging can damage tendons, and the horse can become dependent upon artificial support. Others contend that you should wrap a hard-working horse after exercise to prevent problems. Wrapping legs supports the skeletal and muscular structures. It helps keep the tendons tight, so they don't look filled the next day.

Wrapping legs does require care. The ideal wrap exerts snug, even pressure. A bandage that's too loose can unravel, endangering the horse. One that's too binding could cause a "bandage bow," which results from excess pressure on a tendon.

Grooms traditionally prefer wraps of natural fabrics, such as cotton flannel, to synthetic ones. Even when wrapped snugly, flannel seems to allow the skin to breathe.

To support legs, use two layers of wrapping. The first is a padding of sheet cotton, foam or fleece wraps, or quilted cotton pads; the overlapping layer is a bandage spiraled around the leg.

You can purchase wraps of different thicknesses. Some grooms prefer the puffy wraps, with a center core of foam or polyester batting. Others rely on quilted wraps as illustrated here.

Grooms also debate the height of the wrap. The padding should cover from the base of knee or hock to the fetlock. Some horsemen feel the padding should not cover or bind the fetlock joint, for free movement, while others cover the coronary band. If your horse needs protection in this area, you can add bell boots.

On cloth wraps, you can sew on Velcro fasteners. The fasteners will hold the pad in place while you apply your bandages, simplifying the process.

Fit the pad on your horse's leg, and make two marks on the pad—the first on the outside edge below the knee, and the second where the outside edge overlaps the rest of the pad. On most horses, this will be six to eight inches inward from the outside edge, when you unfold the pad.

Next mark the same locations at the bottom of the pad, above the fetlock. At the top outside edge, below the knee,

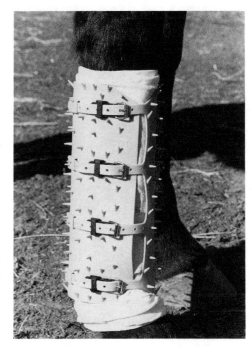

Some horses deliberately tear bandages—protect wraps with the "Bandage Saver." Plastic wraps buckle over the bandage, and the teeth discourage the horse from biting the wraps.

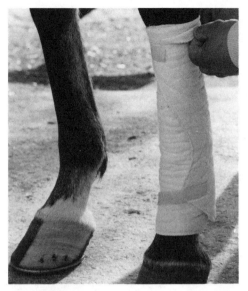

With Velcro closure sections, the quilted padding can be fastened in place on the leg.

With one hand, hold the end of the bandage in place as you begin to wrap downward.

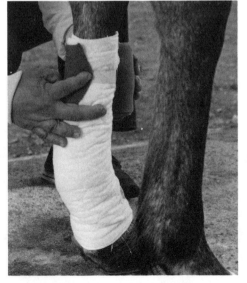

mark a permanent "T" (with felt-tip marker) to indicate the placement of the pad. (You might add further identification such as "TFN" for "Top Front Near" to use the same pad on the same leg each time.) Sew hook sections of Velcro fasteners on the two locations on the outside edges, and loop sections at the inner marks.

For the outer bandage, you can buy polyester knit track bandages in sets of four. A cheaper, traditional choice is to purchase a three- or four-yard length of wide cotton flannel and tear it into long strips, four to six inches wide. Cotton flannel has minimal stretch and is very durable. You'll secure the flannels with duct tape or masking tape.

To wrap, you will need:
- Outer wrap
- Pads
- Masking tape or duct tape

Before you wrap, be sure the legs are clean. Use clean pads to avoid irritating the skin. Your bandages must be tightly rolled, with the outside end rolled inside the bandage so it will end up on top of the wrapping. If you use track bandages with Velcro fasteners, the loop sections should face inward.

A tightly rolled bandage is easier to handle than a bulky, loosely rolled one. It will twine around the leg more smoothly as you unwind the taut fabric.

With your materials ready, place the padding around the leg at the front of the cannon bone or on the inside at the groove. Wrap the padding from the front to the back without any wrinkles pressing against the skin. You can work either clockwise or counterclockwise, whichever is most convenient.

Next start the outer bandage, just below the top of the padding below the knee or hock, and wrap from front to back, counterclockwise. Tucking the end of the bandage under the edge of the wrap will help hold the wrap in place while you begin securing the bandage.

Alternate Methods: 1. Position one corner of the bandage sticking up on your first turn around the leg. On the second turn, fold down the corner and then wrap over it. This helps hold the bandage in place.

2. Start the wrap just above the fetlock joint. Wrap down to just below the fetlock; then spiral back up to end below the knee. Some grooms secure the ankle by wrapping the bandage in a figure eight, down and then up.

Spiral the bandage down the leg, almost to the bottom edge of the padding. Try to overlap the layers by the same amount down the leg, which will usually be about one inch below the top edge of the previous layer.

As you wrap, be sure to maintain an even pressure, without allowing the bandage to form any wrinkles. Remember to pull it snug over the front of the cannon bone, so it remains in place, and lay it flat over the tendon in back. As the horse moves, the wrap shifts slightly. You want the bandage snug enough to remain in place, but not so tight that it causes tendon damage.

Wind the remaining length of the bandage back up to the top. The end doesn't need to reach to the top, but ideally it should end on the outside of the leg so the fastening won't interfere with the opposite leg.

The traditional closing to fasten a flannel bandage is a large safety pin, or two pins crossed in an X. Many grooms prefer the convenience of Velcro fasteners, but a curious horse might unfasten them. You can add a layer of wide masking or duct tape to secure any bandage. Tape is a safe fastener, because it creates equal pressure rather than concentrating it on one spot. Fold the end of the tape so you can remove it easily.

Test the bandage for even pressure by inserting two fingers at the top and the bottom. If any area seems tighter or pinches the leg, remove and rewrap the bandage. With thinner wraps, it's even more important that the bandage lies absolutely flat with even pressure.

Alternate Methods: 1. To relieve temporary swelling, rub legs with a mixture of Vetrolin liniment and water, and wrap legs overnight.

2. Mix a solution of one tablespoon Bigeloil liniment, one tablespoon apple cider vinegar, and one quart water. Rub onto legs and wrap in quilted bandages. Pour the remaining solution in a squeeze bottle. Leave legs wrapped for two hours, keeping bandages soaked by squirting on additional solution.

3. Mix two parts Absorbine to one part baby oil for a mild tightener.

4. For another tightener, rub legs with alcohol before wrapping. This reduces sweating under the bandages, even in the summer.

Angling the corner upward allows you to create a fold for greater security.

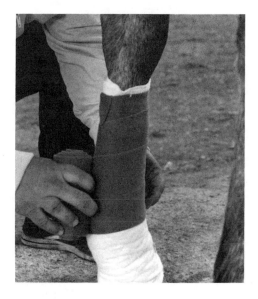

Here the corner is folded over and the next wrap covers it. Pass the bandage from hand to hand as you spiral down the leg. Layers overlap with consistent pressure as you work toward the fetlock.

Do not bandage on a regular basis if the horse has scurf on its legs. If it's prone to rain rot, ensure the legs are dry before you wrap.

To avoid an unattractive rippled effect when you remove bandages, be sure the hair on the horse's legs is short and dry before you wrap them. If it is long or wet, the hair will look ruffled. In a halter class, the hair pattern could make the judge suspect that the horse suffers a soundness problem.

HIGHLIGHTING

Adding artificial shine to parts of the horse's face and legs completes the picture of a well-groomed show horse. However, observe association rules about changing color. The American Horse Shows Association (AHSA) specifies only clear materials.

On the face, Vaseline petroleum jelly, baby oil, olive oil, or equine coat oils can enhance the bone structure. Gleaming highlights draw the observer's eye to the horse's outstanding features.

This procedure resembles applying makeup. Consider the appearance you wish to present, which can be subtle or even theatrical. For example, on a gray, oils will darken the hairs and make the face appear more dramatic. Usually you should aim for a tasteful enhancement, so you don't distract from the horse's beauty.

The areas you plan to highlight must be very clean. Apply equine cosmetics shortly before you enter the ring, because they can attract dust.

Dampen a rag or handkerchief and wipe on a small amount of the product. Then rub onto the horse's muzzle, around the mouth and nostrils. Blend the highlighter into the hairs as you work up toward the nasal bone and jowls.

Alternate Method: Apply a dressing to the palms of your hands, and rub into the horse's skin.

Make the horse's eyes more prominent by rubbing the product in a circular motion around the eyes. You can do one eye at a time, or use both hands on both eyes at once. Don't apply too much "glop" around the eyes, and be careful you don't allow any oil to get into the eyes. Blend the substance into the cheek bones so the eyes look larger but not artificial. You don't want to end up with a "raccoon" look.

Darken and highlight the ears by lightly rubbing the product around and inside the ears. One method is to hold the outside of an ear with the back of one hand, stroking an oil or lotion inside with thumb and fingers of your other hand. Try rubbing alcohol to clean inside the ears, without a greasy result. Avoid excess petroleum jelly, which can heat up and run down inside the ear.

You may also wish to wipe a cream or oil on the top of the forelock, bridle path and mane, to make the entire head look shiny. You can mix petroleum jelly and baby oil for the sheen, or try a product formulated for humans, such as Afro-Sheen hair gel, in the blue shade for gray horses.

Be sure to remove these artificial enhancements soon after you finish showing. If you leave baby oil on skin that has been in the sun, the horse is likely to sunburn. (Some highlighters contain a sunscreen.) Wipe off the oil with a warm, damp cloth. Vaseline petroleum jelly should not cause sunburn, but it's more difficult to remove.

For a final touch, you can groom the chestnuts inside the horse's legs. Depending on the type of class, you may add a product for either a subtle or a shiny effect.

Level the chestnuts with the legs by removing excess layers. You can peel them off, or scrub them with pumice. You can remove the surface more easily when chestnuts are wet, such as during a bath.

Alternate Method: Smear the chestnut well with Vaseline petroleum jelly. Leave on overnight, and rub off with a rag the next day.

To make the chestnuts less obvious, darken with an oil. You can achieve a gleaming effect by greasing them with an ointment. You may wish to match the color of the horse's hooves.

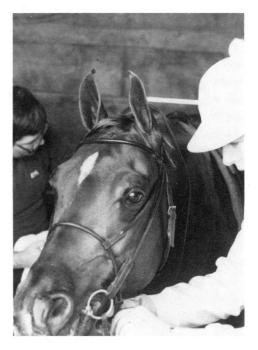

Baby oil on muzzle, ears and around the eyes adds highlights to a classic Arabian face.

11. FOAL GROOMING

Young horses offer a unique challenge to the groom. The textures of their coats, manes, and tails vary from adult horses, requiring a different approach when grooming for show.

SHORTENING THE COAT

If you plan to show a foal in major competitions, you'll need to clip or shed out its fuzzy hair to expose the short coat. With some breeds, like the Appaloosa, foals are shed rather than clipped.

This procedure may be difficult and require several months, especially with a foal born earlier in the season. Keeping the youngster indoors and under lights encourages its coat to shed. The temperature difference affects the coat change, along with proper nutrition and medication. Foals with thinner skin and a finer coat will generally shed out faster than the more cold-blooded types.

Blanketing also helps shed the foal coat. When fitting a sheet or blanket on a young horse, make sure the garment fits properly so it does not rub. A youngster has lower withers and narrower shoulders than an adult, and a too-tight blanket can irritate these areas.

Shaded areas can be clipped to refine the appearance of a foal without clipping the entire body.

Some foal blankets will expand to fit a growing foal. A Velcro front closure allows you to adjust the blanket's size as the foal becomes a weanling.

Clipping the baby hair is the faster, more attractive method. Though some grooms clip before the foal is a month old, others prefer to wait till it is about four months. As with an adult horse, a clipped foal will need to be blanketed and kept indoors for protection.

Results vary after clipping the foal coat. Chestnuts and bays usually look good—grays often end up with a "Brillo soap pad" texture to the coat. These can require reclipping monthly for a smoother appearance.

You can compromise and clip only certain areas for showing at local competitions. Use a coarse blade (#8½ or #10) with the medium clippers. To define the head and throat, clip the head and a V-shaped section down the neck, toward the chest. You will need to blend clipped areas into the surrounding hair.

A sport horse foal has a mane too short for braiding, but the hairs lie fairly flat.

Even when a foal sheds out, it may retain fuzz along its belly. Try clipping with the coarse blade, running the blade with the grain of the hair.

TRAINING THE MANE

Most foals have short, bushy manes that stand straight up. To groom the flyaway hairs into place, you might have to spend several days or weeks training the mane.

Use the same methods on a foal's mane as you would an adult's, with braids, rubber bands, and a neck sweat or mane tamer. The braids will make the mane wavy for the show, but waves look better than a wiry mane that doesn't lie down. You can also use baby oil or Vaseline to smooth the mane in place against the neck.

You may braid the mane if the foal is a sport horse type, in the dressage style for a breed inspection (see Chapter 16). For a foal of a Western breed, consider a banded mane as described in Chapter 12.

Alternate Method: If you're not going to show the foal its first year, you can roach the mane and allow it to grow out. When the foal becomes a yearling, its mane should be thicker and easier to groom.

PART II

SPECIALIZED TURNOUT FOR SHOW

12. QUARTER HORSES

Although horses of many breeds show under Western tack, grooming in this chapter pertains to Quarter Horses and horses groomed in the Quarter Horse style. (Chapter 13 covers the color breeds.)

Grooming and show turnout follow American Quarter Horse Association (AQHA) rules. Horses shown in the Western division of the American Horse Shows Association (AHSA) must conform to its rules. Current styles and regional variations also influence the way you prepare the horse for the show ring.

QUARTER HORSE GROOMING

For halter and most performance classes, horses show with pulled manes. The mane's length influences the look of the neck, with a shorter mane accenting a long, slim neck. On most horses, pull the mane to three or four inches. A five-inch mane may complement a horse with a heavier neck. Be sure to pull it straight so the longest hairs are even. (Some grooms do admit they even the ends of the mane with scissors.)

The mane can lie on either side of the neck. The entire mane must lie flat for a slim appearance, without flapping as the horse moves. A horse may have a cowlick that makes the mane uneven no matter how much you thin it. Trim hairs to even the length of the strands.

You can rely on the mane tamer to train the mane, or braid and wet brush. Section the wet mane into hanks, and place a rubber band at the top of each section. Then pull lower hairs tight so the mane lies flat. When dry, let down and brush.

For a neat appearance before entering the ring, press hairs against the neck with a mane tamer or a dampened towel, pinned under the neck to hold it in place. You can also use an inexpensive alternative, a woman's tube top. The stretchy fabric holds mane hairs flat.

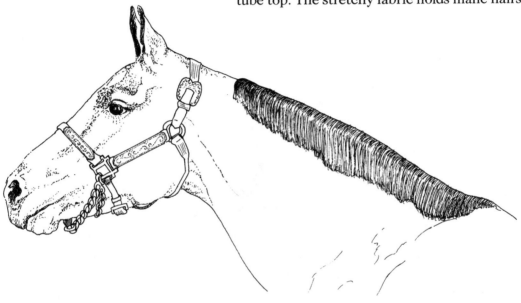

The mane must lie flat, especially on a halter horse. Shown here is a typical show halter, shaped to fit along the cheekbones and decorated with engraved silver and a silver buckle.

Banding the Mane

Currently many grooms band the mane for a neat topline, both for halter and performance classes. Wrapped around the tops of the hairs, the bands are visible only at the roots. A mane banded into many small hanks, neatly lined up in a row along the crest, flatters the horse's appearance.

- To band the mane, you will need:
- A Braid Aid (shown in Chapter 14)

- At least 50 Braidbinders rubber bands
- Hair clip or comb
- Dampened brush or water in a spray pump bottle.

Match the color of bands—black, tan, brown, gray, or white—to your horse. Tan or brown usually coordinate best with a chestnut or sorrel, although some grooms use the white to accentuate an attractive neck.

At the top of the mane, where the bridle path ends, dampen the mane. Starting at the first hairs of the mane, comb with the Braid Aid to separate three equal-size sections of mane. Pin back the rest of the mane with the clip or comb. On a short mane, you'll need to dampen the unsectioned hairs to keep them out of the way.

On the first hank the Braid Aid separated, pull the hair down to keep the mane as flat as you can against the

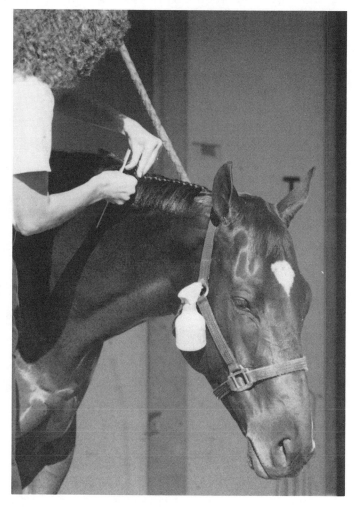

A groom bands a mane. She's hung her spray bottle on the halter's crownpiece ring for quick access. (Be sure your horse will tolerate this short cut.)

neck. Slide a rubber band onto the hairs, and wrap it over itself three to five times. The number of wraps depends on the thickness of the hank of hair. Stack the wraps so the last one is on top without any twists showing. From underneath the banded strands, pull a few hairs to encourage the section to lie as flat as possible. You want the sections to be small and molded to the neck. The sections should not flare out in the shape of an upside-down "V."

Sections must match in size and placement of the band. The Braid Aid helps you comb equal-sized hanks, although the first few sections could be thinner. You'll wrap fewer times on a thinner section, and more on a thicker section. (The bands themselves also vary in thickness.) Watch that each band continues a steady line down the neck.

Banding a mane requires practice and patience. Your first effort could take over an hour. Expert banders can complete a mane in 30 minutes or less.

To handle the many bands, you can stow them in a

A young horse, schooling in the hackamore, has the longer mane of a reiner. This California rider has also fastened a coiled reata to the front of his saddle.

pocket in a grooming apron. Or, place a dozen in your mouth, as chewing will separate them. You can just peel one out for wrapping. (After banding, chew cinnamon gum to clear the rubber taste from your mouth.)

To make the forelock lie flat, shave off the shorter hairs on the edges, or clip about one-half inch under the forelock.

Quarter Horses competing in reining and cattle events wear manes at a natural length. A long, luxurious mane distinguishes the reiner and cutter. Occasionally a roping horse may show with a roached mane, except for the forelock and a tuft of hair at the withers.

The tail flatters the powerful hindquarters of the Quarter Horse. Today's fashion is the long, full, wavy tail, which may be slightly shaped at the top so the hindquarters appear wider.

For a smooth look, separate all strands and spray the tail with a hair conditioner. Wrap with a track bandage to encourage the top hairs to lie flat. Remove after a few hours and brush again. Before a show, wash the tail and fluff the skirt dry with a blow-dryer, to make the tail as thick as possible.

You may wish to pull a few long hairs to make the tip of the tail look smoother. A tail jagged at the end detracts from a neat appearance. Some grooms trim the ends of the tail for a banged appearance.

Current AQHA rules permit tails lengthened by "hair to hair" attachment, *not* a separate false tail.

Rules prohibit the showing of a horse with any alteration of its tail function. "Tail testers" at shows examine horses for any abnormalities, including a surgical procedure (such as cutting the muscle) or injection of any foreign substance. Also prohibited are any other alterations of the horse's body, except those surgical procedures performed for medical reasons by a veterinarian, and artificial appliances.

Trim the Quarter Horse's bridle path to a length of three to four inches. The exact amount depends on the length of the horse's neck and mane. A longer bridle path may visually lengthen the neck and reduce the throatlatch.

You may wish to trim the throatlatch area so it seems slimmer. Clip with the grain, holding the medium clippers upside down to trim only the longest hairs.

Tail Grooming

A Quarter Horse shows the desirable long, lush tail for today's halter, pleasure, trail, and horsemanship classes.

Trimming

A Palomino Quarter Horse shows a short mane and slightly longer bridle path. Its tail is braided and protected in a sock.

Hoof Preparation

Hooves are darkened for performance classes, often with hoof oil. For a halter horse, you'll lightly sand the hoof and paint it with hoof black. It is customary to use black polish on all hooves, regardless of each hoof's natural color.

QUARTER HORSE TACK

Use a Western style headstall, either of the eared or browband type. Don't add a noseband or bosal. For pleasure classes, many horses show in the two-ear headstall, of flat leather with rawhide braid trim or silver trim on the ear loops. The bridle should fit the horse, with the crownpiece buckle fitting below the eye, between eye and ear. You may choose to shorten the tips of the crownpiece for a neater fit.

Bridles

The bridle should be constructed of quality leather, with even stitching. Any decoration should complement the horse's head. A simple style with plain cheeks and silver buckles and tips can accent a fancy head.

Silver decorations are standard on earpieces and buckles. Avoid silver on the crownpiece, which can highlight any up or down movement of the head.

When you choose tack with silver trim, look for hand-engraved sterling silver overlay. This metal will sparkle and reflect light due to its many surfaces. Compare grades of silver, and remember that judges notice the difference in the show pen.

Outfit a Western horse in a standard Western curb bit or a ring snaffle, according to class specifications. AQHA rules specify legal and illegal bits. Most riders use some type of grazing bit, with a maximum shank of 8½ inches.

Rules of the National Snaffle Bit Association (NSBA) and AHSA also list acceptable bit styles. The National Reining Horse Association (NRHA) and National Cutting Horse Association (NCHA) rules also cover acceptable bits. Be sure you outfit your horse according to specifications cited in the current rule book. In many events, the judge or steward will inspect the bit before you enter the ring or after you complete an individual pattern.

Few Western riders currently choose the silver-mounted curb bit, except in Arabian, Morgan and Working Cow Horse classes. These are usually heavy and may overbalance some horses. Most horses do not need the extra weight, since they are schooled to work on a light snaffle. With the influence of cutting and reining, the lighter grazing bit has become the standard.

When you show using a ring snaffle, it must be a single, center jointed style, with a smooth mouthpiece of three-eighths to three-quarters inches in diameter. Styles include the eggbutt, O-ring, and D-ring. Rings can be from two to four inches outside diameter. Some snaffles feature silver engraving on the rings.

Rules may specify a certain diameter of the mouthpiece, measured from the bit ring. Officials in NSBA shows use a bit gauge to measure bits.

You may attach a loose curb strap to the snaffle bit, below the rein attachment. On a curb bit, rules usually specify certain curb straps or chains. The strap must be at least one-half inch wide and lie flat against the horse's jaw.

A hackamore horse, four years or under, may wear only a braided rawhide or leather hackamore, with a non-metallic core. (Show officials may test the core with a magnet.) Mechanical hackamores are permitted by the AQHA in contest events only. With the bosal, riders attach braided horsehair reins, the mecate.

Rules govern the size and adjustment of the bosal. For example, in NSBA, it must be a maximum of three-quarters inches in diameter. The distance between the bosal and horse's nose should measure about one finger. However, NRHA and NCHA specify two fingers between bosal and muzzle.

To attach to the bit, almost all riders today choose split leather reins. Arabian, Morgan, and Working Cow Horse exhibitors follow the California tradition of the romal (closed) rein. Riders using the romal reins usually carry hobbles, attached through the slot for the flank cinch, below the cantle on the near side. AHSA rules require hobbles with romal reins.

Halters and Lead Shanks

In a halter or showmanship class, the horse wears a leather, silver-trimmed show halter. The halter must fit neatly, conforming to the head to complement the horse. Most models feature five buckles, so you can adjust the halter with the throatlatch fitting close behind the jowl. If your halter has a rolled throatlatch with wire inside the leather, shape it to outline the jawline.

Cheekpieces must rest low, placed so they are parallel above the cheekbones. The noseband fits halfway between the nose and the eye. It must be long enough so the cheeks are not pulled out of line with the cheekbones. Some halters feature rounded leather half-moons at the ring where noseband and cheekpiece meet, which break the line of silver decoration along the cheeks.

The tip of the crownpiece should extend to the halter ring joining crown and cheek, but not protrude beyond the ring. Your halter will probably have silver tips, buckles, keepers and trim on the cheeks and noseband.

A horse with a short, wide head can look good in almost any halter. On one with a longer head, choose silver pieces that are short and wide. Less silver is better on a less attractive head. Tiny buckles will not attract attention to poor ears.

If the horse has a head of a solid color, such as a bay with no white markings, more silver accents the head. Use a more conservatively decorated halter, maybe with just two small conchos, on a bald face.

You'll show the Quarter Horse with a chain leadshank. Most exhibitors run the chain through the halter ring on the near side, under the horse's jaw, and snapped to the ring on the off side, under the ear. This is required in Showmanship at Halter classes.

With a young stallion, except in Showmanship at Halter, you may choose to run the chain over the horse's nose. If it is under the jaw, pressure can encourage the horse to be light in the forehand. Increased pressure may signal the horse to rear.

The braided rawhide hackmore is acceptable only on younger horses. This Quarter Horse, shown in hackmore classes, wears the longer mane typical of reining, cutting, and working cow horses.

When purchasing a halter, check it for quality hardware. The buckle should have a short post so it will not bend or break. Nickel with a heavy silver overlay is stronger than solid sterling.

Check that the engraving matches on all pieces of silver. If silver pieces have been added later, they may not be of the same pattern.

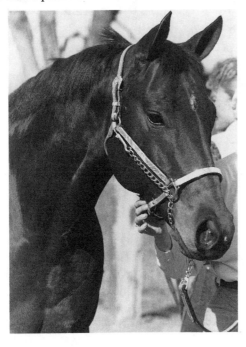

Use a show halter for the Western horse, and attach the chain lead shank as shown here.

Saddles

A stock saddle is required in performance classes. Fashions in saddles change regularly, with trends set by prominent trainers who patronize builders of custom made saddles.

Most saddles are built on a semi-Quarter Horse tree, which fits today's breedier Quarter Horse, Appaloosas, and Paints. Currently in vogue is a flatter seat, as seen in cutting saddles. This places you in the center of the saddle.

For equitation, horsemanship, and reining classes, the saddle must fit you. The seat must be short enough so you don't float forward or back. In one that is too long, your legs will not remain in the correct position.

Some trainers recommend a deeper seat with a fairly high cantle and fenders to allow you to carry your feet underneath your body. If you show in trail classes, look for swells that are not too large—these can make it difficult to bend forward when working obstacles.

In a trail class, this Palomino is tacked with a slick-forked saddle, fleece-lined cinch, breastcollar, and braided headstall and reins, decorated with silver. The braids in the mane and forelock are acceptable in AHSA shows.

Currently, show saddles are a light oil finish. Saddle decorations also change according to fashion. Leather carved in the traditional floral pattern is always correct, but the basket weave is making a comeback. Carving adorns the cantle and pommel, with silver plates seen in both locations as well as the corners of the skirts. Silver lacing and rawhide trim have passed from fashion.

Silver ornamentation makes a saddle flashy, but it is not required. On an equitation saddle, it may even detract from the rider.

The saddle pad changes with fashion, although the traditional Navajo style remains popular. To follow fashion in today's show pen, you'd choose an oversized wool saddle blanket over a felt pad. The blanket's colors can blend with your chaps and match the shades of your shirt. You might match the color to your horse if he "bounces" with a less-than-steady topline. (This probably won't fool a keen judge.)

The current fad dictates a blanket measuring thirty-four by thirty-eight inches, which fits today's large saddle skirts. Look for a thick yet fine weave. A tightly woven blanket lasts longer. If your horse is smaller, such as an Arabian, use a smaller blanket. The large size, made for a Quarter Horse, can overwhelm a more delicate mount.

In the cinch, the traditional woven mohair styles

A Paint models the currently popular type of silver-trimmed saddle and over-sized saddle blanket. This horse also shows a neatly banded mane. (Waiting at the in-gate, the rider has draped a towel over the saddle's pommel.)

continue. New on the scene is a black neoprene girth, which makes a fashion statement and enhances the horse's comfort.

Silver-mounted stirrups are attractive in trail and pleasure classes, but leather-covered stirrups are better for equitation. Shiny stirrups can emphasize any movement of the rider's leg.

OTHER TACK

AHSA rules prohibit tapaderos. AQHA regulations permit them in all but Working Cow Horse classes. The AHSA requires a lariat or reata be carried, coiled and attached to the fork of the saddle. This is optional according to AQHA rules.

Most horses at today's open and breed shows wear breast collars in pleasure, trail, and equitation classes.

Decorated with silver, the leather strap matches the saddle and bridle. In addition to decorating the horse, the breast collar helps to keep the saddle in place. Do not adjust it too tightly for a trail class, since it can hinder the horse from dropping its head while working obstacles.

No martingale, tiedown, or noseband is allowed, except in certain contest events as specified by the AQHA.

AQHA considers leg wraps optional, but not allowed in western pleasure, trail, western horsemanship, or showmanship at halter. Almost all reiners, cutters, and ropers outfit their horses in protective boots. Reiners prefer the white boots on all four legs of the horse. Some feel the bright white accents the horse's fancy footwork. Under AHSA rules, only horses in stock horse classes may wear boots or wraps.

13. COLOR
BREEDS

The color breeds include the Paint, Pinto, Palomino, Appaloosa, and Buckskin. These horses follow Quarter Horse style when shown in Western classes. Exhibited under hunt or saddle seat tack, you'd prepare the horse according to the styles of hunter, jumper, dressage, Saddlebred, or Arabian. For example, groom a Thoroughbred-type Pinto showing in dressage as you would a solid-colored horse. A Half-Arabian Palomino, showing in Arabian classes, would be groomed in Arabian style.

Certain color breeds—Appaloosa, Paint, and Pinto—present unique grooming challenges. To maintain the contrast in these horses' coats, you must groom both dark and white colors impeccably.

Rules of the Appaloosa Horse Club (ApHC) state that you may not alter the coloring of the horse's hide or hooves during show preparation. Striped hooves should be evident, so do not use other than clear hoof polish. Rules also exclude use of any substances to color any part of the horse's body. These prohibit cornstarch, shoe polish, or dye.

The characteristic short tail is still acceptable, falling near or above the hocks. You can roach the mane or leave it natural.

A leopard Appaloosa can have white hair that's thick and bristly. The hair of large peacock spots may be of a different texture than the white hairs of the blanket. This can be advantageous, since a shot administered in a spot will not leave an obvious bump.

If the horse is cold, these hairs will stand up in tufts. Trimming them is difficult, but you can accentuate them by body clipping—surrounding hairs will be shorter and flatter than those in the spots.

An Appaloosa with a colorful head does not need much silver accent on bridle or show halter.

Groom a Paint like you would the Quarter Horse. (Exception: The American Paint Horse Association [APHA] permits the use of artificial tails.) The Pinto may be prepared either as a Saddlebred, Arabian, or Quarter Horse, depending on its ancestry. The Pinto Horse Association of America allows use of artificial tails in all its divisions.

When you band the mane of a Paint or Pinto, use bands of colors that match the dark and white mane hairs. For example, on a mane that's one-third black and two-thirds

An Appaloosa of the leopard coat pattern displays the typical spots over the hips, showing different textures of a natural, unclipped coat.

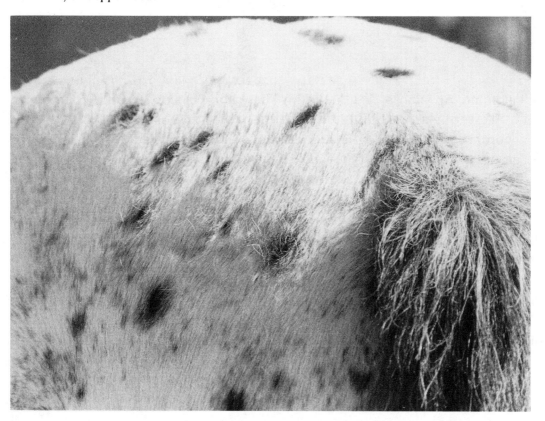

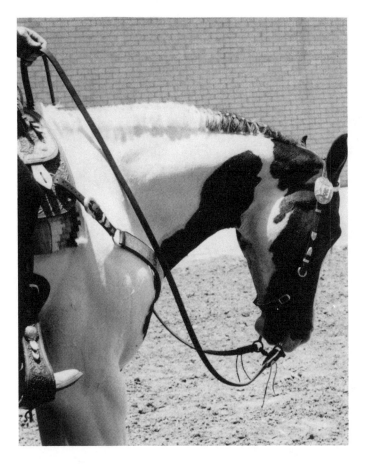

The tricolor mane of this Paint challenges the groom who must band it.

white, you might use ten black bands and twenty-five white ones.

A Paint or Pinto could also have a two-tone tail and the colors may have different textures. Generally white hairs are a finer consistency than the darker ones. Choose a conditioner that works on both textures, or treat the different sections with two appropriate produts.

You must present these flashy horses with perfectly white spots, yet loudly colored Paints and Pintos seem the most difficult colors to keep clean. You may have to bathe your horse almost every day, due to manure stains on the white hairs. The pink skin is sensitive and can be irritated easily, especially after body clipping.

Certain shampoos seem to produce better results on Paints and Pintos. Grooms recommend the Quic Silver and Ultra products. You can also use French grooming chalk, rubbing the block with or across the hair to whiten yellow areas. Some grooms prefer using the old standby, cornstarch.

This Pinto filly shows the result of conscientious grooming of white areas.

The contrast between dark and white areas can produce an optical illusion. White seems to "jump out" at the observer, where dark areas recede.

The appearance can deceive the viewer, with a white back or head appearing bigger or longer. Some grooms consider colors in their grooming of the horse, clipping differently to camouflage certain areas.

With your horse, you can experiment with different clipper blades to adjust the length of hair on certain areas. Leaving slightly more hair on a dark leg may balance how it matches an opposite white leg. Or, clip only the stocking on a horse with legs dark above the knee. The white will draw the observer's eye.

On some horses, the white hair on legs and body differs from the dark hairs. White hair on legs can be thicker and curlier. By trimming white hair closer, you can affect and possibly improve the horse's appearance. Don't expect to hide a splint, but you might improve the look of bench knees by judicious trimming of white stockings.

The Palomino's coat is easier to groom, since it must have dark skin under the golden hairs. To retain the desirable dark color, keep a Palomino out of sunlight so its coat will not bleach. You may choose to keep the horse in a stall during the daylight hours, or blanket it and turn it out into a shaded corral.

Genetics determine the shade of the coat of a Palomino or buckskin. Keeping a light-colored horse indoors doesn't guarantee that its coat will turn dark. Some Palominos and buckskins are naturally dark and rich-colored, where sunlight has little effect on the hairs of their coats.

Rules of the Palomino Horse Breeders of America require a mane at least four inches long. You may not alter the color of mane and tail, and any dark hairs will count against the horse's color score. Don't change white markings by coloring or dyeing them.

A Palomino or Pinto horse or pony shown in the AHSA Parade Division should be presented as a beautiful and stylish animal. The mane should be full, and it may be braided. The tail can be set and fitted with a brace and tail switch.

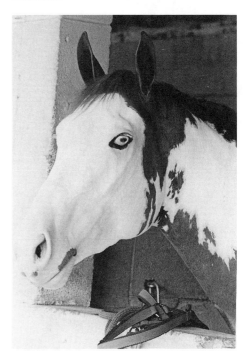

Keep this guy out of the sunlight! His "apron" face makes him a candidate for sunburn.

PREVENTING SUNBURN

White hairs can bleach out, and the pink skin under white hairs is likely to sunburn, especially when you clip the hair short. Paints and Pintos often have white faces, predisposing them to tender skin. Use these methods to prevent this irritation:

1. Rub a sunburn block cream into the skin of the muzzle, around the eyes, and on a white blaze. Try Amway Sun Pacer 15, which contains lanolin and glycerin. Avoid a lotion that contains a high percentage of alcohol, because it can sting sunburned skin.

2. Keep the horse out of direct sunlight and also intense barn lights.

3. Oils applied to the face and bridle path will intensify the effect of the sun. Keep the horse indoors or in the shade during the hottest part of the day. You can place a towel over the muzzle or bridle path to protect these areas temporarily.

14. HUNTERS

Hunter turnout is conservative and traditional. The horse must conform to a certain style. Any changes in hunter grooming or tack are very slight and gradual.

HUNTER GROOMING

Braiding the Mane. Braid the hunter's mane and forelock to lie on the off side. Tightly braided plaits highlight the horse's neck and maintain the tradition of the hunt field.

American Horse Shows Association (AHSA) rules do not require braiding, but judges expect to see every hunter to enter the ring with mane and forelock braided in the conventional style. At a small show, you might take a chance and show your hunter unbraided. If so, pull the mane neatly, at the length described below, and lay the hair down with a dampened brush just before entering the show ring. Realize that this can put you at a disadvantage, because other competitors may show their horses braided.

The number and size of braids can alter the appearance of the horse's neck. You can make a short neck look longer if you put in many small braids. Some people feel braids

A neatly braided mane and clean gray coat make this hunter ready to show.

look better with space between them for a less jumbled appearance. You'd see this style on horses prepared by grooms trained in the British or Continental tradition.

At larger shows, professional braiders prepare many hunters and hunter ponies. Your efforts must match their impeccable results, or your horse will look out of place. Expect to spend many hours practicing to hone your braiding skills.

Before braiding, pull the mane to an average length of four to six inches. As a guide, calculate about three-quarters inches longer than the length of a small mane comb.

For best results, stand the horse in a well-lighted area and gather all your supplies before you begin. If you wear a grooming apron or braiding kit on your belt, stow your tools in the pockets:

- Dampened sponge or brush, or water in spray bottle
- Mane comb, Braid Aid, or a plastic comb with teeth removed for sectioning the mane
- Hair clip or ponytail band
- Pull-through (formed from twisted wire, or a tapestry needle, large safety pin, or hairpin)
- Scissors
- Seam ripper
- Lengths of yarn

Choose wool yarn of a conservative color to blend with the horse's mane or the rider's coat. Navy blue or hunter green, matching the rider's coat, are the most popular choices.

Cut the yarn into pieces ten to fourteen inches long. For an average mane, plan approximately thirty pieces

This hunter's row of neat braids creates the desired line to accent the neck.

for that number of braids. You can buy precut lengths of yarn at many tack shops.

A simple way to measure and cut the yarn is to bend your arm and wrap the yarn around your arm, from elbow to shoulder or thumb to elbow. Snip the loops at the ends to produce pieces about twelve inches long.

Hang your yarn lengths through the horse's off side halter ring, below the ear. You can tuck your sponge in the cheekpiece. Observe your horse's reactions to this storage, and move the items to your grooming kit if the horse objects.

Dampen the first section of mane, adjacent to the bridle path, with your sponge or brush. Avoid wetting the hairs too much, which can make them slippery.

With the mane comb, part a section of mane about three-quarters inches wide, or one-third the width of a mane comb. (British grooms traditionally measure

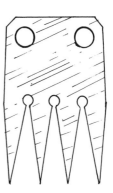

The Braid Aid helps you separate the strands into even sections.

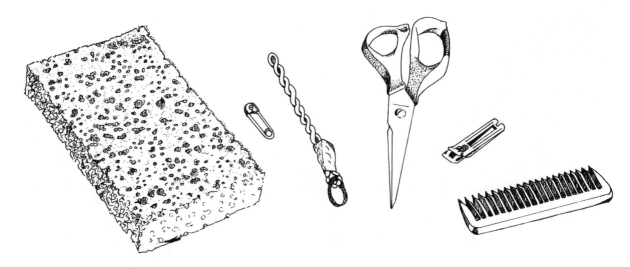

Braiding tools (from left): sponge, safety pin, pull-through made of twisted wire, sharp scissors, hair clip, and mane comb.

each plait as the width of the mane comb, ending up with twelve to twenty plaits.) Run the part straight across the crest. Hold back the rest of the mane with the mane comb, a hair clip, or a ponytail band. Section the strands into three equal parts.

Alternate Method: Use the Braid Aid to part and divide hairs at the same time. Work it down to separate strands, and hold the sections apart with the fingers of your other hand. Slide the Braid Aid out of the mane.

Begin to plait the strands, keeping the hair tight and close to the neck.

Each time you turn one strand over another, hold it tight with your thumb, pushing the hair for a slight twist. Catch as many short hairs as you can, but try not to start the braid too tight at the crest. Too-tight braids may cause the horse to rub. Keep the braid secure by holding it with your thumb while you plait.

Don't pull the mane toward you, which causes tension that stretches and loosens the braid. To produce a tight braid, you can give the hair an extra twist as you cross the strands over one another.

About two-thirds or three-fourths the way down the braid, place the center of a piece of yarn across or underneath the strands of hair, letting the two ends of the yarn combine with the outside sections of mane. Placing yarn behind the braid lets you pull it tight immediately.

Alternate Methods: 1. Thread produces a finer look, but it is harder to handle.

2. You can substitute Braidbinders for yarn, though most hunter grooms avoid them. Bands do not hold the hair as securely, and they may cut hairs. If you do wrap the ends with bands, use two for extra holding power.

Continue braiding the yarn with the hairs. When you reach the end, with only a few hairs left, wrap the ends of the yarn around the strands and tie. For security, tie first with a square knot, then anchor the knot with a surgeon's knot. This is a variation of the square knot, with one extra pass of yarn. After tying a square knot, give the yarn an extra twist through the first loop before you tie the second knot on top. You may wish to fold the short, unbraided hairs under the braided part before tying the second knot.

Alternate Methods: 1. Instead of tying a knot at the end, spread apart the two yarn ends. Gather the ends of the hairs, and wrap each yarn end two or three times around the hairs.

2. Take both yarn ends together and do two tight half hitches around the end of the hair. Tie the first one with the excess hair protruding, and the second after folding the excess hair back on itself.

When you first tie the braid, look to see if it lies flat against the horse's neck. Check it for tightness by folding it underneath itself. If the plait spreads apart, before you've wrapped it, cut the yarn with the seam rip-

Surgeon's Knot: This knot is usually tied with twine. The surgeon's knot is a modified form of the reef knot and the first tie prevents slipping before the knot is completed.

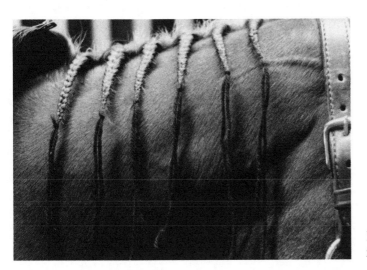

Braid and knot each section of mane from ears to withers.

per and rebraid. A slack braid will loosen more as the horse's neck expands and contracts.

Continue down the crest, braiding each section in the same fashion. Be sure to start each braid the same way, either crossing from the left or the right each time, so braids will match. (After you braid for a while, this sequence will become automatic.)

Watch that all braids repeat an equal size and spacing. It's easy to begin stretching them farther apart when you tire of the procedure.

As you work down toward the withers, the number of strands may be thinner. To maintain even spacing, take a smaller hank of hair for each plait.

After you have completed all braids, begin folding them. Start at the first braid. Insert the bottom of the pull-through downward through the base of the braid, close to the skin. Insert the ends of the yarn through the pull-through. (With a small hole in the pull-through, it helps to wet the ends of the yarn.)

Pull upward on the pull-through so the yarn ends protrude up through the top of the braid. The folded braid should be about one inch long, or slightly longer.

Separate the ends and cross them under the braid at the top. Tie a secure double knot, as you did at the bottom of the plaits.

For extra security, you can also tie an overhand knot underneath the braid. Include any loose hairs in this knot.

To secure the braid and make it lie flat, bring the yarn ends around to the front of the braid and tie securely about half-way down. Press down with your thumb so the braid doesn't slide loose while you knot the yarn. Trim the ends close to this finishing knot, leaving about one-quarter inch on the ends.

Alternate Method: You can add bumps, known as buttons or rosettes, to the tops of your braids for a special effect. After you cross the yarn ends on the front of the braid, push the top of the braid up so it forms a round button-shaped knob. Then tie the top knot below the button, which will lie about one-third the way down the braid.

Though traditional grooms frown on this addition, this does help make the braid lie flat against the neck. It also makes the braid shorter if your horse's mane is somewhat long. You can make a thin neck look fuller if you push the buttons up past the crest.

Plait the three sections of hair and lay the
middle of the yarn across the braid.

A

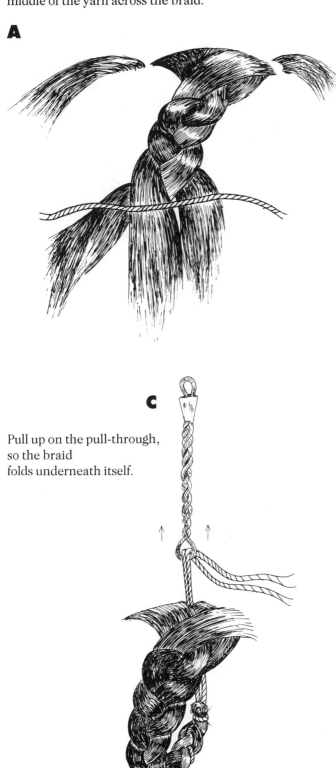

Insert the pull-through, and thread the
ends of the yarn through the loop.

B

C

Pull up on the pull-through,
so the braid
folds underneath itself.

After the braid is folded, it is tied once
on the front.

D

Buttons or rosettes (top left) add interest to the flat braid. Short "porcupine" hairs should be allowed to grow out, even through they detract from the neatness of the braids. If you pull them, they will grow back and still be short! Tie all braids down the mane (top right), then trim yarn ends.

With a flat plait, you can also add another stitch of yarn to hold the hair as flat as possible. With a tapestry needle, catch the yarn ends and make a stitch midway through the braid, from the back of the braid. Stitching through each braid will leave color spots down the center of braids along the horse's neck.

Repeat folding and tying of all braids to complete the mane.

Or, cross the ends of the yarn underneath the braid and pass them over the top, close to the crest. Repeat to secure, and tie off at the top. This creates a line of color along the crest when you've tied all braids.

Alternate Methods: 1. You can make tiny button knots by folding the plaits twice. These buttons stay in place securely.

Using a tapestry needle as a pull-through, make a stitch up through the top of the mane, above the first folded braid.

Stitch downward through both layers of the braid and then through the bottom of the braid.

Fold the braid under itself a second time so it forms four layers. Stitch through the braid toward the crest.

Separate the yarn ends and stitch up through all layers toward the crest. Remove the needle and tie the yarn underneath the braid.

2. You can produce a scalloped effect by tying one braid to another. This style is useful for braiding a long mane

The scalloped mane can attract attention to the neck.

or one that is missing a patch of hair, or when you want to create the illusion of a longer, thicker neck. Consider this a compromise, one not often seen in the traditional hunter classes.

After you've plaited the mane but not folded the braids, pick up the first braid. Pass it underneath its neighbor, and tie its yarn to that of the third braid. If the mane is too short to reach the third braid, tie each braid to its immediate neighbor.

Continue along the mane, attaching braids to form the scallops. For leftover plaits, form them into regular buttons.

Make the mane secure by reattaching each braid to its neighbors. By using the tapestry needle as a pull-through, you can stitch right through the braid. This will not show if your yarn color matches the mane.

HUNTER BRAIDING STEP-BY-STEP:

1. Cut yarn into lengths.
2. Dampen mane.
3. Part and plait first section.
4. Braid in a length of yarn and tie.
5. Pull through the yarn to fold braid, and tie.
6. Braid mane and forelock.

131

7. Dampen top and sides of tail.
8. Separate two sections of hair and cross one over the other.
9. Continue braiding down tailbone.
10. End with a pigtail, tie, and pull through.

Braiding the Forelock

Braid and tie the forelock in the same manner as you did the mane. If it is long, you can double it a second time. Secure all layers together by stitching yarn through the braids with a tapestry needle, working down through the top and back up through the end toward the ears.

Alternate Method: If your horse's forelock is thick or frizzy at the base, you can avoid a lumpy or bushy braid by French-braiding that section.

On the top of each side, separate two small strands of the forelock. Cross the strand on the right over the left one.

Pick up a third strand from the right and cross it to the left, under the strand from the left.

Bring the upper left strand around under the last strand.

Pick up a new strand from the left and cross it under to join the last strand. Catch all the wispy hairs in these braids.

Continue braiding down the forelock, picking up alternate strands from the left and right. The French braid will resemble the tail braid.

When you've completed the base of the forelock, plait the remaining hairs like you would the mane. Tie, pull the braid through, and knot. If loose hairs remain, apply hairsetting gel and tuck them underneath.

When your horse has finished showing, remove its braids by cutting the yarn with the seam ripper. Unravel hairs with your fingers, and brush with a wet brush to smooth the mane.

Braiding the Tail

At major shows and in certain classes, you should braid the hunter's tail. This is optional at local shows.

Overly frequent tail braiding can harm the hairs of the tail. If you show often or braid for every class, you will thin and shorten the horse's tail excessively by breaking off too many hairs during the process.

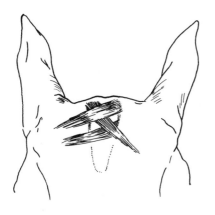

A

To French-braid the forelock, separate one strand from each side of the top of the forelock. Cross the right strand over the left, then pick up a third strand from the right and cross it under the first two.

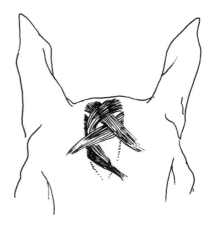

B

Bring the upper left strand around under the last strand. Pick up a new strand from the left and cross it under to join the last strand.

Braiding does accentuate the horse's hindquarters. At smaller shows, you may choose not to braid if your horse has weak hindquarters.

Practice braiding the tail before a show. Again, you must produce a professional result, such as those illustrated here. Anything less will make your horse look amateurish. When you practice at home, also exercise your horse with its tail braided. The horse needs to become used to the feel of the groomed tail; the animal might hold a braided tail stiffly.

The tail should be clean, because any dirt will become evident as you braid. With a clean tail, the horse will be less likely to rub its tail after it is braided. Do not wash it immediately before you braid, since the hairs can be too slippery to handle.

If the horse's tail is bushy at the top, avoid pulling these hairs because you'll need them for braiding. Give them a chance to grow longer before you decide to pull them. If they stick out after you braid, "glue" them down with hairsetting gel.

The method described here is known as an "outside"

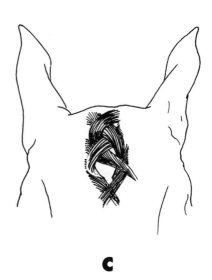

C

Braid the upper right strand under the bottom strands. Continue picking up strands from alternate sides and braiding down the forelock.

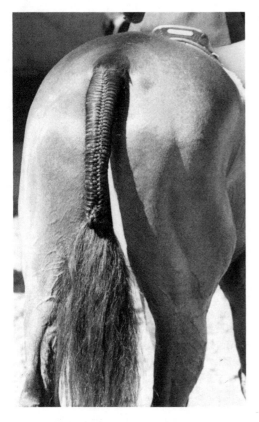

This inside braid is slightly uneven down the length of the tailbone. It features a pinwheel, described on page 136.

or "over" braid, because you create a braid by crossing strands over one another. The less common tail braid is the "inside" or "under" braid, which creates a twist underneath rather than on top. You bring in hair to the top of the strands, so the plait lies flat. This style is more difficult to master, but some feel it produces a neater result.

Gather the same tools you used to braid the mane. For safety, you can braid the horse's tail with the animal standing in a trailer or stall, lifting its tail over the door. You will need to stand on a tall stool if you choose the trailer method.

Brush the tail and dampen the top and sides.

Position yourself so your arms are perpendicular to the top of the tail (stand on a step stool if necessary). Starting high on the top, separate two sections of small, fine hairs—about ten hairs from each side of the tail.

Alternate Method: If the tail hairs are very short at the top, you can make a small braid from hairs on each side of the tail. Add a short piece of yarn, the same color as the tail, to the end of each and use these braids as the first strands.

Cross the left strand over the right at the center of the tailbone. Hold the center of these strands parallel to the ground with one hand.

Pick up a third strand from underneath the right side of the tail, from the very edge of the dock so it can wrap around all the other tail hairs on that half. Cross it to the left, over the first strand and between the first and second strands. Smooth down the loose hairs underneath the section, then braid the strand that is below the other two over the first two.

Pick up the next strand from the left side of the tail, cross it over to the right, and then braid the bottom, righthand strand over the others. Continue picking up strands, alternating right and left, straight down the center of the tail to create a neat, even braid of a uniform size.

Try to pick up strands that are even with the braid and close to the sections above. Keep each section small, twisting the hairs and pulling the braid tight with your thumb. Avoid pulling the hairs so taut that the horse becomes uncomfortable, however.

A

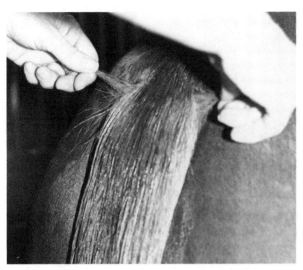

B

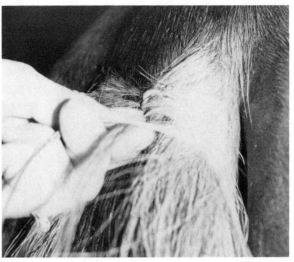

A) Start with strands at the top of the tail.
B) Pick up strands from the sides to form the braid and wrap around the bulk of the tail.

C) At the tailbone, braid the three strands into a straight braid.
D) Pull through and fold, tying off flat or into a pinwheel.

C

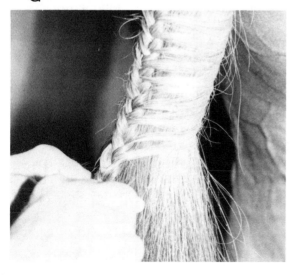

D

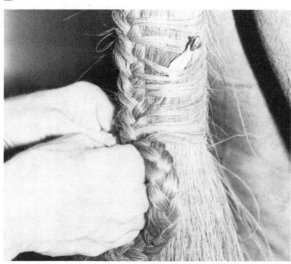

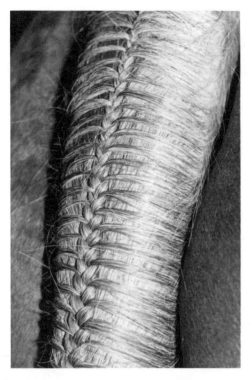

An even pattern is the result of pickup of alternate strands of hair. Wrapping the braided tail protects it from being rubbed.

As you work down the length of the dock, keep your arms perpendicular to the tail so you draw the tail hairs straight across. Though some grooms end up sitting on a box when they reach the point of the hip, it's safer to remain standing.

Many horses get cranky if you take a long time to braid. By working quickly, you will avoid making the horse impatient.

If the horse clamps its tail, you can raise the tail and place a rolled towel underneath the dock. The pressure of the tail will hold it in place.

Near the end of the braid, add a piece of yarn and braid it with the hairs. When you reach below the tailbone, from one to five inches down, tie it off as described for mane plaits. Three times around gives good security.

Alternate Method: Double over the loose ends of hair. Wrap with yarn ends and tie. Double the end over a second time and tuck it underneath.

Insert the pull-through and fold the tail end up underneath itself. Check that the loop is small and not too long before you tie it. If your loop measures more than four inches, it's probably too long.

Wrap the tail with a dampened track bandage as a temporary, short-term wrap. This keeps the hairs lying in place.

Alternate Method: Create a small, tidy pinwheel at the base of the braided tail. This looks best on a horse with a thin tail, with only a small straight braid left on the end.

After you've tied the end of the tail, do not pull it through. Pick up the loose hairs at the end, double them up tightly, and roll the mass of hair counterclockwise.

If the pinwheel looks too large or thick, undo it and finish the tail off in a loop, as described above. An oversize pinwheel—measuring more than three inches across—counteracts the elegant effect of a braided tail.

If you're satisfied with the appearance of the rolled pinwheel, stitch through the hairs at every turn with a tapestry needle, using yarn or thread. Keep the center tight so you maintain the small size.

At the top, stitch the wheel on both sides to attach it to the main tail braid.

A well-braided tail results from practice and patience. While at the show, protect the tail by wrapping it before your class.

You may decide to protect the tail's skirt by putting it up in a mud knot. Part the skirt into two sections. Cross these over each other twice—once in front, then in back. Repeat the crossing back and forth as far as you have hair. Then part the remaining hair into three sections.

Braid these strands almost to the end. Add a piece of yarn and tie.

Insert a long pull-through down through the braid, either from the top or underneath, and thread yarn into it.

Work the braid back down underneath to tuck it in.

Separate the skirt for the mud knot (left). The complete mud knot (right).

Trim a conservative bridle path on a show hunter. It should just fit the crownpiece of the bridle, so two inches is the maximum length.

As a guideline, pull the horse's ear to the side and note how the muscle of the ear creates a line on the neck. Clip right behind that line, which is where the crownpiece rests.

For a horse that has very little forelock, you might start

Trimming the Hunter

your bridle path further back to allow more forelock hairs.

Avoid touching up a bridle path after you've braided the mane, because it's easy to nick part of a braid.

Hoof Preparation

Never polish the hooves of a hunter in AHSA competition. Tradition will permit you to apply a light coating of hoof oil or dressing for a natural luster. In a breed show, polish is acceptable.

Quarter Marks and Stenciling

For a special touch, you can form quarter marks on the top of the hindquarters of a hunter, jumper, or dressage horse. Rarely seen in U.S. shows, these attract the eye to this area. Use these only on a horse with excellent conformation.

For best results, add these marks on a horse of a solid color, with a short, clean coat. If the hairs are too long, the design will fluff up as it dries. Marks will not be possible on a recently clipped coat.

You will need a dampened sponge or stiff brush and a short, one-inch section of fine-toothed comb (either a baby's comb or flea comb for pets). To save time and get uniform results, buy a plastic template to place on the hip. You simply position the template and brush or comb

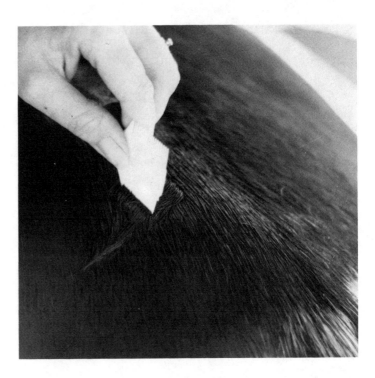

A short, fine-toothed comb is used to make quarter marks.

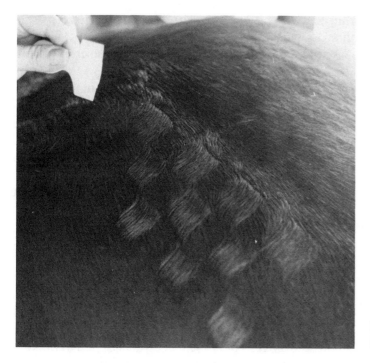

Here three rows are almost completed, forming a checkerboard pattern.

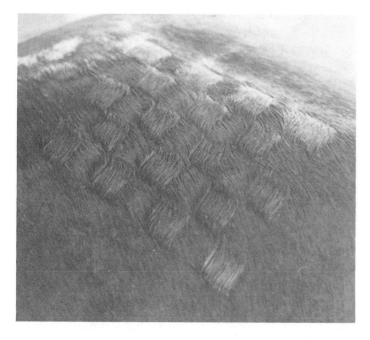

Five rows complete one section of quarter marks.

the coat in the opposite direction for square or diamond shapes.

Without the stencil, start on the top of the croup, about two inches from the spine. Wet the hairs to the skin by sponging or brushing with the grain of the hair.

Begin the pattern on one side of the backbone, starting at a lower corner of your planned square. Push the teeth of the comb down through the hair to the skin, combing across the damp hair. Keep teeth pressed down for one inch, which should be the length of the comb.

You will work upward along the backbone for your first row, using it as your guide for the subsequent marks. Skip the next section for a distance the width of your comb, measuring it to be sure it is exact. Form the second quarter mark in line with the first square.

Repeat forming every other square beside the spine until you reach the top of the hip. Then move down to the first square you formed, and begin a second line of squares adjacent to the first. Your first section should line up directly next to the first space you skipped in the first row. Continue by skipping every other square so the two rows create the checkerboard pattern, keeping the second row in line with the first.

You can erase a mark that is the wrong shape or location by rubbing hairs with your finger. It's easy to drift out of line, so adjust as necessary.

Continue until you have completed the pattern on the first side. Try to end with a full row of squares, so the marks form a four-sided shape.

Repeat on the opposite side, keeping your marks in line with those on the first side so patterns match.

A variation on quarter marks is stenciling. Here you form a mark of one section of hair, not a combination of several. A stencil may look cute, but it's acceptable only in smaller, local shows.

Be conservative in your selection of a shape. Safe choices are a leaf, heart, or square. It should not be too large.

The easiest way is to use a pattern. Draw your shape on a piece of heavy paper or cardboard and cut it out. Wet the hairs on one side of the horse's croup and position the stencil.

Use a corner of your marking comb to draw the outline. Then remove the pattern and comb hairs to fill in the outline.

After you create the pattern, watch to see how well the hairs remain in place as they dry. To help set the shape, you can comb a hairsetting gel through the hairs.

HUNTER TACK

Judges expect to see clean, uniform tack. Leather should be a dark color, not new-looking or a light tan color. Stain light-colored leather before use. With a replacement bridle part, stain it a dark color to match the rest of your tack.

Maintain your tack in good condition. Check your bridle's straps, hook studs on the reins, girth elastics, stirrup leathers, and billets regularly. Besides safeguarding you and your horse, you'll forestall a costly situation arising from tack breaking in the show ring. Unlike some divisions, in hunter and jumper classes you have no opportunity for fixing or adjusting tack once you begin competing.

Bridles

A show bridle should set off the refined head of a well-bred hunter. Crownpiece, cheeks, browband, and cavesson are made of narrow leather, either flat, raised, or raised and stitched. Don't use a browband with metal ornamentation.

Fine accents, such as fancy stitching, make a small head look larger. With a bigger-headed horse, pick a bridle with a slightly wider cheekpiece—possibly up to three-quarters inch on a warmblood. The bridle should fit so all buckles line up evenly, ideally below the eye.

The bit should be a regulation snaffle, Pelham, or full bridle. AHSA hunter rules note that the judge may penalize you for an unconventional bit. Most riders show in a snaffle bit, with the D-ring and full-cheek models most popular. When using a full-cheek bit, you may attach leather keepers that connect the tops of the bit cheeks to the bridle cheekpieces. Clean and polish your bit.

Always fit the hunter with a cavesson. Most riders pick the narrow slotted cavesson to match the bridle. AHSA hunter rules don't prohibit use of a dropped or flash noseband, but these are unconventional and imply the horse has a problem. Rules of the American Paint Horse Association, Palomino Horse Breeders of America, and Appaloosa Horse Club do bar these nosebands.

Fit the cavesson straight and even on the horse's nose. Place it on the nasal bone, about two inches below the cheekbones. You should be able to slip two fingers between the leather and the cheekbones.

Reins may be plain, plaited, or laced. Most riders use the traditional leather reins. Certain classes prohibit the use of rubber reins.

For a snaffle bridle, choose a width that is wide enough to hold comfortably, at least five-eighths inch. Narrower, one-half inch reins are safer as curb reins on a Pelham or Weymouth bridle. Check the metal stud to be sure it keeps reins attached to the bit. Fasten all straps in their keepers for a tidy appearance.

When you show wearing formal hunt attire, the judge will consider your tack for its quality and similarity. The AHSA Rule Book doesn't detail current requirements, so follow tradition with conservative flat leather on the bridle. Stitched-in leather is preferred with formal attire. The judge may penalize you for not conforming to what he considers the accepted convention.

When you show a hunter on the line, fit the horse with a bridle (a weanling is shown in a stable halter). Any yearling or older wears a bridle with a full-cheek snaffle bit with keepers. For precise adjustment, this bridle can be made with three buckles on each side—at cheekpiece, throatlatch, and cavesson cheekpiece.

This bridle can enhance a head by attracting the eye to the horse's finer points. For example, polish buckles so they shine, or even add a browband with a tasteful brass overlay. For a horse with a longer nose, use a wider, plain noseband. If the horse is plain above the eyes, select a wider browband.

SADDLES

Almost every rider uses a close contact jumping saddle. Ladies' sidesaddles are of the plain English type, with fittings specified by AHSA rules.

Use the heavy, flat stirrups of the Fillis style, with white rubber treads. For a child rider, use the Peacock or spring-loaded safety stirrup. A sidesaddle can use a regular or safety stirrup iron, with the large hold to accept the hole of the stirrup leather. Clean and polish the stainless steel of your stirrups.

Though you may use a leather, web, cord, or linen girth, the dark leather model looks best. Most riders choose the Atherstone chafeless girth with elastic usually only on the near side.

This saddle pad frames the close contact saddle in a workmanlike fashion, and the bridle complements a cute face. Some judges might criticize the cloth girth cover, however.

Your saddle pad must fit the shape of your saddle, without being too large or too small. Ideally only an inch or an inch and a half of pad frames the saddle. Most riders use a fleece pad.

AHSA rules permit martingales only in classes over fences. While jumping, almost all hunter riders who use a martingale choose the standing martingale. Fit the martingale at a correct length, so the loop doesn't swing loosely or maintain a constant tension. Either detracts from the desired look of a smooth round. A loose martingale strap causes a safety hazard for the horse; a too-tight martingale indicates to the judge that the horse is ill-mannered.

OTHER TACK

Be sure to add a rubber martingale ring to the martingale strap, which holds the strap snug to the neck. This stops extra slack from sliding down between the horse's front legs. Pull the slack through the ring so it lies above the neck loop. Choose a brown ring that matches the color of your martingale.

A few competitors use the running martingale. Adjust it so the rings barely reach the horse's jowls. With this style, be sure to add rubber or leather rein stops to your reins, so the hook studs don't catch on the rings.

You can use a hunter breastplate with a martingale attachment, though most riders use the martingale. In hunter classes, it's preferable not to show a horse wearing a breastplate alone—this implies the horse has inferior conformation that cannot keep a saddle in place. Sidesaddle riders generally avoid showing with either martingale or breastplate.

Boots and bandages are not permitted on horses in hunter classes. In very inclement weather, judges may permit the use of bell boots. Hunt seat equitation riders may use boots, and the current fashion is to do so. This offers a way to stand out from the crowd in a flat class.

Some judges frown on any flashy name tags on bridles or martingales. Avoid brass tags or plates on your show tack. A brass saddle plate, mounted at the back of the cantle, is acceptable.

15. JUMPERS

Jumper turnout resembles that of hunters, but riders have more opportunity to express their individual style. At the Grand Prix and Federation Equestre Internationale (FEI) levels, you'll see the European influence in the various fashions of grooming and tack.

JUMPER GROOMING

Pull the mane evenly so it will lie flat, with the length appropriate for the horse's type. Only a few jumper grooms braid the mane or tail, except for special Grand Prix events or championships. At a small show or in a children's class, occasionally a jumper will show with a braided tail with pompoms tied along the length, for a more colorful appearance.

To simulate the flattering look of a braided tail, you can shape the top. You pull the side hairs at the top of the tail for a trim, neat appearance. While this style is very common throughout Europe, along with the banged tail, it's not as popular in the United States.

To shape the tail, use pliers, scissors, or thinning shears. You may choose to pull hairs by hand, or use clippers with a coarse blade.

Starting at the top of one side of the tail, part the hairs you plan to pull. Plan to pull

This amateur jumper is outfitted with a full-cheek snaffle, flash noseband, standing martingale, and fleece-covered polo breastplate. The rider uses a close-contact saddle over a fleece pad set on a square saddle cloth.

from the top of the tail down approximately one-half to two-thirds the length of the dock. You'll remove hairs along a line that curves downward toward the underside of the tail.

With one hand holding the rest of the tail hairs aside, use your fingers or the pliers to pull the hairs you have sectioned along the dock. Work from the base, where tail hairs begin, to the point of the hip. Try to pull hairs over a few days time, to avoid irritating the horse. This also gives you a chance to evaluate the results.

Repeat on the opposite side. The bare skin now visible should appear to taper from the top of the tail, as shown in the illustration on page 154.

To avoid a bushy look, you can shorten the remaining hairs close to the pulled areas. If you don't wish to thin the tail by pulling more hairs, cut them with scissors or thinning shears. Trim carefully, holding the edges sideways, so you don't end up with a chopped-off look.

Some grooms shape the tail with clippers. Ask an assistant to hold the horse's tail steady. Use a coarse blade, an #8 ½ or #10, and carefully clip with the direction of the hair. Once you trim this hair, you'll need to continue the task to avoid a bristly effect.

Most horses show in a narrow bridle with a snaffle, Pelham, gag snaffle, or three-ring (elevator) bit. American Horse Shows Association (AHSA) rules do not restrict choice of bit, so a jumper might show in a hackamore or double bridle. American Quarter Horse Association (AQHA) rules limit bits to an English snaffle, Kimberwicke, Pelham, or full bridle. Bits must meet specific measurements.

Choose a bridle of a strap width that complements your horse. A fine-boned Thoroughbred usually looks best in a narrow bridle; a warmblood may require a wider bridle to complement its conformation.

Typical jumper turnout includes a running martingale, reins with martingale stops, and leg wraps.

JUMPER TACK

Be sure the bridle fits the horse in browband and throatlatch, and that cheekpieces accommodate the type of bit you use. Again, with the European influence, some jumpers sport browbands decorated with brass trim.

Many jumpers wear a flash or a figure-eight noseband to stabilize the bit in the horse's mouth and for more control. Riders usually prefer reins with rubber grips for greater security in all weather conditions. Currently popular are the white rubber grips.

Almost all riders use the close contact saddle. When choosing a pad, pick a style that ensures the horse's comfort during exertion. You may prefer to use an easily washable thin quilted pad under a fleece or foam pad, to assure that skin infections don't develop. If your horse has a sensitive back, it may benefit from the new therapeutic pads, either the gel pad or closed-cell foam. For close contact, choose a half-pad that puts less bulk under your legs.

Your preference and your horse's conformation may dictate a breastplate, usually fitted with a martingale. The racing or polo style breastplate, sometimes covered with fleece, will help keep a saddle slipping back while jumping. You might follow the current fashion with an elastic or webbing breast strap. The strong elastic attaches to the girth or saddle's D-rings and fits high on the horse's chest. It stretches to allow the horse to reach with its shoulders, yet it holds the saddle in place during strenuous jumping efforts.

Check association rules for the type of martingale allowed. AHSA rules allow only the running martingale in certain classes—those offering $25,000 or more in prize money. Classes held under FEI rules restrict horses to only the running martingale.

When entering your horse in a competition over high and wide fences, you may add other accessories. An overgirth buckles tightly over the seat of the saddle, the flaps, and the girth to keep the saddle more firmly in place. This wide web strap, with elastic on one end, also keeps the saddle flaps from wrinkling up under your leg and provides an additional measure of security. If your girth should break while jumping, the overgirth would temporarily hold the saddle in place.

Many jumper riders use studs in the horse's shoes, especially when competing on grass footing. (See Chapter 17 for details on studs.)

A stomach guard will protect your horse when it folds its front feet tight against its belly, especially important when equipped with studs. The thick square leather pad attaches over the girth and covers a wider area than the girth alone.

Boots are routine protection for the jumper's legs. You can choose among a wide variety of styles, depending on your horse's needs. Rubber bell boots protect the pastern, tendon and ankle boots guard the horse's front and/or hind legs, and the small rubber fetlock ring prevents the horse from brushing behind very low on the pastern.

You may choose to outfit your horse in the popular open-front galloping boots. These protect the vulnerable ankle and tendon areas, while still allowing the horse to feel a jump pole it may rub. For guarding the hind legs, use galloping boots. Choose boots with fleece lining for a cushiony feel, especially on a thin-skinned

The overgirth, shown on a combined training competitor, secures the saddle during strenuous jumping efforts. This horse wears two saddle pads.

A jumper wears a square saddle pad, close contact saddle, standing martingale (correctly fitted with a rubber stop), and a figure eight noseband in addition to a regular cavesson. It has bell boots and open front galloping boots on its front legs, and galloping boots on hind legs.

horse. The plastic Hampa boots are often used in inclement weather.

You might school a horse in polo wraps, for general purpose protection and support. Few horses show in these wraps, although some do compete in a supportive working bandage if they need extra support. Apply this wrap with extra care, so you don't cause the damage you intend to prevent. The thicker polo wraps are safer to use, because you're less likely to bind the leg. Avoid leg wraps in sand or mud, as grit can work inside and rub the horse's legs.

Fit any boots properly. A too-large or too-small boot can rub sores.

In warmer weather, you may add a crocheted ear net to your horse's tack. Another European import, this headgear protects the animal from irritating insects.

16. DRESSAGE AND SPORT HORSES

The Continental influence prevails in the grooming and turnout of the dressage horse. European methods still set the standard in this discipline, although many techniques for hunters and jumpers also apply to dressage horses. In general, aim for a look of understated elegance in sport horse turnout.

DRESSAGE GROOMING

You'll show the horse braided, so pull the mane to a braidable length. If your horse has a thin mane, you may decide to use the thinning shears instead of pulling. The mane may lie on either near or off side of the neck.

Braid the mane in the same style as a hunter's mane. Dressage horses usually reflect the Continental look of fewer braids spaced further apart.

When you've tied all braids, you might choose to wrap each braid snugly with a piece of white or black adhesive tape, one-quarter inches wide and one-half inches long, covering the knot of yarn. Some tack shops stock a special sticky vinyl braiding tape, or you can buy reusable white plastic sleeves that curl around a braid tied with Braidbinders rubber bands.

A dressage horse shows the currently popular style of braided mane, with fewer braids than a hunter.

White accents highlight the shape of the horse's neck, so ensure that you place each section in the same position on the braid. If you add a bump to the top of each braid, position the tape just below the bump. Also space braids evenly down the crest. Spacing is more crucial than a standard size or thickness of the braid, because the tapes make the braids stand out.

Most grooms use the Braid Aid to measure the distance between braids. You can also measure with a marked mane comb, either one with a mark painted or taped on it, or an old plastic one with a missing tooth. Starting at the first braid, measure with the comb and part the hairs for the second braid.

You can pull the forelock either to a point or straight across, or you can leave it natural. Braid it also, in the same style as the hunter, and wrap it with tape.

Most dressage riders don't braid the horse's tail, feeling that the horse will move more freely with its tail unbraided. To simulate the neat, straight appearance of a braided tail, you can pull or clip the top of the tail.

The braided mane of the dressage horse is taped with white adhesive tape.

The narrow top accentuates the shape of the tail-bone. It refines the outline of the horse when viewed from the side and the back. The finer the tail, the wider the hindquarters appear, and the fanning of the full skirt below the pulled dock enhances the look of the swinging tail so desirable in the dressage horse. A swinging tail implies a swinging back.

Grooms usually clip the sides of the dock. Fit a #10 or #15 blade on the medium clippers (some grooms prefer a #30 for a finer result). Starting at one side of the top of the dock, clip down about five or six inches, with the grain of the hairs.

At the end of the clip, taper the trim to a point, not

A groom has protected the dressage horse's braids by wrapping a leg of dampened pantyhose over the braids. This covering also acts as a mane tamer.

153

Photographed in Germany, a sport horse shows a neatly clipped tail.

DRESSAGE TACK

Bridles

a straight division between clipped and unclipped hairs. Blend the line of clipping into the tail.

Carefully clip along the edge to catch any loose hairs from the top of the tail that stick out to the side. Do not clip off any of the top hairs.

Repeat on the other side. If you feel you've clipped too close, or the heat of the blade may have irritated the skin, rub a soothing ointment into the skin. Also apply baby oil into the roots of the hair to the tailbone.

Alternate Method: You can pull tail hairs as described for jumpers.

The amount of facial trimming depends on your orientation. If you follow the Continental look, you'd leave long hairs on the muzzle and trim only the hairs that protrude from the ears.

The bridle path should be short—one inch is adequate.

You may oil hooves in a hunter manner. Few grooms polish the hooves of the dressage horse.

American Horse Shows Association (AHSA) rules specify what type of bridle and bit are permitted in dressage classes. For Training through Third Level, the horse is shown in a plain snaffle bridle with either a regular cavesson, a dropped noseband, a flash noseband, a crescent (lever) noseband, or a crossed (figure-eight) noseband. Rules illustrate the acceptable bits. The loose-ring snaffle is a popular choice for many competitors.

Many people prefer the flash noseband, which is easier to fit than the dropped style. The top edge should rest on the tip of the nasal bone, not the cartilage. The bottom edge just touches the corners of the horse's mouth.

In Fourth Level, you may show in any of the above bridles, or use a simple double bridle of bridoon and curb bit with chain, with a lip strap optional. Use a regular cavesson with the double bridle.

If you show in FEI classes, realize that some rules vary from AHSA's. The "Krank" and jawband nosebands are acceptable, and Federation Equestre Internationale (FEI) rules require the double bridle with specific bit measurements. FEI rules prevail in international classes, even in a show recognized by AHSA.

This dressage horse models a white-lined bridle, loose-ring snaffle, and flash noseband.

Because dressage is an artistic sport, the fashion of the bridle is important. Try different looks on your horse to judge which best complements its head. Like the hunter world, a conservative choice of headgear is always correct.

Most competitors show in a narrow bridle of flat or rolled leather. Add elegance with a raised browband and cavesson. Fancy browbands are popular, either of woven plastic or overlaid in brass or silver.

155

Now in vogue is the European style padded browband and noseband. This complements the head of a warmblood, which may have a larger head than a Thoroughbred. (Measure your horse's head when fitting a dressage bridle. A "warmblood" size may fit a head forty-four inches long, compared to a "horse" size of forty. The throatlatch, browband, and noseband can measure up to six inches longer.)

Leather padding in contrasting white or brown frames the dark leather. This catches the eye of the observer, and it may tend to balance out a larger head. You can select from different widths of padding, ranging from a narrow edging or a wider contrasting strip overlaid on the dark leather. If your horse has a bigger head, you can try a wider bridle with more white. If the horse has no white on its face and an attractive though large head, a bridle with narrow white lining may enhance its appearance.

A bridle in all black leather may be the most attractive choice on a gray horse or one with a large white blaze. (Black does go in and out of fashion in the dressage world.) Fancy stitching adds interest to plain leather.

Many dressage bridles show the Continental fashion of cheekpieces and reins attaching to the bit with buckles, not hooks and studs. Buckle ends add interest and color, either in brass or silver tones.

Reins are usually flat leather. Laced reins or reins with hand stops help you maintain contact. You may also use web reins or those with rubber hand parts, for a better grip. You can choose among reins with full rubber grips wrapped around the rein, leather reins with a rubber lining on the inside only, or web reins embedded with rubber elastic.

Saddles   Almost all riders use a dressage saddle, although AHSA rules permit any English saddle with stirrups. Like riders in any other division, dressage competitors follow the leaders in choosing a brand name or style.

Under the flaps of the saddle, you'll try to use minimum padding to maintain your leg contact. Place a natural cotton or wool layer against the horse's back, usually a quilted design that helps the pad hold its shape. You may use a pad that fits the shape of your

The foregirth can be seen ahead of the regular girth. Both are padded to provide cushioning. Robert Dover on "Romantico," preparing for the 1984 Olympic Games at Santa Anita Park.

saddle, or the popular square pad. If necessary, you may fit a fleece saddle-shaped pad on top of the square white quilted pad, or use a half-pad (of gel or closed-cell foam) to absorb concussion. A new design of quilted square pad features a pocket for inserting a square or tombstone-shaped gel pad.

Traditionally riders show with the white square pad.

You'll also see the white pad bordered in colors, or a black pad bordered in white. Some riders purchase a style featuring the horse's breed brand on the pad's corners—this advertisement may be considered somewhat pretentious.

Many pads feature loops for the girth and billets, which secure the saddle onto the pad. Thread the girth through the loops at the bottom of the pad. Fit the first billets through the billet loops.

If your saddle has the long billets, which place the buckles out of the way of your thigh, you'll normally use a short girth. For a saddle with flap straps, use a girth with three buckles on each end.

For some European horses, the foregirth is a helpful accessory. This additional girth of web or leather prevents the saddle from riding forward on a horse with round withers. You might also use this on a horse with a long back, to hold the saddle farther back. In this position, you can make the back appear shorter.

Made of web, leather, or plastic over a metal wither bar, the foregirth features tabs that hold the saddle back. Place the foregirth on top of the square pad, and slip the saddle behind it. The regular girth should overlap the surcingle of the foregirth to avoid pinching the horse's skin. When schooling, you may wish to cushion the skin by placing a thin pad underneath the two girths.

Be sure your saddlery meets the appropriate AHSA or FEI rules at the show, both in and out of the ring. Rules prohibit showing or schooling in certain tack, and the technical delegate or steward will examine your turnout.

PRESENTING THE SPORT HORSE IN HAND

Either at a competition or a breed approval, outfit your sport horse in the correct tack for presentation. In shows, you can compete under Dressage/Sport Horse rules of AHSA or the U.S. Dressage Federation (USDF). Breed associations follow European traditions in the turnout of animals for inspection into a studbook.

In these events, the simple act of leading a horse assumes major importance. Fifteen minutes at a breed approval affects a horse's worth and future career, so aim to present your horse's quality in its appearance as well as its gaits.

For an approval, groom the horse well. Don't use

any cosmetics on the horse's face, or polish the hooves. The horse does not need to be shod, and you don't have to body clip if you're showing a horse in the fall. Some exhibitors do clip a patch on a foal's left hip, for easier branding at an approval in the winter months.

Pull the mane short. In most cases, you'll braid the mane as you would for dressage, as a braided mane accents the horse's neck. Clip or shorten the tail at the dock, and bang the tail.

You'll show a horse aged two or older in a snaffle bridle. (USDF rules allow bridles on yearlings; AHSA rules require a horse younger than two to show in a halter.) When showing a horse of European breeding, follow the style by choosing a dressage bridle with buckle ends. Many handlers use a flash noseband, and a contrasting browband completes the look. AHSA rules specify that the bridle must have a throatlatch.

At a mare show in Germany, a Hannoverian mare models a snaffle bridle with decorative browband and a flash noseband and a braided mane accented with white tape.

Rules of the Appaloosa Horse Club specify the type of snaffle bit, permit a dropped noseband, and prohibit decorated bridles and silver halters.

You will receive a badge with the horse's number. Secure the badge to the offside of the halter ring, or to the bridle, where the browband meets the crownpiece.

Tradition and rules affect your decision to carry a whip or not. In a breed approval, you'll present your horse to a commission of predominately European authorities. Few European handlers traditionally carry a whip. If your horse shows better with a whip, the unwritten rule usually allows an assistant to follow the horse and crack a whip on the each leg of the triangle. (Check with the approval's host to confirm this option.)

When showing a horse under AHSA or USDF rules, you may carry a whip. (AHSA rules permit an assistant.) Ideally, you won't need to worry about this extra aid, as you've trained your horse at home.

The Trakehner and Holsteiner associations require you to first present the horse in hand, then release it to run at liberty to display its canter. Other associations may observe your horse, usually only a stallion candidate, free-jumping. In this situation, use reins that snap or clip to the bit, so you can quickly turn your horse loose and regain control after you catch it. In free-jumping, you'll probably be allowed to present the horse equipped with wraps or galloping boots on the forelegs.

17. COMBINED TRAINING

T he competitor in combined training competes in three phases: dressage, cross-country, and stadium jumping. Events vary in their levels of sophistication. A horse trial, which does not include the prolonged endurance phase of the three-day event, is often less formal. American Horse Shows Association (AHSA) rules govern combined training events except for the CCI (Concours Complet Internationale). In a CCI, you must follow Federation Equestre Internationale (FEI) rules.

GROOMING

In general, you'll groom your horse in a utilitarian style, like a jumper. You may braid for the dressage test.

If you present your combined training competitor in a veterinary inspection, prepare the horse as you would a sport horse. Again, the braided mane is optional. You may decide to oil the hooves.

For the cross-country phase, you may equip your horse with studs in its shoes. These steel projections help your horse "grab" onto the dirt, grass, or mud while galloping and

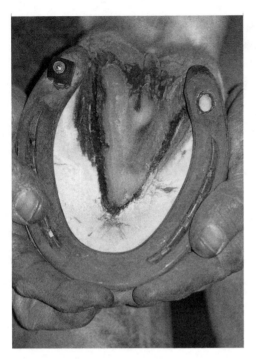

A farrier places a shoe ready for studs, with a stud fitted in the hole on the left.

jumping at speed. Some jumper riders use these for traction, depending on the weather and terrain.

On your horse, the farrier will apply shoes about five-sixteenths inch thick. The shoes contain threaded holes on each heel to accept the studs. You may choose to use studs on both inside and outside heels of the shoe, or only on the outside.

Studs screw into the holes on the shoes. Usually only five machined threads will seat a stud, so you must protect the threads with plugs. Rubber or cotton plugs fit into the holes when you're not using studs.

Plug holes immediately, right after the farrier nails on the shoe. You can coat the threads with a lubricant, like WD-40 or ichthammol emollient, before inserting the plugs.

You can choose among a range of studs, with the shape and length depending on the terrain and weather. A stud can project a minimum amount, like a small, square road stud, or reach as much as five-eighths inches into the ground like an Olympic stud.

Use a screw tap to clean the holes after you remove the plugs. Screw the studs in and remove them later with a wrench. Be sure you protect the horse's legs with boots, so it doesn't accidentally cut its leg with a stud.

For the more demanding competitions, some grooms rub a coating of grease such as wool fat or soft paraffin on the fronts of all four legs. This lubricant can help the horse "slide" over the top of a solid fence, if it miscalculates the height or width of the obstacle.

Tack   For cross-country, plan for stressful jumping efforts. The tack must remain in place during the test, without endangering either horse or rider.

Use reins with rubber grips, so your hands won't slip. Keep the bridle in place by connecting the crownpiece to the horse's mane. Tie a shoelace to the crownpiece, and tie the other end to a lock of the mane. In case the horse falls, the bridle should remain on its head even if you pull on the reins.

In certain events, you and your tack must meet a minimum weight. If you need to make up weight, you'll use a weight pad, which fits under your saddle and on top of your regular saddle pad. Lead weights slip inside pockets on the pad.

In the stadium jumping phase, this rider's horse wears tack that meets AHSA rules: snaffle bridle with flash noseband, reins with rubber grips, standing martingale, and open front galloping boots.

Use a breastgirth of leather, web, or stretch elastic. A web overgirth assures that the saddle remains firmly in place, a precaution in case your regular girth breaks.

Protect the horse's legs with boots that won't slip or turn on course. If the going is wet or the course includes water obstacles, avoid a boot that will absorb water. Some

This eventer has equipped her horse with a breastgirth.

grooms wrap with exercise bandages, but you must secure these to endure the stress of jumping.

For the less arduous dressage and jumping tests, observe association rules that specify tack for the schooling and competition. According to AHSA rules, dressage saddlery essentially follows the Dressage division, with a breastplate permitted. For jumping, you may use only a running martingale or Irish martingale. FEI rules also cite saddlery, almost the same as AHSA lists. A technical delegate will inspect saddlery before you begin each phase.

18. AMERICAN SADDLEBREDS

Known as the peacock of the show ring, the Saddlebred competes in three-gaited, five-gaited, and pleasure classes. These elegant horses are turned out immaculately and require diligent daily care to maintain their show ring style. Judges penalize a horse with a rough coat and consider neatness in grooming and tack in pleasure classes.

American Horse Shows Association (AHSA) rules currently list five under saddle divisions for Saddlebreds. In the Performance divisions, three- and five-gaited horses traditionally show with high tails, the result of tail sets and braces. Their feet are specially shod and prepared for the show ring. Horses in the Pleasure division—Country, Show, and Park—show with less animation and unset tails.

Saddlebred turnout also applies to the Saddle type of Pintos (showing under rules of the Pinto Horse Association of America) and the Golden American Saddlebred (the Palomino Horse Breeders of America).

SADDLEBRED GROOMING
Mane Grooming

Most Saddlebreds show with a full mane, which you cultivate to grow to a flowing length. Except for horses showing in Country Pleasure, you'll follow tradition and braid these Saddlebreds, with one long braid attached to the first section of mane and to the forelock.

Before braiding the horse, you can place a small towel over its muzzle, tucked into the noseband of the halter. This will keep the horse from being tickled by the ribbons, or attempting to nibble them. You will need an assistant to help start the braids.

You will braid satin ribbon, five-eighths inches wide, into the first section of the mane and the forelock. You can use one color or two complementary shades. You will also need a pair of sharp scissors.

When you choose ribbon colors, you can match or contrast with the colors of your browband and cavesson, or use your stable colors. On a dark horse, red and white look good, or one solid color will enhance a stunning, flashy horse with a white face. The color of the braids can help pull together an entire outfit.

Cut three lengths of ribbon, each approximately two feet long.

Dampen the first three inches of the mane, and separate the hairs into three parts.

Instruct your assistant to hold the three ribbons on top of the hairs, at the crest.

Then begin to twine a ribbon around each section, braiding as you wrap. You should twist the ribbon so it covers the hairs totally.

When you have secured the ribbon partway down the hairs, your assistant can remove his or her hand. Continue braiding down about eighteen inches. With the scissors, trim any loose hairs that protrude beyond the braid.

At the bottom of the braid, tie a knot. Fold the ribbon ends in half and cut on a slant. Fluff the ends so the tufts form a star shape.

Repeat this fold and cut at the top of ribbon ends, on the crest.

Repeat this process for the forelock braid. Tuck the end of the forelock braid underneath the crownpiece of the halter so the horse does not nibble it. When you bridle the horse, you can wrap the forelock braid around the throatlatch three or four times to prevent it from flapping as the horse moves.

You can add glitter to the mane by rubbing brillian-

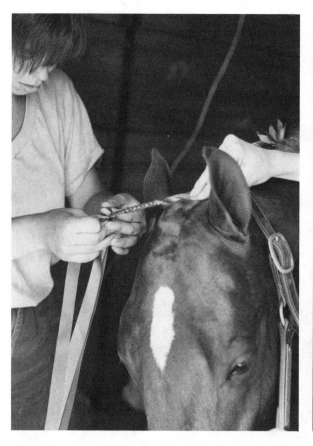 

The assistant holds her hand on the ribbons as the groom braids the ribbon onto the forelock (*top left*).
The completed mane ribbon features tufts at both ends (*top right*).

tine over it. Rub a light amount on your fingers, then wipe it on the hairs.

Other enhancements permitted on the mane are artificial coloring and the addition of more mane hair. You may not add mane hair to a Country Pleasure horse.

On the three-gaited horse, also called the walk-trot horse, you roach the mane. You should clip it about once a month with the medium clippers, using a #10 blade in the off season. For a neat show ring appearance, clip it with a #40 blade, the day before the show.

You may show a two-year-old of any division with a full mane and tail.

The set tail is distinctive of the breed, adding to the horse's beauty. The high-set tail is traditional, but rules don't require it in any Saddlebred class. Pleasure Horses must show with a full tail, with tail carriage unaltered by any artificial means. (You may show a Pleasure Horse that

Grooming the Tail

167

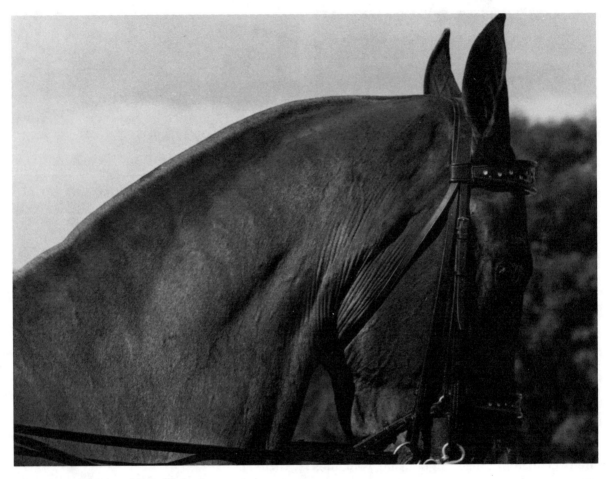

This three-gaited Saddlebred displays a roached mane and cleanly trimmed ears.

previously had its tail altered but is no longer kept up in a tail set.)

The high-set tail is the result of the horse wearing a tail set while in the stall. The tail fits through a crupper, with a spoon fitted under the dock. A tail set harness holds the set in place, usually worn over the horse's sheet or blanket.

When the tail is in the set, you must keep it clean so it doesn't begin to itch. Use a tail set whose spoon is padded with sheepswool lining. Some grooms apply baby powder to the skin under the spoon, and cushion it with cotton padding.

A cover protects the top of the tail while in the set. The rest of the tail is usually kept braided up to protect hairs from breakage. Tail boards in the stall, placed along the walls at the height of the horse's shoulder, prevent the horse from rubbing its tail on a flat surface.

When the show season is over, you can let the horse down and leave its tail out of the tail set. Replace the tail in the set about one month before your first show. This gives you time to work up the tail muscles to get the horse comfortable in the set.

Remove the tail set before the horse enters the show ring. Take the tail out of the set about thirty to forty-five minutes before your class is called.

Don't remove the tail from the set too soon. The tail muscles can become cold if the tail is out of the set too long, and the horse will become uncomfortable when you position its tail.

To maintain the high tail carriage when the tail is out of the set, you may choose one of three methods. Use a tail brace, a device that holds the tail steady and avoids the undesirable crooked tail. It fits underneath the horse's tail and ties onto the tail and saddle girth with shoe strings. The hairs of the tail cover the brace. For a horse that will be shown in several consecutive classes, the brace may be the most comfortable appliance. It does not interfere with the circulation as a lace might. You can choose one type of brace to use on a horse whose tail has not been set.

In place of the brace, wrap a lace around the doubled tail, to hold it vertically. Or, the horse is gingered to carry its tail high. This acts as a mild irritant to encourage the horse to hold its tail away from its body.

To ginger the horse, use ginger salve. You can purchase this product, a blend of aconite and ginger root in petrolatum (petroleum jelly) and glycerin. Or, mix a small amount of ground ginger root into a dab of petroleum jelly. Lightly rub a small amount of the mixture under the dock, around the horse's anus, about five or ten minutes before the horse enters the show ring. (You might choose to wear a rubber glove during this procedure.) After the class, be sure to wipe off the salve with plain petroleum jelly.

On a Saddlebred shown with a full tail, you may add a tail cap, switch, or full tail for additional fullness. (Country Pleasure prohibits any false tails.) These enhancements also help cover up a tail brace.

The additional hairs must match the horse's tail, and you must be sure they're clean and well picked out, just like a tail.

It's an art to attach a switch so it appears natural and

Waiting for its class, a Saddlebred still has its tail in the set. The tail is braided up to keep it clean. In the background are a wardrobe of tail switches, each colored to match the tail of a different horse.

inconspicuous. The usual method is to tie it to the tail with a shoelace. Braid the lace inside a few strands underneath the top of the tail, under the tail brace. Then wrap it around both tailbone and the switch, and knot it for security. Be sure the additional hairs are attached firmly—a loosened switch ruins the look of an elegant tail.

You'll usually roach the tail of the three-gaited horse, shaving four or five inches down the dock. Don't trim the tail close with a fine blade, because it can make the horse's tail resemble a mule's.

A recent trend is the "feathered" tail for the walk-trot horse. If the horse does not carry its tail correctly, leave the hairs unclipped for a more attractive appearance.

Walk-trot horses used to carry their tails at a 45° angle from the body. The fashion now is vertical, carried straight up off the horse's back.

With a long tail, knot the hairs so the tail does not drag on the ground before the class. To avoid the undesirable wavy tail, you can tie a ribbon on the end of the tail, loop it up, and tie the ribbon under the tail to hold it off the ground.

AHSA rules permit dyeing the mane and tail, but not any other part of the horse's body.

The feathered tail is more attractive than the roached style on many three-gaited horses. This tail is held in place with a lace.

Saddlebred trimming enhances the horse's crisp appearance. To emphasize the desirable sharp-eared look, leave diamond-shaped tips of unclipped hairs on the ears. Oil this hair lightly before a class, which makes the horse look more "hook-eared."

Trim a bridle path of about six inches on a horse with a full mane. Because the forelock is braided, many grooms save time by clipping off most of the hairs underneath the forelock. You may leave a short tuft of hair for anchoring the braid. To clip this area, part the forelock, lift up hairs you wish to retain, and protect them with your thumb while clipping.

You may want to try trimming a "V" on the front of the forefeet. This design creates the appearance of slimmer ankles and pasterns, making the horse look straighter in the leg.

Grooms who wish to avoid body-clipping a winter coat have devised alternate clips. For a horse with fuzzy hairs on the backs of the ears, you can shave the entire outside of the ear and the top of the head down to the browband. Called a skullcap trim, this gives a neat appearance. Any change of color is less obvious since the bridle covers the line between clipped and unclipped.

Another clip to emphasize the forehand runs from mid-neck, at the base of the windpipe, up to include the throatlatch and head.

Trimming

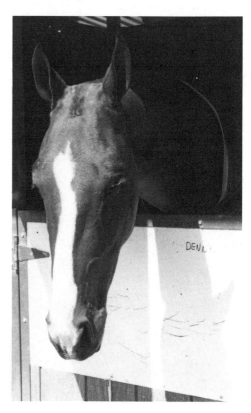

This Saddlebred's forelock is closely clipped.

Shoeing

Because Saddlebreds are so athletic and perform precise disciplines with animation, shoeing is an integral component in show ring performance. The farrier seeks to achieve proper balance, so the animal can perform its gaits correctly. Shoeing affects speed, action, and length of stride.

Shoeing requirements vary, with the three- and five-gaited horses shod with long toes and weighted shoes. Most Saddlebreds wear pads, a leather pad between shoe and foot that protects the sole. The pad helps to hold the shoe in place and may alter the angle of the foot.

The Country Pleasure horse must be plain shod, without pads, and weanlings and yearlings must show barefoot.

Sand and polish hooves. Use black on dark hooves, and clear on white hooves.

Hoof length and polishing enhance the horse's movement.

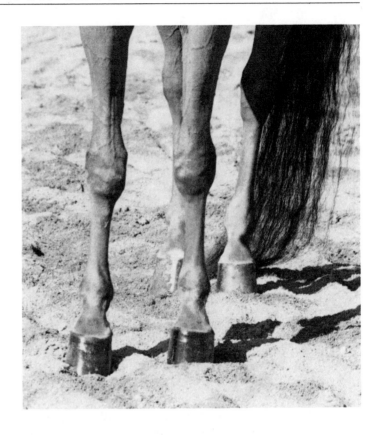

SADDLEBRED TACK

The Saddlebred wears a flat, cut-back show saddle, which emphasizes the horse's forehand. (Certain Country Pleasure classes specify Western or hunt seat equipment.) Most riders use a brown saddle.

Saddles

The flat saddle should sit horizontally on the horse's back. The seat size should fit the rider, allowing the knee to lie flat against the stirrup leather while the hips rest in the deepest part of the seat. A popular style is the Helen Crabtree saddle, which features an equitation seat with a deeper seat to hold you in place while protecting the horse's back. This saddle popularized the adjustable stirrup bars. You can place the leathers at an individual position to keep your leg underneath you.

Stirrup irons should measure about one inch wider than your boot. Choose Fillis stirrup irons for weight to increase your security. Grooms used to blacken the white rubber treads to conform to tradition, but now this color is acceptable. To save time polishing stainless steel, you can choose irons and bits that are chrome-plated for a sparkling appearance.

Saddlebred riders traditionally didn't use saddle pads. A pad detracts from the horse's beauty, and most types would show beneath the saddle. Yet you may choose to protect the horse's back and the saddle by using a felt pad shaped to fit the saddle's contour.

White girths are traditional, and most people choose vinyl or leather. Clean these with Formula 409 cleaner. If you use the older style web or tubular linen girth, you will have to whiten it with shoe polish. New girth styles are made from vinyl, in solid colors or in a combination of two complementary colors. AHSA rules specify a leather or web girth in the three- and five-gaited performance divisions.

Bridles

To enhance the beauty of the horse's head, choose a narrow bridle, usually with straps three-eighths inches wide. The horse generally shows in a full bridle, made of flat or round leather. AHSA rules do allow you to use a Pelham bit in Pleasure Equitation classes. The leather bridle, like the saddle, must be stained dark; don't show with light-colored tack.

A matching browband and cavesson set decorates the bridle. You can pick from a wide variety of colors and patterns, though red patent leather browbands remain fashionable. A current trend is to match the colored browband with a plain, unstitched leather cavesson.

Also seen are the shaped browband and cavesson set, which are flared in the front. The browband allows a narrower shape at the ear, which is comfortable for the horse, but it may not lie flat against the horse's head. A browband that bulges out from the horse's face is unattractive; try exchanging it for one that fits, or possibly have one made to fit your horse.

Cavessons are either the slotted or spike ring styles. Most of the plain leather cavessons are of the spike ring design. Fit the cavesson so it rests on or slightly above the ring of the bridoon when you shorten the reins.

Laced snaffle reins are often seen in the show ring. These help the rider maintain steady control on a sweaty-necked or pulling horse. Narrower than the similar reins used on hunters, the lacing is finer.

Other Tack   In a model or in-hand class, show the Saddlebred in a bridle, usually with only the curb bit, or a halter. AHSA prohibits the curb bit for weanlings and yearlings.

Rules also exclude the use of any artificial training devices on horses entered in pleasure classes, at any time on the show grounds. These include chains, shackles, rubber bands, or blindfolds.

Martingales or breastplates are not permitted.

The five-gaited horse wears quarter boots on the front feet. These protect the back of the pastern, as the horse could overreach when it racks.

Made of leather, these two-part boots must fit snugly, but not too tight. You should be able to fit one finger between the strap and pastern. They must be shining white, so paint them with white shoe polish before each class.

In inclement weather, show management may permit the use of polo boots or bandages in other classes.

19. TENNESSEE WALKING HORSE

The grooming of the Tennessee Walking Horse and Walking Pony resembles that of the Saddlebred, although the two breeds are handled and shown differently. Rules of the National Show Horse Committee, Inc. (NSHC) govern the breed. At shows, a Designated Qualified Person will officiate to see that rules of the Horse Protection Act and NSHC are enforced.

TENNESSEE WALKING HORSE GROOMING

Show the horse or pony in a long, full mane and forelock. You'll braid the first strand of mane and the forelock like the five-gaited Saddlebred, except in Western classes. Some exhibitors add ribbon "butterflies" along the length of the braid as additional ornamentation. (This is not allowed in Equitation classes.)

To present a coordinated picture, equitation riders blend the color of ribbons with their habit and the horse's browband. Dyeing of hairs is permissible, but you may not change the color of hide, hair (markings), or hoof.

A full, flowing tail enhances the distinctive gaits of this breed. Horses in Pleasure classes must show with natural, unset tails. The Show Tennessee Walking Horse usually has a full

The Tennessee Walking Horse is shown with mane and forelock braided.

tail, prepared in the same fashion as the five-gaited Saddlebred. Most horses show wearing a tail brace. Hairs may be dyed. Though switches are permitted, only horses with very short tails wear this accessory.

Rules prohibit braced tails in the Pleasure division. Weanlings and yearlings shown in halter classes may not be fitted with a tail brace or switch.

As with the Saddlebred, trim the horse regularly. Trim the bridle path to eight inches, on both Show and Pleasure horses.

Trim the hairs of the fetlock, but clip hair on the front of pasterns or coronet with a coarse blade, about two weeks before the show. This hair protects the ankles from being rubbed by action devices during training and showing. You can trim the hairs on the back of pasterns with a close blade.

A champion Tennessee Walking Horse, "Coins Bad News," typifies the breed's qualities and perfection in grooming. Photo courtesy of John Feltner; photographer: Jack Greene

Hooves

The hoof and shoes, if any, must conform to official measurements. The length of the toe must exceed the heel by at least one inch.

Any horse may show barefoot. Weanlings shown in halter may not be shod.

In the Plantation Flat-shod Pleasure classes, you show

your horse either plain shod without pads, or Lite-shod. NSHC rules describe specific measurements.

Feet of horses in the Show division and Park and Show Pleasure classes are padded up, with oversized pads (not more than 50 percent of the natural hoof length) anchored to hooves with metal bands. Bands must be placed at least one-half inch below the coronary band.

Sand the hooves, and polish the hoof, pad, and metal band.

You may apply only specific substances to the pastern area at the show, for only the Show and Show Pleasure horses. Lubricants allowed include glycerin, petrolatum, and mineral oil, or a mixture of these. Check with show management before applying any lubricant.

You may not show any horse that shows any evidence of previous soring of pastern or coronary band, such as a scar, callous, or granulated tissue. This applies to all horses foaled after October 1, 1975.

TENNESSEE WALKING HORSE TACK

The bridle is a narrow show style in black or brown leather with a colored cavesson and a matching browband. (Rhinestone or sequined browbands are not allowed in Pleasure or Equitation classes.)

Show the horse in a Walking Horse shanked bit, with narrow leather reins. Bit shanks measure from six to ten inches, but they may be no longer than 9½ inches for the Plantation Pleasure Horse. On all horses, the curb chain or strap must be at least one-half inch wide and lies flat against the jaw. In Pleasure classes, judges will penalize a tight curb chain, and the cross chain cavesson is prohibited.

In breeding classes, show a mare or stallion over two years old in a bridle. Weanlings and yearlings must show in a halter, with a snaffle bit optional. On any show equipment, you may not attach a nameplate or display a name.

Use a cutback saddle. Often a black horse is fitted with a black saddle, and a sorrel or bay with a brown one.

Don't use any boots or action devices, except on horses showing in the Show division and Equitation. Place these on the front pasterns to encourage the extreme action of the breed. The type of device must conform to official regulations.

You may choose any one of these three types: a boot, with no rough edges contacting the horse; a smooth single

A Plantation Pleasure Tennessee Walking Horse is presented with an unset tail and a natural foot. This mare is performing a running walk suitable for trail riding.

chain with a maximum weight of six ounces; or rollers of hardwood, steel, or aluminum, with a maximum weight of six ounces.

Most exhibitors choose the chain or the rollers, as grooms consider boots to be harder on the horse's skin. Boots must be a leather or unlined rubber bell boot, a hinge bell or Walking Horse hinge, or a heel boot. They may be of any weight, but the judge will ask your groom to remove one boot when your horse stands in the lineup.

Many Tennessee Walking Horses are also outfitted in a breast strap, one-half to one inch wide. The horse carries itself with hindquarters lowered. Attached to the first billet on each side, this helps hold the saddle in place. It may be black or brown leather to match the saddle, or white vinyl with colored accents that match the girth.

No martingale or tiedown is permitted.

20. ARABIAN

Groom the Arabian and the Half-Arabian to highlight their natural elegance and beauty. Enhancements may be clear polishes only, with no colored solutions applied to the body. Prohibited are white shoe polish on white socks, or brown polish on the chestnuts.

ARABIAN GROOMING

The mane should be long and full. Ideally the hairs feel soft and silky, with a fine texture.

Some grooms shape the forelock by pulling or trimming off the top and sides. Others prefer it to be as fluffy as possible.

When you show the horse under saddle, usually you'll tuck the forelock under the browband. This holds it in place as the horse canters. To do this, wet the forelock with a dampened brush. Twist it to the side.

Spray the forelock with a hair spray to hold it in place, then tuck it securely under the bridle's browband or ear loop of a Western headstall.

Braid the mane only for hunter, jumper, dressage, or English Show Hack classes. Because the mane is long, you may braid it into a French, or continuous, braid. This style is attractive, although it is flexible and may work loose.

At the top of the mane, part a section into three strands about one-quarter inch thick. Braid them down an inch, holding the braid so it lies across the neck at a ninety-degree angle.

You might need to braid down less or more, depending on the thickness of the mane hairs.

Holding the braid in one hand, use the other to pick up another strand from the crest. Braid it into the original strands for another inch or so, still holding the braid at an angle across the neck.

Continue working down the neck, picking up strands so you collect the entire mane in the braid.

At the withers, braid in yarn, tie, and use a pull-through to fold the braid. Or, tie the braid with a rubber band. Wrap and tie several times so the end lies neatly, forming a round bump.

The Arabian's distinctive tail should be long and natural, never set or gingered. You may braid the tail only for the classes that permit a braided mane.

You may brighten the color of a white or gray tail with a rinse to make it look silvery white or gray. Don't apply glitter to the tail, mane, or hooves.

Close trimming can bring out the lines of the facial bones. However, a recent American Horse Shows Association (AHSA) rule change forbids "balding" around the eyes and clipping off the tips of the eyelashes.

Cut the bridle path to an average length of four or five inches. To make a throatlatch appear longer and slimmer, you could trim it to a maximum of six inches. This will also exaggerate the look of a long mane on a slim neck.

Sand and polish the hoof, with the ideal look resembling patent leather. You may apply clear, black, or brown hoof polish.

The groom has tucked this Arabian's forelock under the bridle's browband. Narrow leather and minimal silver accent the horse's delicate face.

Preparing for a side saddle class, this gray shows a long, natural tail.

181

Horses under the age of two must show barefoot. The toe may not be longer than 4½ inches, with a fourteen-ounce shoe the maximum weight. AHSA rules detail the use of a single pad.

ARABIAN TACK

In Park, English Pleasure, and Country Pleasure classes, show your Arabian in a flat show saddle. The forward seat style is appropriate only in the hunt seat classes. An English Show Hack may use any type of English saddle.

You might use a felt saddle pad under the flat saddle, because some Arabians tend to have sore backs. This can detract from a neat appearance, as it raises the saddle and causes the neck to look shorter and head lower. Choose a pad that doesn't show when you're in the saddle.

The girth may be leather, web, string, or vinyl, with the colored vinyl type currently popular. You can select a white girth with a vertical stripe of color, which coordinates with your outfit and the horse's browband and cavesson.

In Western classes, use a standard stock saddle. To fit the Arabian's shorter back, many riders choose a model with rounded skirts. Unlike the Quarter Horse exhibitors, Arabian showmen continue to prefer show tack in dark colors, such as chocolate brown.

When showing aside, choose either the English or Western sidesaddle. Show officials will separate the class into the two styles when the number of entries warrants a division.

Bridles match the type of saddle. With the flat saddle, rules specify a light show bridle with a single curb, curb and snaffle, or Pelham. Almost all riders choose the double bridle with a colored browband and cavesson set, similar to those used on the Saddlebred. You will also see a leather browband and cavesson, occasionally ornamented with silver.

Hunters and jumpers show in regular hunt bridles with cavessons. The gag bit is allowed only in jumper classes, and judges may penalize unconventional headgear.

Outfit a Western horse in a regulation bridle, in either the split ear or browband style. Currently the browband type of flat leather is more fashionable. Both bridle and reins are decorated with considerable silver. Most riders prefer the romal (closed) reins, except in reining classes.

The French braid can keep a long mane contained while the horse is being schooled.

A stallion shows the typical length of bridle path for the breed, which highlights a slim throatlatch. Cosmetics on the muzzle add an elegant, tasteful glow.

Here they follow the style of split reins, influenced by the reining style.

When you show an Arabian at halter, rules require a suitable halter with a throatlatch. The choice of style should enhance the horse's head, attracting the observer's eye to the horse's expression.

You can choose to emphasize the horse's eye or muzzle. A red browband will bring out the eye, while detracting from the muzzle area. Large silver conchos also attract attention to the eye.

Accent your horse's elegant throatlatch by using a gold chain or a fine black string. If your Arabian has a heavier throat, you can use a standard style and adjust it loosely. The leather may look floppy, but it makes the throatlatch seem longer and slimmer.

A noseband tends to cut the horse's head in half, making it appear shorter. A halter without a noseband acts to lengthen the head. On an extreme head, the halter with a snaffle bit accents the clean look.

Choice of color also influences the total image. On a

The browband and cavesson match on this Arabian's double bridle.

gray, black with silver decoration looks good. Choose black with red trim for a bay.

Some exhibitors prefer the extra control of the iron noseband for a lively stallion. Made of metal tubing, with or without a cable core, this slim halter is a strong device. Combine it with a control bar to "bump" the nose if you need to.

The snaffle bit can also control a stallion. Use it with sensitivity to cue the horse to stretch its neck and bring its nose out. Used too roughly, the horse may tuck its nose and squeeze its throatlatch, which shortens the appearance of the neck.

Martingales and tiedowns are not allowed, except with regulation hunt tack in a class over fences. Breastplates are popular on horses shown in Western classes.

Rules do not permit boots or bandages. In inclement

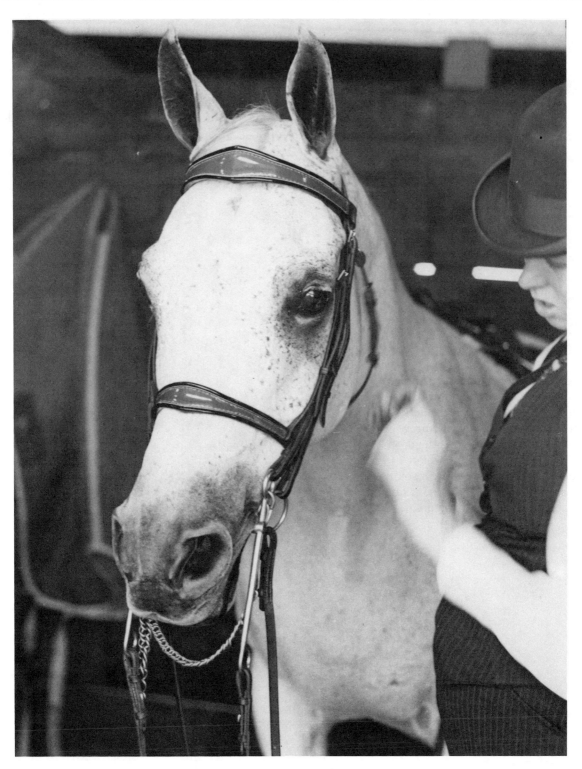

Muzzle, ears, and eyes are highlighted by expert trimming. Cynthia Burkman prepares "Corjet."

weather, however, show management may allow the use of bell boots.

Riders in the Mounted Native Costume classes must choose appropriate tack and attire. Colorful fringes and tassels decorate the tack and clothing. The bridle may be of any style that will control the horse, and riders usually choose an English saddle (cutback or forward seat) that the costume covers. The outfit consists of a cape or coat, pantaloons, headdress, and scarf or sash.

Competing for National Championship honors, a mare shows an extreme amount of facial cosmetics to highlight her eye. Check current trends at the shows you attend, as this look may fall from fashion (hopefully). The halter has a gold chain throatlatch, and close trimming accents a fine facial structure.

21. NATIONAL SHOW HORSES

Across between the Arabian and the Saddlebred, this unique English horse expresses the beauty of both breeds. Under American Horse Shows Association (AHSA) rules, you may show the National Show Horse as a Half-Arabian, governed by rules of the Arabian division, or under National Show Horse rules. If you expect to show in both divisions, usually held in separate shows, realize that some regulations vary.

NATIONAL SHOW HORSE GROOMING

In general, prepare your National Show Horse as you would an Arabian. Rules require a natural appearance, with a full mane and tail. The mane usually lies on the off side. You don't show the horse with a set tail, artificial tail, or glitter.

Shoeing regulations do differ from the Arabian. If you compete in Half-Arabian classes, you'd conform to the shorter toe length required by the Arabian division. In its own division, the National Show Horse may have a foot as long as 5½ inches, with pads. Shoes may contain no foreign material, which includes any use of lead screws.

A champion English Pleasure National Show Horse displays the breed's animation. Photo by Howard Schatzberg.

Exhibit the National Show Horse weanling in a halter of the Arabian style. Photo by Howard Schatzberg.

The weight of shoe and pad can total sixteen ounces. A horse showing in Three- or Five-Gaited classes may carry shoes of any weight.

NATIONAL SHOW HORSE TACK

The National Show Horse competes in pleasure and gaited classes. For English Pleasure, Country Pleasure, and Three- and Five-Gaited, outfit the horse in English tack, with a flat saddle and full bridle. As an English Show Hack, you can use the full bridle or any show bridle with a snaffle, Pelham, or Kimberwicke bit. This class forbids nosebands other than the simple cavesson.

No National Show Horse shows in a breastplate or martingale.

Competing in Five-Gaited, this National Show Horse wears quarter boots. Photo by Howard Schatzberg.

In halter classes, use an Arabian style show halter. On a horse one year or older, you may opt for the Saddlebred fashion of showing the horse in the bridle fitted with a curb bit.

The Five-Gaited horse may wear bell boots or quarter boots, both unweighted.

22. MORGANS

Though Morgan breed is groomed to emphasize its elegance and trim appearance. Styles in English classes show Saddlebred influences, but the breed must be shown naturally, without any added hair, tail brace, or ginger. Morgans show in Park and Pleasure sections under American Horse Shows Association (AHSA) rules.

MORGAN GROOMING

Show a Morgan in its natural beauty, with a full mane. Maintain a long and flowing mane, never trimmed or pulled.

The breed's trademark mane is often wide, averaging about two inches. It should lie on the offside; if not, you can "undercut" the mane. Clip a narrow width of hairs under the mane to train it to lie correctly. With a bushy mane, you may need to undercut it as much as half its width.

For a clean look, tuck the forelock under the bridle. This keeps the long hair from blowing into the horse's eyes or ears, and gives a cleaner look. Grease the strands to keep the hairs together, or wrap a rubber band around the hairs. Conceal this band under the browband.

A Morgan's wispy forelock is tucked under the bridle browband. He shows the breed's full mane.

Some grooms trim the horse's bushy forelock, shaving it to a one-half inch square. This results in a wispy forelock, about a thumb's width in diameter. If you don't want to trim the forelock so drastically, just trim the outer, wispy hairs that fluff to the sides when you lift the bulk of the forelock.

You may braid the mane and tail only in hunter, jumper, or dressage classes. To avoid shortening the long mane, braid in the French braid (described in Chapter 20) or the scallop style (described in Chapter 14).

The tail must also be full and natural. In the Park division, tails are long and floating, with several inches or even a foot of hairs resting on the ground when the horse is standing. Protect the long, full tail by braiding and wrapping.

This length of tail can become entangled in the horse's hind legs. Morgans showing in the Pleasure division usually carry a shorter tail, barely touching the ground.

The bridle path accentuates the length and curve of

This pleasure Morgan displays typical breed characteristics in its short face and long, full mane and forelock.

the horse's neck. Clip the length an average six inches, according how it complements the position of the horse's throat. The length can vary according to the type of class and personal preference—from a short three inches to ten inches. Trim a Western horse's bridle path shorter than an English horse's.

Leave diamond-shaped tips of hair on the ears after clipping. If desired, make the eye look larger by clipping a circle around the eye with a surgical blade. Apply black facial highlighter to enhance the look of "mascara."

You may need to body clip the Morgan's winter coat. Avoid clipping the summer coat, by not clipping when the horse starts to shed.

AHSA rules specify three different weights and lengths of shoes according to Morgan show sections. You may show your horse barefoot, and weanlings and yearlings must show without shoes. Shoes and pads on performance horses must be open heeled, without bars, turnbuckles, bands, or external weights. At all Morgan shows, officials must measure one foot of each champion and reserve champion as horses exit the ring.

Hooves are sanded and polished.

MORGAN TACK

In English Pleasure and Park classes, most horses show in the flat show saddle. Use the appropriate styles in hunter and Western events.

The full bridle with colored browband and cavesson properly matches the flat saddle. If you're showing the horse with a forward seat saddle, AHSA rules list the appropriate bits.

To emphasize the distinctive small muzzle and wide-set eyes, you can fit a Morgan with a wide browband and cavesson. These shorten the face, especially across white facial markings.

In hand, show the Morgan in a Weymouth bridle, with the snaffle bit and its reins removed. Young horses up to two years old are shown in a show halter with chain lead shank, usually of round or flat patent leather.

Boots are allowed only on jumpers and stock horses. Show management may allow the use of polo boots or bandages in inclement weather.

While on the show grounds, you may not school your horse in any rubber or elastic devices attached to its legs or hooves. Rules do permit schooling in vertical half-cup blinkers.

23. ANDALUSIANS

This ancient breed is groomed to highlight its proud appearance. Because Andalusians have an abundance of hair, grooms concentrate on the lush mane and tail.

ANDALUSIAN GROOMING

In most classes, leave the mane long and flowing. For special occasions, grooms braid the hairs into elaborate styles. One is the traditional bullfighting braid, practiced in Spain and Portugal.

Bullfighting Braid. Gather these tools:
- Scissors
- Hoof pick
- Hemostat
- Dampened brush (a finishing brush will hold more water than a stiffer brush)
- Braidbinder rubber bands
- Two rolls of contrasting colors of polyester ribbon, three inches wide, of the single face, bordered satin type.

The long mane of the Andalusian is usually braided to preserve the hairs. "Arrogante," a stallion owned by Rainbow Farms.

Measure and cut the ribbon. For a length appropriate to the horse's neck, drape it over the poll so the ribbon touches the ground on both sides. Cut on the diagonal for easier threading, and set ribbon aside.

Wet both on top and underneath the mane with the dampened brush.

Use the tip of the hoof pick to part the mane into two sections, evenly down the middle of the crest, so half falls onto each side of the neck.

French braid both sides of the mane (see Chapter 20), using Braidbinders to secure the ends. Braid the forelock in a regular braid.

Place the ribbon on top of the crest, where the mane begins. Arrange it so both ends are the same length. With the hemostat, pick up one end of ribbon to thread it through the very top of the braids, holding the ribbon shiny side up. Avoid wrinkling the ribbon.

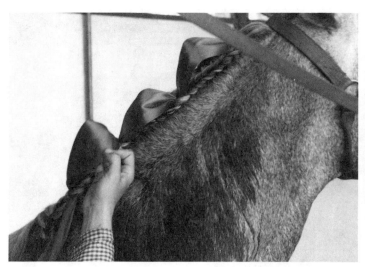

Three red puffs have been added to the mane.

Alternate Method: Traditionally, grooms use a needle to thread the ribbon. This must have a large eye to avoid wrinkling the ribbon. You can use a carpet needle or a special type imported for Portugal for this style of braiding.

Four inches down the mane, work the ribbon through another braid. Don't pull it tight, but lift it into a puff, so it stands up from the crest with the shiny side up.

Continue down the mane to create a series of four or five puffs.

At the pigtail that ends the French braid, form a loop of ribbon, and work the ribbon back through to the beginning of the last puff.

Secure the end by repeating this loop. Complete the braid by running the end of ribbon through the loop of the last puff.

Use the other side of the ribon to repeat the braid on the other half of the mane.

Add a second row of puffs on both sides, with the contrasting color of ribbon. Thread the second color of puffs through different sections of the mane to show off the colors.

When you've threaded all ribbon through the mane, trim all the ends at an angle, about three inches below the loops.

Using the hemostat is one way to thread the ribbon through the braids.

A row of white ribbon contrasts with the red.

The completed braid adds an authentic flavor to the horse's appearance. "Aploma," a filly owned by Rainbow Farms.

Alternate Method: You may choose to use three lengths of narrower ribbon in two colors, which will cover more of the mane hairs.

Cut another ribbon for the forelock, measuring about four times the length of the braided hair. Thread it straight across the top, then thread it again at the bottom to make one loop that pulls the forelock up under itself.

Make another loop to form a puff similar to those in the mane. Trim ribbon ends.

Continental Braid

Another braid for the Andalusian, also seen on some Arabians, is the Continental or macrame braid. This appears complicated, but it is actually quite simple. The striking pattern is effective for costume classes and breed exhibitions.

You'll need Braidbinders and one-half-inch wide tape. You can buy black electrical tape in a dispenser, or use a roll of colored adhesive tape.

Part a section of mane behind the ears that measures about two fingers wide. Apply a rubber band over the strands and wrap it three times. The band should rest a short way down from the crest.

Continue parting and banding the entire mane. Other sections will be thicker, so you will only need to wrap the band twice around the hair.

Alternate Method: If time is short, make sections thicker. The final effect will not be as attractive, but you can complete the braid in thirty minutes.

Wrap each band with a piece of tape 1¼ inches long. Don't try to save time by taping the hairs without banding them first; the tape alone will not hold the mane in place.

To form the second row, split the first two hanks in half and band half of the first to the adjacent half of the second.

Continue parting and banding down the mane to complete the second row, forming diamonds between the two. Try to follow the curve of the first row, banding as high as possible. As the horse flexes its neck, the bands may slide down the hairs.

Tape the second row. Include the first and last hanks, which are narrower strands not connected to another.

Repeat to form at least four rows so you create a pattern of two complete diamonds.

When the mane is finished, spray it with an oil-based product to add shine.

Braid the forelock, either in two sections with ribbons, or one long braid. The style varies according to the type of bridle the horse will wear.

You can improvise a variation by first braiding the mane part way into a series of narrow braids, then finishing with the macrame pattern.

Fit bands near the crest.

With three rows banded and taped, one set of diamonds has been created.

This divided forelock braid was inspired by the Saddlebred style.

Remove the braids by sliding the tape down the hairs. Because this tape isn't very sticky, it shouldn't pull out hairs.

A bridle path is optional, because the horse should grow as much mane as possible. If you trim one, it should be no more than one inch long.

ANDALUSIAN TACK   In English and Western classes, you'll use tack similar to Arabians and Morgans. When competing in a costume class, you may select an authentic Spanish saddle and attire.

24. PERUVIAN PASOS

The two easy-gaited breeds, the Peruvian Paso and the American Paso Fino, are groomed in similar style, with the emphasis on their natural beauty and presence, known as "brio." These horses should never seem as if they have been prepared with any cosmetics.

They share a distant, common ancestry, but the two breeds have developed separately. They are shown quite differently in the United States. The Peruvian Paso is unique among show horses in that it has been imported to North America with its authenticity intact. Its cousin, the Paso Fino, has developed to please northern tastes, as described in Chapter 25.

Two associations set rules for the Peruvian Paso: the American Association of Peruvian Paso Horse Owners and Breeders and the Peruvian Paso Horse Registry of North America.

PERUVIAN PASO GROOMING

Many breeders and judges from Peru serve as judges at U.S. shows. These authorities prefer the horse to be groomed as naturally as possible, and they will criticize the exhibitor for excessive clipping or use of products.

Mane and tail of the Peruvian Paso should be full and fine-textured.

The horse has a fine coat, which you should groom through rubbing rather than coat dressing. Because the judge wants to feel the coat's natural texture, don't use any oil on the face or any artificial coloring. (Cornstarch is acceptable to whiten leg markings.)

The mane and tail of the Peruvian Paso must be long and flowing. Both should be fine-textured. In Peru, grooms often fashion the tail to be narrow at the dock and wide at the base, with the bottom banged. This creates a broomlike appearance and produces a pleasing effect when a group of Pasos are ridden abreast in the traditional "barrida," or sweep.

A Peruvian Paso showing under the rules of the Peruvian Paso Horse Registry of North America may have a bridle path up to two inches long. The American Association of Peruvian Paso Horse Owners and Breeders allow no bridle path, following the Peruvian style except geldings. You may trim a gelding's bridle path down three-fourths its neck, with not less than one-half inch of mane standing up. The last one-fourth of the mane is not clipped, to aid in mounting, and you shave the forelock. If the horse is eligible for showing under both sets of rules, do not trim any bridle path.

With no bridle path, you must divide the hairs of mane and forelock carefully, laying each section in place.

Don't trim the legs too close. About six weeks before the show, trim from the knee down to the hoof, so the color will return before the show.

The Peruvian Paso is traditionally shown barefoot, with a hoof not more than four inches long. You scrub the feet clean, but usually don't paint or polish them. Be sure to clean the horse's feet before a class—an embedded pebble could affect the quality of the horse's gait.

PERUVIAN PASO TACK

The handmade tack must be authentic, as judges will inspect it in performance classes.

Show the Peruvian Paso with the distinctive Peruvian saddle. This is handmade of intricately carved leather, covered by the "pellon," a heavy leather-backed tapestry of strands of black wool. The stirrups of the saddle are pyramid-shaped, made from carved wood. Silver often decorates the stirrups.

Always use the saddle's traditional leather tailpiece, or "guarnicion." This accessory consists of a crupper, tailcover, and straps to connect it to the skirts of the saddle. The Peruvian Paso shows in classes with either the bozal or the Peruvian curb bit. The bridle, reins, and romal are made of intricately braided leather, decorated with silver fittings. Under the bridle, the horse also wears a braided leather halter. Fit a horse shown in the bit with a leather or metal "bozalillo," a narrow bozal, adjusted in a position similar to that of a drop noseband.

In a breeding class, you may show the horse in either a leather stable halter, the Peruvian bozal, or an Arabian-type halter. The shank is long, averaging sixteen feet, to allow the horse to work loose. It is equipped with a chain, which you can thread under the horse's chin or clip to the halter ring.

Mane and forelock are divided to lie in place.

PERUVIAN PASO ATTIRE

The traditional outfits of the "chalanes," or horse trainers, dictate the clothing worn in Peruvian Paso classes. In breeding classes, handlers all wear white long-sleeved shirts and pants. Some add a small white towel worn on the right hip, tucked into the pants or belt.

Authentic gear for the Peruvian Paso includes handmade bridle, Spanish-style saddle, wool pellon, and wooden stirrups. The rider is wearing the traditional poncho, scarf, and hat.

When mounted, riders add a wide-brimmed straw hat, in the Peruvian planter's hat style. Boots are low-heeled, similar to a jodhpur boot.

According to Peruvian custom, only riders of finished horses (shown in bit and spur) wear the traditional poncho. The large garment is usually of white cotton or wool, though cream and beige are also acceptable. The finest ponchos are of a brown shade, woven from vicuña or a blend of vicuña and silk.

With the poncho, the rider wears a white or cream scarf around his neck and a wide-brimmed planter's hat. On the finished horse, silver spurs with large rowels complete the authentic attire.

25. PASO FINOS

The Paso Fino shows under rules of the American Horse Shows Association (AHSA) and the Paso Fino Owners and Breeders Association. As with the Peruvian Paso, the aim in its grooming is a natural look.

PASO FINO GROOMING

Judges consider the horse's appearance, or finish, in the Bella Forma, or conformation and gait, class. The coat should be slick to intensify the overall refinement of the Paso Fino.

The mane and forelock must be long and flowing, so don't pull hairs to shorten or shape the mane. You may not color any hair artificially.

Leave the tail natural, brushing it well so hairs flow free to accentuate the horse's movement.

Hairs should cascade from the tail bone as the horse moves in its distinctive gait. To accentuate this look, you can part the tail hair down the middle, separating the hairs into two sections. Apply a small amount of baby oil down the part. At the base of the tail bone, pick up a few hairs and loop them into a slip knot to hold the part in place. Just before entering the ring, untie the knot and fluff the hairs.

The Paso Fino may have a four-inch bridle path, but most grooms trim it only the width of the clipper blade.

Trim the ears and the whiskers on the muzzle and around the eyes. Cut only the tips of hairs on the jawline to accentuate the contours. On the legs, highlight the refinement of bones and tendons by trimming with the grain of the hair. Clip the feathers close under the fetlock to define the line, and trim the hairs on the coronet.

Most Paso Finos are shown barefoot. The hoof may not measure longer than four inches. If you shoe your horse, the limit is 4½ inches, with a plain ten-ounce shoe.

Hooves are usually painted in only the natural color, although some exhibitors do polish hooves with hoof black.

You may level chestnuts with the leg. On the muzzle and around the eyes, apply baby oil.

PASO FINO TACK

Tack should be plain, so it will not detract from the horse. In Classic Fino and Performance classes, you'll usually show the horse with an English saddle. (Most riders choose a dressage saddle.) Although Colombian tack is not allowed, some exhibitors use a Colombian saddle pad under the dressage saddle. A standard stock saddle is used in Western Pleasure classes.

The bridle matches the saddle. English bridles should measure from three-eighths to five-eighths inches wide, with matching cavesson (not a dropped noseband) and browband no wider than one inch. Reins must be plain, not braided, leather.

Most riders show with a curb bit, generally of a loose-shanked style with a rubber or leather mouthpiece. Some horses go better in a spoon mouthpiece, with or without a roller.

You cannot add a noseband to the Western bridle. The bit can be of any type, with the curb limited to a six-inch shank and equipped with a curb strap or chain.

Horses shown for schooling can wear any humane bit; the Colombian bosal, in which the throatlatch ex-

The Paso Fino is prepared with a full natural mane and tail. "Volcan Lace," stallion owned by Melody Oaks Ranch.

erts pressure on the chin; or a combination of bosal and leather-mouth snaffle.

In "Bella Forma" (conformation) classes, show a horse less than two years old in a halter, with one long lead line. Outfit a horse two or older in a plain leather halter, with two long (sixteen feet) lines.

The halter is made of flat leather in a narrow width, with a browband and throatlatch. It may be brown, black, gray, or white to match the horse's color. The judge checks the noseband for smoothness, and the horse's nose for any scars, which are prohibited.

On the Paso Fino, the rider in Western Pleasure classes

must carry a lariat or reata, and a breastplate is allowed. English riders may not use a breastplate or martingale.

PASO FINO ATTIRE

Clothing is subtle yet elegant. The official dress, allowed in classes except Pleasure and Western Pleasure, is a long-sleeved bolero-type jacket with pants. These usually match in color, with conservative earth tones such as white, tan, or black preferred.

With this dress, wear a white or pastel shirt, decorated with trim or ruffles, and a small triangular tie. Boots, an optional cummerbund, and a flat-brimmed Spanish hat complete the outfit.

Wear a more casual outfit in pleasure classes, such as a long-sleeved shirt, trousers, boots, hat, and jacket or vest. A tie is optional. Western riders should wear a Western hat and shirt, chaps, and cowboy boots.

26. PONIES

Many ponies are groomed according to their breed type. For example, prepare a Walking Pony like a Tennessee Walking Horse, a Quarter Pony like a Quarter Horse, and a Connemara like a hunter.

PONY GROOMING

Manes and Forelocks. Some ponies have naturally bushy manes and forelocks. The mane can be so heavy that its weight pulls the crest to the side.

To train the mane and forelock to lie flat, you can save time by clipping off part of the underside instead of pulling individual hairs. Some grooms consider this shortcut appropriate only for local events, not recognized shows.

Lift up the mane and part off a section of about one-third of the hairs lying underneath. Hold these apart, and with large clippers shave them close to the neck. Clip part of the forelock hairs as well. The rest of the mane should lie flat.

Prepare a hunter pony as you would a hunter, pulling its mane short for braiding.

Some breeds, such as the Shetland, the Welsh Pony, and the Pony of the Americas (POA), must abide by specific regulations in their show turnout. The first two breeds are affiliated with the American Horse Shows Association (AHSA).

A Welsh pony models the typical full forelock and mane. "Ardmore Active," mare owned by Pony Cross Farm.

Shetland show ponies may have their tails set, but they may not be fitted with a switch or metal tail brace. A shoe string tied to the tail can hold the tail in place.

A Shetland may show with shoes as a yearling or older. Foals must be shown barefoot.

A Welsh Pony should have a natural full tail that you may never set or ginger. Section B, Hunter, and Pleasure ponies may show with a tail braided in hunter style.

Fanciers prefer a natural mane on this breed. Hairs may be pulled to keep the mane neat and in proportion to the size of the pony.

Show the Welsh Pony with its ears unclipped. On a Welsh Cob, leave the trademark feathers on the legs untrimmed.

This rider is just the right size for her pony hunter.

If you need to braid the mane, the scalloped style (described in Chapter 14) produces a clean line for hunter and halter classes.

According to AHSA rules, the Welsh Pony may be shown barefoot, and foals and yearlings must show without shoes. A two-year-old may be fitted with an unweighted shoe without pads. Toes of the Section A pony are limited to four inches, with a ten-ounce shoe. For Section B, the limit is 4½ inches, with a twelve-ounce shoe.

The Pony of the Americas follows rules similar to the Appaloosa. You may roach or pull the mane to a five-inch length. Pull the tail so it reaches near the tops of the hocks.

POA hooves must be naturally colored, with no artificial polish added.

PONY TACK   Pony tack is naturally smaller in size to fit both pony and rider. You may have problems locating quality equipment, which might need to be custom-made. In response to the growing numbers of hunter ponies, several firms offer a range of saddlery designed for ponies.

Bridles   Pony-sized English bridles are readily available, proportioned to fit. On a large pony, you might try a cob bridle. If the throatlatch is too long, have a saddler add a second buckle to the off side. Reins should measure about forty-eight inches long.

Most ponies wear a bit with a 4½-inch mouthpiece, though a large pony may take a 4¾ and a small one as narrow as 3½ inches.

Ponies may be shown in breeding classes wearing a halter or bridle.

Saddles   A pony's saddle should be proportionate to the animal. Many ponies have backs rounder and wider than horses, and the saddle tree must fit the pony's conformation. An English saddle should have smaller flaps, so they cover less of the pony's back.

It must also fit the rider, so a child's saddle should be proportioned differently from an adult's. A twelve- to fourteen-inch seat should be made deep, with a somewhat straight flap and high cantle. This design will accommodate the young, short-legged child who often tends to ride with her legs out in front of her body. Pony saddles of these small sizes can fit children aged four to ten.

Look for stirrup leathers forty-two to forty-eight inches long. You may need to add a crupper to keep the saddle from sliding forward.

Few Western saddlemakers craft quality pony saddles. You might choose to have a saddle custom made. A large pony may be able to wear a small model built on a short Quarter Horse tree. You'll probably have to special order a Western cinch to fit a pony.

Under AHSA rules, specific regulations apply to certain tack of some pony breeds:

In breeding classes, a Shetland stallion aged two years or older may show in stallion tack. This consists of a leather surcingle with a crupper and with check reins attached to the bit of a snaffle bridle. A Welsh stallion must be three years old to show in stallion tack.

POAs aged four and under may show wearing a rawhide hackamore. Over five, a bit is mandatory. In English classes, a POA may not be shown with a Pelham bit converter. A cavesson is required, with a drop noseband allowed in jumping classes.

THE PONY PICTURE

Ponies are appealing, and the total picture should reflect their unique characteristics. You can accentuate a cute face by highlighting a tiny muzzle and large eyes with baby oil or Vaseline.

A rider suitably proportioned to the pony will not detract from the appearance. On a pony shown hunt or stock seat, the rider's feet should be at or above the horse's belly line, with the leg about three-quarters of the way down the barrel. An adult can look suitable on a Section A Welsh Pony, if proportioned correctly. (Usually a person five feet or under will fit the smaller pony, unless the torso is long.) An adult riding saddle seat, which requires a longer leg, can create a pleasant picture.

A hunt or stock seat rider will appear overbalanced if the bottoms of her boots rest below the pony's bellyline. Shortening the stirrups may raise her feet, but she will look ridiculous if her knee angle is too abrupt. AHSA rules in the Pony Hunter division note that the judge must penalize an entry where the rider's height and weight don't seem suitable to the pony.

PART III

ATTIRE

INTRODUCTION
TO ATTIRE

Your horse is ready, and your show schedule's in hand—now consider preparing yourself. Clothes do not a horseman make, but they do contribute to a winning image.

You're in a horse show, not a fashion show. Yet, you must wear correct attire that complements your performance. Association rules specify the basic appointments and occasionally some details of your turnout. Follow those rules when you pack for a show, to ensure that your clothing conforms to current specifications. A show official, either a judge or equipment steward, could disqualify you from a class. In some shows, officials will not allow you to enter the ring wearing improper dress, so read those rules!

As an equestrian, you dress the part to respect the centuries-old traditions of fashion. The horseman has always displayed a certain cachet, a style sense that set him apart from earth-bound humans. Today you perpetuate this custom through a confident presence, or "class."

Horsemen display class by conforming to equestrian fashion, and outdressing the competition. You fit in and show your good taste by trim, workmanlike dress. At the same time, you also display a "fashion forward" flair without overwhelming other riders. You

A custom outfit gives you the confidence you need in today's competition. Photo courtesy of Hobby Horse Clothing Company.

stand out from the crowd in a subtle way and influence the judge with your professionalism. If two horses are equal, the image that you present could make the difference in the placings.

In the show ring, you dress for success. When you know you look sharp, you'll act the part. Choose attire that inspires you to show your best, and flatter your body shape with clothing that accentuates your positives while minimizing any negatives.

Selecting the winning attire does require building your wardrobe. Dressing up can be part of the fun, unless you dread shopping. The time you spend organizing your outfit should increase your confidence in the show ring. Combine the right look with a winning attitude, and you'll exude that show ring presence that tells the judge, "I'm a winner."

Quality show attire does make a difference. You'll be showing before horsemen who have scrutinized thou-

Pulling together the right outfit presents a positive first impression in quality show attire. Photo courtesy of Hobby Horse Clothing Company.

sands of riders, and these experts recognize distinction. Judges make instant assumptions, and they might judge your equestrian skills by the image you present.

For that positive first impression, buy the best items you can afford. Choose garments of quality fabric that are well cut and sturdily constructed. Verify that every item fits you well, whether you're in the saddle or holding the lead shank.

Build your wardrobe from head to toe, or start with the basics and work up and down. You'll consult various sources while acquiring different garments. You may purchase items at department or specialty stores, tack shops, Western wear stores, or through custom tailors.

27. WESTERN ATTIRE

Of the three primary styles of show attire, Western is the most colorful. You may choose to attract the judge's attention by wearing flashy outfits that are also neat and workmanlike. Current trends favor sophisticated, tailored apparel.

Western attire includes a long-sleeved shirt, Western hat, and cowboy boots. Rules of the American Quarter Horse Association (AQHA), American Paint Horse Association (APHA), Appaloosa Horse Club (ApHC), and American Horse Shows Association (AHSA) specify these basic requirements; in performance classes, chaps are optional in most associations but required in ApHC and AHSA.

Currently colorful fashions abound in all types of shows. Previously, riders of Arabians, Morgans, and those competing in West Coast open shows displayed more colorful dress than Quarter Horse, Paint, and Appaloosa competitors. With the impact of the Quarter Horse Congress and national championships like the World shows, dress among the various breeds has become more standardized across the country. These events set fashion trends, as the industry tends to copy what the champions wear.

This plaid shirt is appropriate for the informality of a trail class.

Western dress changes more than hunt or saddle seat. Fashions go out of style quickly, and you have to keep up. Be sure you match current styles, so you don't look outdated.

SHIRTS

You'll wear a long-sleeved shirt, which AHSA and AQHA require to have a collar. The style can range from a standard white dress shirt to many variations on the traditional yoked design. Women riders often choose the pleated tuxedo shirt with a wing collar as a basic, to dress up with Western accessories.

To flatter your body, wear a trimly fitted shirt. Current blousy men's styles, influenced by the preferences of rodeo riders, are so full the extra fabric floats in motion. You need to decide if the billowing movement distracts from your riding or the horse's performance.

Your shirt should fit well at the collar and have sleeves of the proper length. When you hold the reins, your wristbones shouldn't show. Be sure the shirt has shirttails long enough to stay tucked in.

Women riders need a smooth, polished look in pleasure and horsemanship classes. Extreme motion distracts from that image, so choose a shirt constructed to fit closely through vertical darts in the front, bust darts, and a contoured center back seam. Keep your profile trim by tucking your shirttails snugly, possibly inside your underwear. If the shirt still looks too blousy, pin the front to your pants waistband, just behind your belt buckle.

When wearing a form-fitting shirt, a woman can avoid that distracting "bounce" by wearing a sport bra with

A shirt must fit at the collar and have sleeves long enough to cover your wrists. Matched with a vest and chaps with tooled tops, this outfit makes you look like a winner in pleasure classes. Photo courtesy of Hobby Horse Clothing Company.

wide straps or a body shaper made of nylon and spandex. This smooths the torso and helps create a leaner, Western look. It also helps if you're short-waisted, by minimizing the pushed-up look created by chaps.

Shirts usually fasten with buttons or snaps. A custom-made shirt may feature a front or back zipper, which improves the fit and prevents gapping between the buttons. The shirt might be constructed as a body shirt, with snaps at the crotch, so it won't ride up.

Women's shirts may feature a yoke in front and back. Look for trim that flatters you. A curved yoke creates a line which can emphasize the bust, or possibly makes shoulders look rounder. Some younger riders might look cute in lace-trimmed shirts.

For more definition of the arm, the shirt may be puffed at the top of the sleeve, but still fitted on the arm. The leg of mutton sleeve, possibly considered improper Western attire, has lost popularity.

Some slim youth riders wear a turtleneck body suit, accented with appliques. This fitted look flatters a trim rider.

Though most shirts are made of cotton or polyester blends, silk or silk and rayon give an additional sheen. A silk plaid shirt will make you more visible, especially in an indoor arena. A shirt made of a lighter fabric should be lined for a better shape. Dry cleaning is recommended for quality shirts, which will maintain the crisp appearance of the trim.

For those special occasions, you might choose a shirt that sparkles. Sequin trim or appliques add highlights when you show indoors, and an all-over sequined shirt definitely catches the eye.

AHSA rules specify that you must wear a necktie, kerchief, or bolo tie with the shirt. Whatever the show, you'll wear some Western accessory at your throat. Men rely on a scarf or silk tie tied in a square knot. In less formal shows, you'll see riders wearing scarves around the neck with the top button of the shirt undone. The scarf should not stream in the breeze as the horse moves.

Young girls may pick a ribbon as a tie, to enhance the feminine look of their shirt. Another unusual tie is a length of Ultrasuede with rounded ends, which can be stretched to tie in a square knot. The ends fit under the collar, or one can be pinned in place over the other. This heavier material will not flap like cloth, and it can match the shirt buttons or piping.

Recent innovations include a pre-folded silk bow tie and the rosette tie. Some riders choose a bolo tie with a silver slide, or simply a brooch if rules don't require a tie.

Reining, cutting, and Quarter Horse riders choose simpler outfits.

You may add a tailored vest, sweater vest, sweater, or short jacket over the shirt. With a shirt like the tuxedo style as a base, you can layer your look and change your appearance for different classes.

Vests and jackets in a feminine cut flatter the figure. A vest trims and ties you together at the waist. Its tapered body gives you a clean silhouette and matches well with a tuxedo shirt.

Cut properly, the vest should fit you smoothly, without gapping in front, back, or around your arms. It should have no excess fabric and make you look sleek. Look for a vest constructed of several shaped pieces rather than two pieces with darts. The vest can have a V-shaped

VESTS AND JACKETS

Showmanship is one of the more formal Western classes. A jacket of hand-woven silk over a tuxedo shirt and rosette tie broadcasts the message that you are a winner. Photo courtesy of Hobby Horse Clothing Company.

Jeans are usually correct, since they are covered by chaps.

neckline with or without lapels, or a horseshoe-shaped neckline. Its length should cover your belt in back when you're in the saddle, and the front points should fit over your belt to allow your buckle to show.

If you choose a jacket, pick one with a fit tailored like the vest. Choose a style with or without lapels, or with a shawl collar. Military and double-breasted styles are also popular.

A jacket, especially one with slightly puffed sleeves, can widen your shoulders for a V-shaped silhouette. Sleeves must cover your wristbones, and waist length flatters most body shapes. If you're heavier, try a V-neck. A slightly longer hem, down to mid-hip, might camouflage or accent what you'd like to hide. Try on different styles to pick one that looks best when you're in the saddle.

Designers make vests and jackets in solid and patterned fabrics, of silks, wools, cottons, linens, and brocades for an elegant look. Textured fabrics add interest, and vertical stripes can lengthen you through the body.

For that show ring sparkle, you can select a fabric with iridescent metallic threads, or go for the "glitz" of beads or sequins. Choose an appropriate amount of glamour, so you don't look overdressed for the occasion. Check the construction of spangled jackets, to be sure the accents are sewn to durable fabric and will survive dry cleaning.

In cooler weather, you can wear a sweater over your shirt.

PANTS

In performance classes, you'll usually wear chaps, so your pants show only in front and rear. Most Western riders still prefer jeans, which are appropriate in any size show. Cowboy-style Wranglers give you a proportioned fit, trim and flat in the front. Jeans should be plain, with no pleats or decorations, and high-waisted.

You'll conform to the majority with dark blue or black Wranglers. Your show jeans should not be faded in color. Have them laundered and heavily starched at a dry cleaner or shirt laundry.

For a unified look, a few women equitation riders wear a one-piece suit, with shirt attached to matching pants. This design prevents the shirt from pulling free from the pants. It's gone out of style in most breeds, but may come back.

Dressy Western pants are also appropriate and may feel more comfortable in the saddle. If you compete in showmanship, you can choose smooth-fitting black knit pants or black Rockies. Men might choose fitted frontier pants.

CHAPS

Chaps attract the eye, being the largest article of clothing, and you might build your outfit around your chaps. They're probably the most expensive item you'll buy.

Shotgun chaps enclose your legs. These should fit trimly. Ideally they fit close along the thigh, with a slight ease at the knee and flared over the boot. You should see only a slight wrinkling at the knee and lower leg, with no other creases, when you're mounted.

Chaps need to fit at the waist so the chaps belt covers your belt and the waistband of your pants. This forms a visual line upward to "lengthen" your leg. They should not rest on the hips, which can make you appear shorter, or gap in front.

Long chaps fringe swings as the horse moves, detracting from the quiet appearance of a pleasure horse.

With the chaps cut at an angle, the chaps belt will curve in front. While this covers your belt, the chaps buckle will lie right under your belt buckle. In the back, the chaps buckle also dips slightly at the center. When you're fitted for new chaps, wear your show pants, belt, and buckle.

For comfort, the zipper should be placed slightly toward the outside of the leg rather than straight behind the leg. Otherwise, the zipper will press into your skin, and also look more obvious.

The basic pattern of chaps is symmetrical, and it is harder to fit a rider with a small waist and heavy thigh. To fit this body type, the chapmaker straightens the outside curve, with the inside curved more to present a cleaner, straighter line along the thigh, from the knee to the hip.

Chap length can accentuate a long leg and add inches to a shorter one. They should reach long enough to cover the boot heel. Full-length zippers should extend to the bottom of the cuffs to prevent flapping. Chaps by Hobby Horse Clothing Company feature a spur slot, so your spurs poke out through the chaps.

The designer can finish the yokes at the cuffs in two ways. The gusset of the chap falls almost to the arch of your foot, so it curves in a moon shape. Or, you can have a double yoke that rests at the top of the instep. Cut longer through the yoke, it makes the leg look longer.

Most riders choose the fringed chap. Fringes also create the illusion of length, though fringe hanging six inches below your heel can draw unwanted attention to your foot. Realize that fringe will emphasize any leg movement, as it can swing along with your leg, so choose chaps with thin, "quiet" fringe.

As an alternative to fringe, you can wear plain chaps. Scalloped chaps add decoration and a touch of femininity. They look better than fringe on heavier legs and won't swing if you have to use your legs on your horse. However, fringe continues to be more popular.

If you show in cutting, you'll probably choose batwing chaps. These fit over your pants, without enclosing your legs. Buckle the straps at the backs of your legs to fit the leather chaps in place.

Put on chaps correctly by buckling the belt around your waist higher than where they will sit. Slide them down a little, tug them into place, and make sure they are straight in the back and sitting at the same height on both hips. If your chaps have a point on the back, center this over your middle belt loop.

Pull the insides of the legs around to the outside to help zip up smoothly without gapping. Zip down three or four inches and tug the chaps down to smooth the fabric. Also tug them from above the knee for a smooth appearance. Turn up the cuffs after you complete zipping the chaps.

Some riders find it easier to put on their chaps after they are sitting in the saddle. You can lift one leg off the saddle and tuck one chap around yourself, then do the other.

Chaps are traditionally cut from garment or top grain leather, with most riders choosing roughout over smooth side out. Split leather is heavier, sueded on both sides. You can also choose pigsuede.

Chapmakers also fabricate chaps from Ultrasuede, a

Plain chaps make the leg appear motionless. Light colors build a unified look.

brand-name synthetic material that replicates the look and feel of suede. Ultrasuede has become popular with slim female riders, due to its wide range of 150 colors. This fabric is thinner and less durable than leather.

On the back of the chaps belt, you can have a button the same color as the chaps. Many riders add silver conchos or a large three-piece buckle set to the back, which contrasts better on darker colors. The flash of silver will attract attention to your waist, so be sure your chaps fit correctly so both legs rest at the same height, parallel to the cantle of the saddle.

You may decide to choose chaps with tooled tops— tooled or exotic leather sections stitched at the hips. These generally look better on men, as the accents make women look heavier at the waist and hips.

Store chaps on a hanger, right side out. You can machine-wash Ultrasuede, using liquid detergent in cool water on a gentle cycle. Dry cleaning is possible, but not recommended. Be sure to remove any silver before washing, since tarnish can stain the fabric.

Don't wring wet Ultrasuede. Air dry your chaps until they are almost dry, then put them in the dryer for ten minutes, on the fluff or cool setting, to restore the nap. You can also press Ultrasuede, on the reverse side with a cool iron. Brush the fabric to bring up the nap, and stiffen fringe with spray starch on the reverse side.

BOOTS

For riding, you select Western boots for comfort rather than fashion. Under chaps, very little of the boot shows.

Many riders choose the roper style. A black boot will match anything, or you can choose a color to match your chaps. If you can afford an exotic dress boot, such as ostrich, these are also popular.

HATS

You must wear a Western hat in all classes. Choose a hat of the correct size, shaped to flatter your appearance.

The crease of the crown, the curve of the brim, and the width of the brim differentiate styles of show hats. Most riders wear a felt hat with a four-inch brim, with little curve on the sides and a wide, flat cattleman's crown. This size can overwhelm the face of a woman or child, so ask a hatter to trim the brim and shape the hat to fit. The hatter will steam and stiffen your hat. An expert will "sculpt" the hat for you, by adjusting the height of the crown and shrinking or stretching the hat. He can

A young showman wears a hat appropriate for her head, along with a fitted jacket.

shape the brim so it curves to enhance your face. You might look better in a brim that's square in front, or slightly dipped forward.

A young child can be difficult to fit for a hat. The large crown and brim look out of proportion, and the child may not be able to see from under the brim. Unless you can locate a quality child-size hat, you might have the brim trimmed to 3½ inches.

In today's show ring, you can wear a felt or straw hat. Most riders choose fur felt, usually in a neutral color like black or silverbelly. Realize that a darker hat casts a shadow over your face, while a lighter color brightens it.

Felt hats vary in quality, rated according to X. The X describes the quality of the interlocking hairs that constitute the felt. A 5X hat would be average, with a 30X or higher of a fur like beaver or mink. Fur felt is considered better quality than wool or rabbit hair. Fur is more tightly packed, so it resists stains better. It also has good substance to wear better and stay crisp in its shape. Beaver, the best material, interlocks in all directions and also breathes.

Riders traditionally switch to straw hats in the summer months. Choose a straw by the number of stars. A 6* or 7* straw hat is good, and 15* is a high-quality hat.

Look for a tightly woven straw in a natural, ivory, or cream shantung. Most feature a four-inch brim, and the Cattleman's crease is standard.

Help retain your hat's shape by handling it gently. Never push or pull the brim or crown. Use both hands to set it on your head, holding the hat at the front and back of its base, at the ribbon. Press it carefully into position without handling the brim, so it rests level from the front to the back. Remove the hat with both hands, wiggling it loose to lift it off.

When you're not wearing your hat, store it in a cool place. Heat softens a hat, and the felt can warp. Either let it hang from the back of the crown, or store it in a hard plastic hat carrier.

Clean your hat after every wearing. Brush the dust off in a counterclockwise motion, with a quality camel hair or horsehair hat brush. The soft brush won't pull hair from the felt and make the texture rough. Use a light-colored brush on lighter hats, and a dark one on dark hats. After brushing, rub the hat lightly with a dry towel, then brush again. Brush a straw hat with a damp cloth.

A hatter can professionally clean, block, and shape your hat if necessary. A few experts renovate worn hats.

You may want to wear a felt hat colored to match the rest of your outfit. Hatters sell hats from permanently dyed felt, or they color white hats to order by chalking or spraying. Spraying is more durable than chalking, though any colored hat is more delicate and requires extra care. A colored hat shows dirt more easily, so brush it after every wearing. The hatter can touch up worn spots with oils and powders.

HAIR AND ACCESSORIES

Details pull your outfit together. Women should wear their hair neat and out of the way. Pull your hair back into a bun, and place it into a snood like the Show Bow. For short hair, you can pin your hair up and secure a separate bun, made of crepe hair (purchased at a craft store) or lengths of your own hair, made by a stylist after a haircut.

Hair should never cover your number. You might pull your hair back and wear a scrunchie. If you have long hair, you can braid it, tie it with a ribbon that matches your chaps, and pin it to your back so it stays in place. Or, if your hair is too long for a medium-sized bun, pile most of it on top of your head and make a bun out of hair below your hat. Make sure your hair is not so high you can't get your hat on straight. (You may need a hat one-eighth-inch larger.)

Accessories complete the Western outfit. A belt is not mandatory, but all riders wear one.

Choose a Western belt that matches the color of your pants or chaps, so it won't cut you in half visually. You can use one made of the same material as your chaps, in a width appropriate to your height.

A silver trophy buckle adds a touch of flash. A good choice would be an oval shape, measuring four or five inches across, or a silver buckle tip and keeper.

Gloves that match the color of your shirt add a dressy touch to your outfit. Try to wear gloves that are long enough so your skin does not show in the gap between glove and sleeve.

Tasteful earrings and barrettes add interest. For example, burgundy earrings can complement an equitation suit of the same color. Many riders wear earrings in a silver concho style. Or, gold or silver earrings or posts can match a barrette of the same color. They should not dangle.

When choosing accessories, realize that the judge will stand a distance from you. For most of the class, he or she watches you from fifty feet away. The judge observes your whole image rather than every detail.

WESTERN SIDESADDLE

AHSA rules describe sidesaddle attire under the Equitation division. Ladies may show aside in all sections of the Arabian division and in AHSA Stock Seat Equitation classes for adults (not juniors).

You'd wear the same outfit you would astride, from the waist up. A vest or short jacket looks smart. Cover your pants with an apron, instead of chaps. As you would with chaps, match the color of your apron to the rest of your attire. (See more details about the apron's cut and length in Chapter 28.)

AQHA rules specifically prohibit riding aside. ApHC allows this dress (and tack) only in the sidesaddle class.

PUTTING IT ALL TOGETHER

Many experts advise that you dress for your horse by choosing a color scheme that flatters the animal. When you and your horse match, you present a unified, pleasing picture. Color catches the judge's eye and can influence his opinion, unless he happens to be color-blind.

Determine which colors go with your horse. He presents a large block of color, so your outfit should complement his coat. Soft earth colors seem to match coats of red tones. Earth tone color combinations that catch the eye include rust and green, and taupe with just about anything.

Many riders stick with the flattering dark colors. Greens and navy are coming back, which can match any color of horse. Black is a conservative color, which is correct in almost every situation. With black chaps, you can dress down for equitation with a dark shirt, or dress up for other classes, maybe wearing a colored tuxedo

A fully sequined jacket, matched with white chaps and hat, perfectly coordinates with a cute chestnut mare. Photo courtesy of Hobby Horse Clothing Company.

shirt, or a plaid shirt of bright colors, with a short black jacket.

Black is also dull, because so many riders rely on it. Some shades of deep wine and very dark purple complement bay and chestnut horses.

For a more dynamic look on a horse of brown, white, black or Palomino, you might pick a brighter, stronger contrast that attracts attention. Red or blue catch the eye. If you have a perfect leg position, you can look spectacular wearing white chaps on a dark horse. Wearing red or white can broadcast the message "I'm good!" as these colors indicate you have supreme confidence in your ability. Wearing darker colors can suggest that you

This rider chose earth colors to match a Palomino: tan chaps, white shirt, and black hat.

don't want to show off your weight or your horse's gaits.

With a loud-colored horse, like a Paint, Pinto, or Appaloosa, try not to clash your outfit. Your horse has a lot of chrome, so tone down yours. In this case, a solid colored fabric may look better than a pattern.

Experts advise you to select the color of chaps first, then coordinate the rest of the outfit with that shade. Chaps can match the shirt or accent a color in a plaid.

Consider sticking with two basic colors in the outfit. For example, red and black can highlight a bay horse. The same Ultrasuede used in the chaps can trim the shirt, both as button coverings and piping.

Some equitation and horsemanship riders wear a solid colored outfit, with chaps the same color as shirt and pants. If you appear to be all of one piece, so you fade into the color of the horse, you seem to eliminate excessive motion. With no contrast between the color of chaps and pants, you de-emphasize the hip.

Preparing for an Arabian Stock Seat Equitation class, this young rider has chosen a solid colored outfit in classic black.

When choosing colors, consider the show environment. If you'll be indoors under artificial light, you need a brighter look. Don't choose a fabric that's too shiny, because you might create a blinding effect under lights.

Keep your colors in mind when you shop for your wardrobe. Whenever selecting a color for either leather or Ultrasuede chaps, view it in the light in which you will be appearing. Colors may appear different in sunlight than under flourescents in the shop.

When aiming to match a color to your horse, bring a recent picture. You can also collect paint chips from a paint store. Hold the chips up next to the horse in the sunlight, and then match them with the chap colors right away so you know you've picked the right shade.

Once you have your chaps, you'll work around them when choosing your shirt, vest, jacket, or sweater. Bring your chaps with you while shopping, and again compare shades in the appropriate lighting.

Your hat can contrast with or match with the colors of chaps or shirt. Like the chaps, check the hat color in the light of the show ring.

If you need ideas, study the photos of winners in recent breed magazines. With a horse similar to yours, what colors did other riders choose? You could bring photos to a shop, to discuss with a consultant.

Find a shop where expert staff can assist you. A show-wise consultant will ask you about your horse, your favorite colors, the classes you'll enter, and the show environment. Find such advice at a local custom shop that specializes in show attire, or attend a major show to meet with vendors exhibiting at the trade fair. These retailers set (and follow) horse show trends, and they'll help you keep up with the ever-changing fashions.

Match your attire to the class, following both written and unwritten rules. Some general guidelines for popular Western show disciplines appear on the next page. The first two classes are considered more informal than the latter two.

BE FASHION SMART

	Pleasure	Halter	Showmanship	Horsemanship
Objective	A workmanlike appearance	Almost invisible	Eye-catching yet professional	Quiet, clean, tidy look
Chaps	Yes	No	No	Yes
Pants	Wranglers	Dress Pants	Dress pants Rockies	Wranglers Dress pants
Vest or Jacket	Either	Jacket optional	Jacket	Either
Gloves	Optional	No	Yes	Yes
Hair	Up under hat or tied back	Up under hat or tied back	Up under hat	Up under hat

28. HUNT
SEAT ATTIRE

The hunt seat rider must dress in traditional, dignified fashion. All aspects of rider turnout should be neat and workmanlike in this most conservative riding style.

With the popularity of hunt seat riding, competitors in all levels and regions have become sophisticated in the quality of their turnout. East Coast riders used to be considered the most outstanding. Now style has standardized on all "A" show circuits, and all riders are groomed identically.

This chapter incorporates attire for the hunter, jumper, and equitation divisions, along with specifics for dressage, combined training, sport horse, and sidesaddle exhibitors.

COATS

The coat must be tailored to fit you. A custom-made coat will look better than one off the rack. The differences are subtle, but they mark a top-class rider.

A tailored coat may consist of as many as eighteen separate pieces on the outer shell alone. On a correctly fitted garment, the shoulders should mold smoothly from the neck to

Waiting for her jumper round, this amateur rider models a well-tailored pinstriped coat in charcoal gray. Her choker is properly fitted, close to her neck, and it matches the color of her shirt.

the top of the sleeves, with the shoulder meeting the sleeve at the top of your shoulder bone. Look for the fabric to drape straight from your shoulders to the hem with no evident bulge or wrinkle. The side seams start at your armpit and fall directly down the sides. Seams on the tops of the shoulders are in line with your neck, about one-half inch behind your ear.

For that polished look, a coat should fit smoothly across your back, yet with enough fabric to enable you to stretch forward. One that is too wide at the back can cause the shoulders and collar to be out of place. The collar shouldn't gap, but fit comfortably at the appropriate height. Armholes are large enough for comfort. They

Side vents on a hunt coat flare when you jump a fence.

don't bind, and they're not so big that the coat bunches up when your raise your arms.

A tailor can alter a manufactured coat to fit you better. Taking in the bust seams or shoulder seams can improve the way the coat shapes to your build.

The sleeves should reach partway down your hand when you're standing. They just cover the wrist bones when arms are slightly bent. The outsides may be slightly longer than the insides.

The coat's waistline should fit at your waist. A hunt coat will close with three buttons, buttoning to the left in a woman's coat and to the right in a man's. Buttonholes should never gap when you move.

Correct coat length is when the hem just covers the bottom of the buttocks with you standing. A coat that is too long hides your leg. In the saddle, the hem barely brushes the top of the cantle, or the pommel when you lean forward. For most hunter riding, you'll probably choose the double vented style over the single vent, with the coat's skirt subtly flared at the cantle. A skirt that flares too much will detract from the neat picture you want to portray. It floats around you while you're jumping.

You may decide on the placement of the vents, either at the side or farther back. Vents allow you to move comfortably with the horse as it jumps over a fence. When you close the angle of your hip over the fence, a coat with side vents shows your hips where the vents gap. Placed more to the rear, the vents flare apart over your buttocks.

The coat's collar should be of the same fabric, not velvet. The pockets are flapped, moderately sloping, and set below the waistline at the hips.

Wool is the classic fabric, with the traditional variations of tweed or melton (a closely woven wool with a slight nap). Although some riders choose polyester or a wool/polyester blend for easier care, wool gives a better shape.

The most fashionable colors are navy blue, charcoal gray, dark hunter green, and black, in solids and very subtle pinstripes, one-sixteenth-inch wide at the most. For summer, you may choose a coat in a lighter weight and shade, though few of today's riders choose colors other than those listed here.

Look for a coat lined in silk or rayon. A full lining drapes better and gives a firmer shape. It should feel slightly elastic when you stretch your arms. The color of the lining should be subtle, to match the coat or be of a slightly lighter or darker shade. Interfacing also adds body at the cuffs, hem, collar, and chest.

Certain classes require that you show in formal hunt attire. Even if you haven't joined a hunt, your coat and all other articles of clothing must conform to American Horse Shows Association (AHSA) rules.

Formally dressed women wear a frock coat with rounded skirts, a cutaway, or a shadbelly. The frock coat is a longer coat constructed with separate skirts that are sewn to the coat at the waistline. The shadbelly and cutaway are both tailcoats. Rules in certain divisions permit the wearing of the tailcoat in the English Show Hack classes (Arabian and National Show Horse) and Hunter Pleasure (Morgan). These divisions note that the coat is appropriate after 6 P.M. and in Championship classes.

Select a formal coat in a dark fabric, with melton a

good choice. These coats usually feature a single center vent. The collar is of the same material and color of the coat, unless you're a member of a hunt who has received an invitation to wear a collar with hunt colors. Buttons on a black coat are of black bone. If your hunt has invited you to wear them, the buttons are engraved with the hunt's emblem.

To wear hunt colors or buttons in a class, AHSA rules require you to present an official letter of permission from your hunt. The letter must be dated in the current year and signed by the hunt's Master or Honorary Secretary.

Men wear the same styles, unless they are permitted by the Master of their hunt to wear the traditional scarlet with four brass buttons. Only the Master of the hunt is allowed to wear the square cornered, single breasted frock coat in scarlet.

In jumper classes, you may wear any hunt coat. Under AHSA and Federation Equestre Internationale (FEI) rules, certain special classes require both men and women

USET rider Greg Best wears the scarlet coat while showing the famous "Gem Twist" in the 1990 World Equestrian Games.

riders to wear black, dark blue, or dark green coats. Some riders wear scarlet coats (cut in the regular hunt style, with a single vent). The coat with the blue and white collar of the USET, however, is restricted to those riders who have ridden as members of the U.S. Equestrian Team.

Preserve your wool coat by having it dry-cleaned, preferably after each wearing. It will need to be pressed, either by a professional cleaner or tailor, or at home. You can do it yourself, taking care not to stretch the fabric. Use a dry, medium hot iron. Dampen a pressing cloth and place it over the wool while you apply the iron. Don't press until the wool is dry, or you will add a shine to the fabric.

Store your wool coat on a wooden hanger to retain its tailored shape. Wool needs to breathe, so air it occasionally and avoid storing it in an airtight container. Be sure you protect the fabric against moths and mildew.

SHIRTS

Wear a fitted riding shirt under your coat. Choose a shirt that won't create bulk and stays tucked in your breeches or jodhpurs. Roomy shoulders should let you put your arms forward without feeling a pull across your back. You may substitute a turtleneck, but only at local or winter schooling shows.

Quality shirts are either 100 percent cotton or a cotton broadcloth, although many riders choose a cotton/polyester blend. Colors are whites, pastels, and pinstriped. Only the solid white shirt is traditional with formal attire. Check the construction, looking for flat seams with a high number of stitches per inch. Interfacing at collar, cuffs, and placket prevents puckers and wrinkles.

Sleeve length is an individual choice, according to the weather and the type of show. Generally in more formal situations, a long sleeve shirt is more appropriate. Sleeves should cover your wristbones when you hold the reins.

If you attend a summer show with the temperature in the 90s, expect show management to announce that jumper riders may dispense with their hunt coats. Plan for this situation by bringing a neatly tailored white polo shirt, with short sleeves and a collar. You can substitute this for the traditional riding shirt, neatly tucked in your breeches.

Women's shirts feature a stand-up collar. You wear a

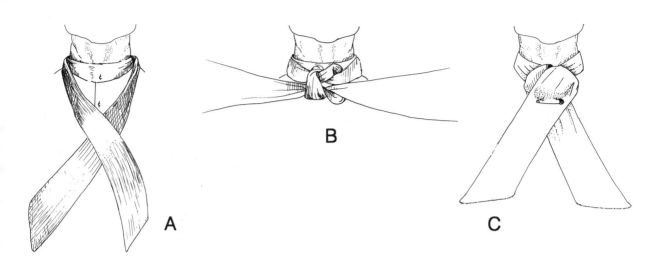

choker over the collar, which matches the shirt color. It should be wide enough to cover the entire collar, adjusted snugly around the neck. A quality choker is cut in a curve to mold to the contour of your neck. You may decorate the center of your choker with a small monogram. A button under the front holds the choker in place so the monogram remains centered.

Men wear white dress shirts, with a four-in-hand tie coordinated to match the coat. When outfitted with the scarlet coat in special classes, men follow the custom of wearing a white tie over a white shirt.

In place of a choker or tie, the white stock is correct for both men and women. Usually riders wear stocks only when required, like in appointments classes or a more formal type of hunter class, such as a hunter classic. Tie the stock neatly, secured with a plain gold safety pin (always placed horizontally,) and the ends tucked into the tied portion. If you prefer, you can purchase a white bib with a pre-tied stock, so you simply slide the bib in place. Your coat covers the bib.

Although current AHSA rules don't require it, formal attire traditionally includes a vest. Canary yellow is the preferred color. Some riders choose plain white or buff.

Hunt seat riders show in breeches and tall boots. Made of a nylon/spandex four-way stretch fabric, breeches must fit well. They must not be baggy, but you don't want them too tight. Some riders wear Underalls underneath for a smoother look.

One way to tie a stock: (A) Bring the ends around your neck, pulling the looped section snugly in place. (B) Tie a loose square knot. (C) Spread and flatten the cloth in the knotted sections to cover the knot. Carefully fold one end over the other, and pull each end to the side. Secure with stock pin.

BREECHES

Breeches of cotton blends may be more comfortable, adding a cool breathability to the stretch fabric. European fashions have introduced different styles and fabrics. You may prefer the comfort of a pleated front, slight flare, or side zipper.

Breeches must withstand the stress of your movements in the saddle. On stretch fabric, check the stitching to be sure the seam will stretch along with the elastic, either through elastic thread or a zigzag stitch pattern. Especially examine where the fabric and leather knee patches meet. You should see a flat seam for comfort and durability.

Most riders wear light beige, buff, or a very light gray. In a less formal event, you might choose rust or a darker gray. White, buff, or canary breeches are correct with formal hunt attire. American Quarter Horse Association (AQHA) rules add the colors of buff, gray, and rust; the American Paint Horse Association (APHA) lists buff, gray, rust, and canary.

In Grand Prix jumper classes, you'd wear white or light beige breeches. Only white breeches accompany the scarlet coat.

Young children who ride ponies are more properly outfitted in jodhpurs and jodhpur boots. The total picture of rider and pony determines the suitability of this attire. Tradition sets no specific age when a child grows into breeches and boots, but a small child on a pony looks better in jodhpurs, even if she's as old as eleven or twelve. A large eight-year-old may look more appropri-

This young rider is correctly outfitted in jodhpurs. Her coat is too short, however.

ate in breeches and boots, as does any child on a horse.

Jodhpurs may be of the same colors as breeches. They should be worn with brown leather garter straps, which fit just below the knee to keep the jods from slipping up or wrinkling. The low jodhpur boots should be brown to match the garter straps.

With breeches, tradition demands tall boots. The height emphasizes the length of your leg, so boots should reach to the top of the crease behind the knee. Boots that are too low are unattractive and mark you as a novice in the hunter ring. If your boots are too tall, the leather will develop an unsightly fold at the top, where your leg forces the leather downward.

The difference between a good boot and a perfectly fitted one is a close fit at both calf and ankle. You should never see a gap between your leg and the top of the boot. The narrow ankle design is apparent in custom-made boots; if you purchase a stock boot, you'll probably need to have a bootmaker alter it for the slim look. A few manufacturers offer a stock boot that looks similar to a custom boot, made of side leather and tapered to fit. If you have the right size of foot and leg, this boot can look as good as a more expensive model.

The boot's leather affects its appearance. A fully lined calfskin boot is generally stiffer and harder to break in. Some styles are lined with a softer leather around the ankle to help mold the leather to your leg. A cuff-lined boot of baby calf leather is more pliable and will form itself to your foot and leg more easily. This boot also tends to slip down much more than a lined or partially lined boot—order it tall enough to account for this tendency.

With new boots of stiffer leather, you need to work diligently to make the boot form a correct drop at the ankle. A fully lined boot should reach to the middle of the back of your knee when new, in order to drop to the proper height. The amount of drop may vary among boots from one-half to three inches.

Expect this breaking-in process to take about two weeks. While you walk around in the boots, the leather should gradually form a supple fold at the ankle. (Most shops will start the fold for you.) You may need to protect the front of your ankle by wearing a tennis sock, folded twice to pad your leg.

Most riders today buy black boots, though brown was

BOOTS

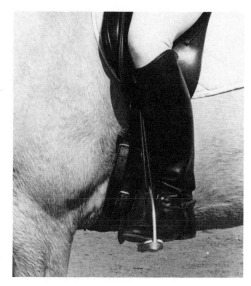

The boot may be shaped at the top, being higher on the outside. Ahead of the boot of this dressage rider can be seen the short dressage girth.

a popular color in recent years. Field boots continue to be fashionable. One of the few recent changes in hunt seat dress was the acceptance of field boots in black leather.

Wear boots with cuffs (tops) with formal attire. Women riders may wear black boots with patent leather tops, with tabs sewn on the boots. Men wearing the scarlet coat generally choose black boots with tan calfskin tops, also with tabs. When a man wears a bowler, then he must match it with plain black boots.

Bootmakers offer these formal foxhunting boots with attached or detachable cuffs. Waxed calf leather is traditional.

Formal attire includes boot garters. Black garters are correct with black boots or boots with patent leather tops. If the boots have brown or colored tops, garters are the same color as the breeches.

Keep your show boots in top condition through proper care. Wear socks that absorb moisture rather than allowing sweat to soak into the boot lining. Avoid wearing nylons in place of socks. Even though they permit the boot to slide on and off easier, they will allow more moisture to seep into the boot.

Use a padded boot jack to remove your boots. Insert boot trees into both the foot and the calf areas before you store your boots.

After wearing, wipe boots with a damp cloth and clean them with castile soap. Use a cream polish, and polish boots with a brush. Avoid wax, which can seal the pores and prevent the leather from breathing.

HEADWEAR

Headwear varies according to the rider's age and the event. While jumping, you must always wear protective headgear.

Most riders wear the velvet-covered hunt cap. If you're an adult rider (over eighteen), you may choose any type of cap. For riders under 18, AHSA rules require you to wear properly fitted protective headgear. AHSA encourages junior riders to wear a hat certified by the Safety Equipment Institute (SEI) to meet American Society for Testing and Materials (ASTM) standards of protection. This hunt cap must be secured with its attached harness. APHA rules require all juniors to wear ASTM-approved headgear at the show.

It's imperative that your hat stays securely on your

These young hunt seat riders wear hats that meet ASTM standards.

head, to protect you during a fall. Sizes do vary, especially with the cushioning inside the ASTM caps. Take the time to shop for a hat that truly fits the shape of your head. At the tack shop, fix your hair as you will for show, and try on various styles and sizes. Secure the harness and test the hat's fit by putting your head down and shaking it vigorously. It should not slip at all. Wear the hat for at least five minutes to confirm its comfort—if a hat presses too hard against your skull, you'll find excuses to avoid wearing it.

If you're fitting a hat on a child, be sure the hat fits comfortably and securely. At an AHSA show, the child must wear the hat whenever mounted. Show officials observe junior riders and will promptly correct any who mount without wearing correctly fastened protective headgear.

The bowler, or hard hunt derby, is considered out-dated in hunter classes, except with formal attire. Riders prefer the hunt cap in either black or very dark navy. Brown is permissible, to match brown boots, and only the occasional jumper riders wear this color.

Both velvet and velveteen are now made from synthetic fibers. Velveteen is less expensive, and it's difficult to discern from velvet.

Hunting tradition dictates specific hats with formal attire. Here only the Master or a junior rider may show in a hunt cap. Men and women wear a hunting silk top hat with a scarlet, shadbelly, or cutaway coat. The bowler matches a black coat.

Formally attired men and women must wear hats equipped with a hat guard. This cord connects to the brim of the bowler or silk hat, and it attaches to a ring inside the collar of the coat. Its purpose is to prevent the rider from losing the hat if it comes off.

Under any hat, your hair must be neat, never flyaway or wispy. Very young girls may style long hair into two braids, tied with ribbons. All other women should pin hair back or up underneath the cap, then secure a hairnet over all the hair before putting on the cap. The hairnet should match the color of your hair. You may choose to put your hair back into a snood like the Show Bow.

OTHER ATTIRE

Although not required, dark leather gloves add to your elegant appearance. You may wear rings under your gloves, with the stones turned to the inside to prevent damage to settings or gloves. Formally attired riders usually wear brown gloves.

If you anticipate riding in wet weather, purchase a pair of dark, sweat-proof gloves. Manufacturers treat the leather so the dye won't transfer to your skin when wet.

Choose spurs without rowels, with straps matching the color of your boots. Fit a spur to rest on the heel seam of your boot. Buckle the spur strap so the end points toward the outside; tuck the end underneath the strap, or trim it close to the buckle.

You may wear a belt with your breeches or jodhpurs. Suspenders are a colorful alternative, which your coat conceals.

If you carry a stick, it should be short (18 inches or less) and of the same color as the horse. A dark stick is acceptable on a light-colored horse.

In hunt seat riding, you should not add any jewelry. Some judges even criticize riders who wear earrings in pierced ears. The formally attired rider wears only a stock pin.

When showing a hunter on the line, you may correctly wear regular hunt seat attire, complete with coat. Some men prefer to wear a business suit. At some shows, women handlers occasionally wear sportswear, such as a blouse with a skirt or culottes.

DRESSAGE ATTIRE

Dressage riders must also dress conservatively. Hunt seat attire is appropriate in AHSA levels, which are not governed by FEI rules.

The dressage coat resembles the hunt coat with a few variations. To conform, you'll wear a black wool coat, usually with a center vent and four buttons. The coat can feature a waist seam for a sleeker fit. As in hunter seat classes, the better show coats are custom-tailored. Most riders wear a white stock in place of the choker.

You may choose to wear cotton stretch breeches with a full leather seat to help sit close to the saddle. Look for a high, wide waistband for support. Some models have a front control panel. White is the usual color, although you may pick beige or light gray.

Black boots are fitted the same as for hunt seat, though dressage riders prefer a slightly higher boot. Riding with a longer stirrup, you'll have less of a problem with a crease behind the knee. You may choose a stiffer boot, which has less breakdown at the ankle and helps hold your leg

Competing on a Half-Arabian, this rider wears a bowler. Shadbelly, white stock, and top hat are appropriate at the FEI levels of dressage.

correctly. It has a stiffer shaft, equipped with a full lining and back stiffener.

You'll probably choose a hunt cap, although some riders wear a bowler. You usually wear dark gloves when showing. When you're competing through Fourth Level, AHSA rules permit you to carry a whip measuring a maximum of four feet. You may not show with a whip in AHSA and USET Championship classes, FEI classes, and other USET competitions.

For all tests above Fourth Level, you must follow the dress code: White or light-colored breeches, and a black coat with a derby, or a black or dark blue wool tailcoat with a top hat. For the tailcoat, you'd choose a shadbelly with brass buttons and attached vest points (sewn to the front hem of the coat to simulate the appearance of a full vest). Weighted tails lined with a sweat-resistant fabric enhance a quality coat. Tails can reach slightly above or to the backs of your knees when you're standing.

Choose a top hat of silk or fur felt. Fit the hat so the top is absolutely level, never tipped back on your head. Requirements include stock, gloves (usually white with the shadbelly), black boots, and metal spurs.

In FEI classes, you may wear the shadbelly with a top hat.

To show a sport horse in hand, follow the written and unwritten rules. Conformity indicates your respect for tradition. Rather than riding attire, you should dress in neat, comfortable clothing that looks inconspicuous and permits free movement. Don't wear a T-shirt, jeans, or riding boots.

Recommended attire:

SPORT HORSE ATTIRE

Association	General Recommendation	Shirt	Pants	Shoes
AHSA	Conservative sportswear Vest, tie optional	Trim, tailored	Dark slacks	Running
USDF	(Same as AHSA)			
Appaloosa Horse Club	Conservative Vest, tie, gloves optional	White (collared polo acceptable)	Trousers	Running or paddock
European breed associations	Breeds follow traditional color combinations:	White (Trakehner, Dutch) Yellow (Hanoverian) Red (Holsteiner, Oldenburg)	White (Hanoverian, Holsteiner, Dutch) Black (Trakehner) Blue (Oldenburg)	Running

COMBINED TRAINING ATTIRE

Observe AHSA rules for attire appropriate to each phase. In the dressage test, you wear hunting dress or dressage attire. At horse trials, you may wear a shadbelly only at the Advanced Level, and spurs are required at Intermediate and Advanced Levels. Unrowelled spurs must conform to specified limits.

Whenever jumping, all competitors must wear protective headgear secured by a retention harness. On the endurance test, riders dress casually. Over boots and breeches, you may wear a polo shirt, turtleneck, or pullover sweater.

You'll layer the recommended back protector vest over this, zip it closed, and then place your pinny on top. The back protector, also called body armor, reduces impact in case of a fall. Foam panels allow you to bend normally,

Olympic rider Mike Huber wears a
back protector vest while competing
over cross country.

yet absorb shock. Padding guards the spine, kidney, and
coccyx areas, with some models also protecting the col-
larbone.

Wear hunt seat dress in the show jumping test. You
can wear the same attire as during the dressage test,
matching breeches with black boots, or black boots with
brown tops.

SIDESADDLE ATTIRE

Rules in the AHSA Hunter Division list exact specifications for ladies sidesaddle dress. When showing in the
under saddle class in Ladies Sidesaddle classes, you must
adhere to these details for formal attire.

In general, a properly fitted, severely tailored habit is
always appropriate for an elegant turnout. It consists of
a form-fitted jacket that shows off a trim waistline, with
a matching apron that covers your legs and the saddle's
pommels. The jacket resembles a hunt coat, without being cut away in front.

An apron is correct attire. It hangs more neatly than a skirt and adds safety to your outfit. (A skirt or divided skirt can catch on the pommels if you fall.) Its hem hangs parallel to the ground, level from front to back when you're mounted, at or slightly above your left ankle bone to reveal a portion of your hunt boot. The hem completely covers your right foot, hanging two to four inches below it.

Rules specify a melton or other heavy cloth, in black or dark blue. A thick, heavy fabric holds its shape and hangs well without billowing as the horse moves. Under your habit, you wear breeches. A loop inside the apron secures around your right leg so the apron lies flat.

Riding aside, pin your hair back into a bun with no loose wisps. Wear a collared shirt with a tie, and a hunt cap or bowler with a veil. Carry a leather-covered cane. AHSA rules describe explicit details of formal attire.

Period attire is acceptable only in the Arabian division, in Ladies Sidesaddle classes. Although rules encourage authenticity, some exhibitors continue to dismay traditionalists by choosing lavish, colorful outfits.

Showing in the Arabian division, this sidesaddle rider doesn't meet the specifications for dress in the hunter division—but her attire does display the elegance of this riding style.

29. SADDLE SEAT ATTIRE

Like hunt seat attire, saddle seat clothing reflects a heritage of distinction and prestige. The elegant rider dresses neatly, with good taste. Observers note more evolution in this division than in hunt seat, with greater variations among riders.

Riders showing Saddlebreds, Tennessee Walking Horses, Arabians, Morgans, Andalusians, and National Show Horses wear basically the same three-piece saddle suit, with each breed type slightly different. In general, Saddlebred exhibitors set the standard for saddle seat attire in both informal and formal styles.

SADDLE SUITS

A flattering saddle suit is tailored to fit the rider, and it is never styled like a costume. Menswear inspires styles, and trends often follow those set by the men's fashion industry. A classically tailored formal saddle suit should make you feel superbly dressed, able to glide from saddle to limousine for an after-show ball at a sophisticated hotel.

The coat should fit well, yet create a flowing line to accentuate your seat on a handsome horse. Its construction forms functional wrinkles for comfortable riding. You sit in the saddle with arms forward, so these wrinkles should occur in the back, at the shoulder, and near the waistband.

The informal coat closes with a single button. Changes in current fashion concern the width of the lapels and the length of the hem. A medium width peak lapel should stay in fashion better than a thin or wide type.

Length of the coat varies according to your stature. It should look proportionate to you and your horse, the hem slightly above your knees in the saddle. Some people choose to accentuate a long torso with a spectacularly long coat. Be sure the sleeves are long enough to cover your wrists when you hold the reins.

You may decide to pin the coat back, especially when you're showing in equitation. Adjust the pinning for the length of your leg, so the coat flatters you when you're in motion.

As with the hunt seat coat, the custom-tailored model

Warming up a three-gaited horse, a rider models a derby and a coat that contrasts with darker jodhpurs. Her horse wears action chains and has its tail tied with a lace.

255

This young rider is well dressed on a three-gaited Saddlebred.

will denote the rider of top quality. It can conceal figure flaws and accentuate your waistline, without appearing at all baggy. If you are the right size, you can find a manufactured suit of coat, pants, and vest to fit. Or, you can purchase clothing off the rack and have it altered by a tailor.

Wool is the best material for a saddle suit. Wool tailors correctly, producing crisp corners on the coat's lapels, and it wears well when properly maintained. Since it is a natural fabric, it breathes and is actually more comfortable than polyester on hot days. Though polyester and wool/polyester blends are also used, the experts don't recommend them. They claim these suits don't look or wear as well as the more expensive wools.

A saddle suit has coat and pants of matching colors. The suit is proper attire in any pleasure or equitation class. You may choose a black tweed coat over black pants, or a tasteful brown plaid with brown pants.

For an informal suit, a coat and pants in earth tones are the best colors, though choice is personal preference. There are about fifteen shades that are most often seen, which coordinate with the rider and the horse.

You can follow one of two approaches when choosing a color: a shade that becomes you, or one that coordinates with the animal's color. The color can make a statement while flattering your body type. A one-on-one look, where hat and suit match, gives an illusion of height. Or if you're tall, a light tan suit with a navy vest and navy hat presents an elegant appearance. The contrasting vest is popular in pleasure classes; it's also seen in equitation.

Choosing your outfit is an individual decision, although you should listen to the clothier and your trainer. In general, a beginner should stick with the more subdued shades. You don't want to overdress for your level of skill or your horse's ability. When you're more seasoned, you can show off your talents with flasher colors or fabrics.

Look for a harmonious picture. Dress for a mirror to see how a color suits your complexion and body type. Consider the visual effect you'll present as you sort through color and fabric choices. Different alternatives will change your aspect. If you look your best, you will help make your horse look good, too.

To accent the horse's color, earth tones generally highlight or echo a chestnut, brown, or brownish-gray horse.

Bright, pure colors such as blue, red, black, or green may look better on a bay or blackish-gray. Peach looks good on a bay, but it is more striking on a chestnut.

Another consideration is where you will be showing. For an outdoor show, you can wear a darker color. In indoor arenas, pick a lighter or paler shade so you will show up better. In a dark suit on a plain bay horse, you can "disappear" in a vast arena.

Equitation riders must always choose a solid, matching look, both for a refined appearance and to conform to prescribed rules. American Horse Shows Association (AHSA) Saddle Seat Equitation rules specify conservative colors for both informal and formal wear. Herringbone and pinstripe patterns are allowed, if they appear to be solid from a distance.

A dark color makes the rider look smaller; a light color highlights the rider's posture. An outstanding equitation rider may choose a light gray suit to attract attention.

Popular in many breeds is the day coat, or "odd" coat, which contrasts with the color of darker pants. Usually tailored with a shawl collar, this informal look extends the wardrobe of the saddle seat rider in pleasure classes. If you have a dark brown saddle suit, you might wear a light-colored (not white) coat, especially when showing indoors. Some coats are made in a silk or silk blend, for an iridescent look. One example of an attractive outfit is a cream coat, brown pants and vest, and a cream hat on a black horse, possibly accented by cream on browband, cavesson, and girth.

This variation is acceptable, yet again you must exercise good taste. A gaudy, too-bright color or bold stripes will detract from the elegant appearance of horse and rider. If you're short, the contrast may not flatter you, because it will make your body appear to be cut in half. Try to attain a balance of color with the horse, without overdoing the effect.

An attractive coat lining enhances a refined appearance. As the horse moves, the lining shows as the coat flows back. It should be a subtle color, preferably coordinated to the your tie and boutonniere. You might even link the color to the horse's browband, cavesson, and/or girth.

The three-piece saddle suit includes a vest. It must fit snugly and usually matches the color of the coat. A reversible vest, which can provide two different looks, is a good investment.

For Arabian English Pleasure, this rider has chosen a day coat matched with plum-colored jodhpurs and derby.

Under the day coat, some riders choose a striped or patterned silk vest to match the tie. Although permitted, this may be considered too flamboyant.

Formal attire is only proper after 6 P.M., usually only in important Three-Gaited classes in major shows. The classic informal suit is also proper (required for Saddlebred Pleasure Equitation classes). In other equitation classes in the evening, you must wear formal attire according to AHSA rules.

Authorities do not consider the day coat correct for evening wear. However, in some prestigious championships, riders wear shimmering brocade coats of colors contrasting with their jodhpurs.

The one-button tuxedo-type coat is part of formal attire, and it must fit well. It is made of a wool worsted, with lapels of the same or silk material. Wear the coat with a matching waistcoat or cummerbund of silk, velvet, or the same material.

Traditionally, formal attire is conservative. Though black is the traditional color, equitation riders may select dark gray, dark brown, or midnight blue. Collar and lapels must be of the same color.

Shirts

The design of your shirt is not as crucial as the suit, as only a small area will show between your tie and vest. You may choose a regular dress shirt, with a plain or pleated front, for both formal and informal wear. What is important is the fit of the collar and length of the sleeve.

A collar has to fit snugly around the neck, never gapping. It should be tall enough so one-half to one inch shows above the collar of the coat. Look for a tuxedo shirt with a wing collar (now offered by several equestrian retailers). Avoid a shirt with a too-large collar, which can ruin an otherwise perfect appearance.

The cuffs of shirt sleeves should extend just barely beyond the coat sleeves. From one-eighth to one-quarter inch is correct. If a shirt fits well except for the sleeves, fabric can be trimmed from the shirt tail to extend the sleeves.

A slim rider might want to have tucks taken up on a shirt so it will not bunch or ride up under the vest. Shirts are often difficult to hold in place and the tails tend to pull free, whether you tuck them in before or after closing your pants. Another approach is to pull the waistband of your underpants over the shirt tails, which helps keep the shirt tucked in.

Choose a white shirt of broadcloth, pique, or silk. You can wear a shirt with a regular or wing tip collar with either informal or formal wear. In informal classes, you could choose a pastel shirt, following fashions in menswear.

Jodhpurs

For pants you'll wear the Kentucky jodhpurs, fitting close but not tight. The cuffless leg is tailored to flare over the boot. Well-tailored jodhpurs show a flattering bell shape to the hems.

Length is important—when you sit in the saddle, the pant leg should cover the boot heel, with subtle wrinkles over the instep. Custom-made "jods" feature an offset hem, a dropped heel that is shorter in front and longer in the back. The hem breaks slightly at the front and slants toward your heel. When you sit on the horse, the rear of the trouser hem appears angled. Hems of ready-made trousers are either straight or cut at a slight angle. If hems are long enough, a tailor can alter them.

A suit includes matching jodhpurs. When you buy a suit, it's a good idea to buy two pairs of jodhpurs. The pants endure more wear than the coat.

Parents of young riders sometimes feel it's less expensive to purchase a suit in a slightly larger size to allow for growth. Experts recommend against this since the purpose of a suit is for the current show, not one sometime in the future. You can make sure the hems of coat and pants, and seam allowances in the coat, are wide enough to allow for alterations. Some shops rent children's saddle suits for a special show or the entire season.

When you dismount, always turn up the hems of your jodhpurs. In the saddle, wear elastic jodhpur straps, or underpasses, which connect on each side of the hem. They button or clip in place to hold the pant legs down over the boot. Without the strap, pant legs tend to ride up. The strap should be dark to match the boot, and it must not look obvious when in place, covered by the hem of the trouser. As the elastic stretches with use, replace the strap for a neat look.

The trousers of a formal suit match the coat in fabric and color. They feature single stripes down the leg of black or blue satin, which should match the lapels.

Extra features on a custom suit are knee patches of Ultrasuede. Self-patches, made of the same fabric as the jodhpurs, are standard, but they will eventually wear through. Ultrasuede material will protect the trousers from wear and saddle oil, and they add slightly more grip.

If you show in both saddle and stock seat classes, you can wear jodhpurs under your chaps for quick changes between events. Have custom trousers made with Western style belt loops. The loops won't show under your saddle seat coat, but they'll add to the Western appearance when you wear your fancy belt and buckle. One tip: Be careful you don't zip your jodhpurs into the zipper of the chaps—the teeth will cut a perfect circle in the pant leg of your expensive tailored trousers!

Maintain your saddle suit by having it dry cleaned immediately after each wearing. Body odor and perspiration harm wool fibers. You can also wipe the arm panels with a damp sponge as soon as you remove your coat. Avoid insect damage by storing wool properly.

BOOTS

Many saddle seat riders wear highly polished black jodhpur boots, made of calfskin in the elastic-sided design. For a long line, the color of boots match the pant color. Brown boots would go with brown pants. Patent leather boots are also popular, both with informal and formal suits. "Ripple" soles help you keep your feet in the stirrups.

You may wear spurs on your boots, with spur straps of a color that matches your boots. If you show in equitation, you may wear only unrowelled spurs. A whip is optional. AHSA rules limit its length to six feet, including the lash.

HATS

The hat must fit squarely and securely on your head. A soft hat is standard in informal classes, with popular choices the derby, Homburg, or snap brim.

Equitation riders generally pick a felt derby colored to match the suit, continuing the solid look. When you show wearing a day coat, you may choose a hat to match the coat, or contrast, such as a light blue hat with a navy coat. The derby is shaped, with a rolled brim that softly curves on the sides and back.

Men and boys select either the Homburg or snap brim.(Ladies may also choose these styles.) The Homburg resembles a man's street hat. It has a lengthwise crease on the crown, a brim rolled up on the sides, and a drop in the front and the back. The brim should not be flat or too large.

The snap brim has a thin, crisp brim that you can snap into various positions. Both this and the Homburg are most proper in black or dark brown or blue, and both feature a grosgrain band that is usually of a darker shade than the hat.

Saddle seat hats (*from left*): the Homburg, the top hat, and the snap brim.

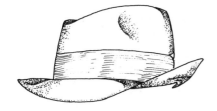  

Waiting for the announcer to call their class, two riders model the derby.

A quality hat, one that will hold its shape, is made of fur felt. Wool felt, which can be dyed to a matching color, will not retain its shape as well.

Some riders, usually men, prefer to wear a straw hat in the summer. In a vanilla color, you can accessorize this hat with a band that matches your saddle suit or day coat. Wear the straw hat in informal classes only.

With formal attire, you'll wear a silk top hat. The color matches your suit.

OTHER ATTIRE

Women's hair should always be neat and controlled, either pulled back into a bun or under a hair net. Some riders place a bow on top of the bun to match the color of the horse's browband, cavesson, and girth.

Choose gloves that relate to the colors in the rest of your outfit. Equitation riders usually pick a dark glove, close to the color of the coat sleeve, or a quiet look. In pleasure, you can wear gloves of the same color as your hat, having them sprayed with fabric dye to match.

In informal classes, all riders wear a man's four-in-hand tie. Women can select an appropriate design from the boys' department, but it shouldn't be a clip-on type.

Choose a quality, colorful tie that visually unites your outfit. A tie that goes with your vest gives you an uncluttered look and a leaner line. Secure the tie so the long end conceals the short end. Your vest and jacket will hide both ends. A collar bar will maintain a neat appearance.

The formally attired rider wears a bow tie, either a butterfly or straight club style. Neither end should show, and the material may be satin, velvet, or grosgrain. Black is most correct, but you will see riders with ties in white or a color matching the suit.

Other accessories can help unify your look. A small artificial boutonniere, placed in the lapel, can be of the same color as the horse's browband. Your hat can also blend with your shirt, if you trim it in the same color. Wrap a length of grosgrain ribbon around the band, secured with a safety pin.

With the formal attire, hold your trousers in place by suspenders. Studs, matching cuff links, and a small fresh red carnation in the lapel complete the look.

Since a horse show is an event, women may wear discreet makeup. Your eyes won't show much under your hat, but extra lip and cheek color will create a more dramatic appearance. Remember that indoors your face will wash out under the light, so add a touch more color.

Equitation riders may not wear earrings, bracelets, or rings.

IN-HAND SHOWING

You can choose to wear your regular saddle suit or the suit without the coat to show your horse in hand. The coat is uncomfortable buttoned, and it can flap unattractively when you raise your arms to cue the horse.

You might prefer a tailored vest, designed for arm movement. The vest fits snugly around the waist so it does not raise up, and the outfit is styled to emphasize a fitted look from the back and sides. The judge will most often be looking at your back, checking for the horse's number.

Clothiers offer high-waisted pants, which keep the shirt tucked when you raise your arms. The waist-

This Arabian exhibitor wears a shirt, vest, and jodhpurs of a shorter length for an important halter championship.

band is shaped similar to a cummerbund, with no belt loops.

Some men choose sportswear, such as slacks topped with a sweater, or a sweater vest over a shirt and tie, or even a business suit. Sleeves and shoulders should permit free movement, so you can hold your arms high to show the horse.

You don't want a jacket whose coat tails swing when you lift your arm. Look for one styled like a Western jacket, with a sleeve cut so the fabric won't crawl up around your neck. A hat and gloves are optional.

You may decide to wear formal attire, without the coat, for halter classes in the evening or daytime. Study the effect, as a bowtie and cummerbund can make you look like a waiter.

SIDESADDLE ATTIRE

Add an apron to your saddle suit when riding aside. A conservative day coat is acceptable. Under the apron, you may wear jodhpurs or breeches. You might choose the taller hunt boots, if the apron hem flaps or doesn't quite reach long enough, as revealing the top of the short jodhpur boot detracts from your appearance. Or, with the jodhpur boot, extend the apron's hem so it covers the heel of your left foot. Combined with the longer coat, this elongates your frame.

Seen from the offside, an Arabian rider wears a white day coat and matching derby while showing side saddle.

BREED VARIATIONS

Morgan. Riders in park classes must wear saddle suits of solid, conservative colors. In pleasure classes, an informal saddle suit is suggested when a flat show saddle is used, though the day coat is often worn.

Arabian. Riders of Arabians are considered more adventurous in their choice of colors and fabrics. Women often wear day coats in colors such as peach or cream. In park classes, formal dress is suggested, with the time of day, locale, and weather modifying the outfit. Peach- or copper-colored formal attire is considered an acceptable shade for this breed.

Informal attire is recommended for pleasure classes, usually the saddle suit in conservative colors. Many pleasure riders wear the day coat.

Tennessee Walking Horse. In classes where the horse is judged, riders wear informal saddle suits. Some women show without hats, with their hair pinned back and fastened. Men generally wear the snap brim.

Equitation riders are required to wear neat, well-fitted suits of a solid, conservative color. Coat length must measure at least three inches below your fingertips when standing. In the saddle, jodhpurs, fitted with jodhpur straps, must reach to the top of the boot and the bottom of the heel.

The vest is not required, but if worn may match or contrast with the coat. The shirt is white or pastel, and a four-in-hand tie and hat (snap brim or derby) match or coordinate with the suit. Gloves must be worn, either off-white or matching the suit.

Informal attire is acceptable in the evening. The tuxedo type one-button coat is permitted only after six, and it must be of dark blue, brown, gray, or black.

265

National Show Horse. AHSA rules specify dress for specific classes. In Pleasure, Three-Gaited, and Five-Gaited, wear a saddle suit of conservative colors. The day coat is permitted.

When showing in halter, you may wear a saddle suit. Rules require a pant length for standing, admonishing not to roll up the hems of jodhpurs. (However, in a pinch you could fold the hem to the inside and tape it with duct tape.)

Though this is a gray pinstriped suit, it appears solid-colored from a distance.

PART IV

SHOW
STRATEGY

30. SHOW GROOMING MANAGEMENT

By grooming your show horse regularly, you'll need few additional preparations for an upcoming event. Yet you'll also plan your strategy to bring him to the ring in a peak of perfection.

To succeed, you must develop an organized approach. For the horse, schedule any procedures, such as bathing, clipping, or a visit from the farrier. Check his shoes daily, and attend to any blemishes. You will also gather all the clothing, tack, and equipment, and enlist at least one assistant for show day.

During your planning, remember that Murphy's Law applies to horse-show grooming. If anything can possibly go wrong, it will—so be prepared. Producing the perfect horse and rider at the ideal moment is never as easy as it looks, and everything will take longer than you've anticipated.

BEFORE THE SHOW

Checking Clothing. First, gather your show clothing. It's wise to plan a test run of a new outfit at home before the show. You might need to punch an extra hole in your chaps belt, or wear a thicker pair of socks inside your new hunt boots.

Some clothes will fit more tightly on the horse than they did at the shop. When you purchase new chaps, jodhpurs, or breeches, test the fit by straddling a chair or saddle. Check them at the barn in your saddle, to see if you need to return them for necessary alterations.

As you pack your show clothing, be sure you have the correct items for the classes you enter. Experts recommend you explore any regional or breed variations before you select attire for a show that's unfamiliar to you. For instance, if you've always shown under American Horse Shows Association (AHSA) rules and plan to enter a class governed by Federal Equestre Internationale (FEI) rules or a show in Canada, study the appropriate rule books.

Ensure that each article of clothing is clean, neat, and in good repair. Your outfit for halter or performance classes should look crisp, not necessarily new or expensive.

In addition to your show gear, plan for the time between classes. You may choose to wear jeans or overalls over your show attire, to keep clean. Take a variety of safety pins for emergency repairs, or pack an extra shirt or pair of pants—buttons fall off and zippers break at the most inopportune moments.

Plan for quick changes at ringside, or last-minute substitutions. When you scan your competition in the warm-up ring, you might see five other riders in day coats of your shade of blue. With a spare coat in your garment bag, you can quickly change so you won't get lost in the crowd.

WARDROBE PACKING	
Transparent vinyl garment bag	Coat, pants, vest, chaps
Boot bag	Boots
Hat carrier	Hat
Tote bag	Spurs, spur straps, ties, gloves, belt, show underclothes, boot care kit
Cosmetic bag	Hair care, hat cleaning brush, sewing kit, jewelry, hair net, bobby pins, sunscreen
Duffel bag	foul weather gear: rain slicker, vinyl hat cover, boot rubbers

Make a checklist, and routinely store your show-ready wardrobe in bags dedicated to show gear.

Fit your horse's tack before the show. Study the entire picture to decide what items best complement your horse.

Checking Tack

Give all your tack a good cleaning, and remember to condition all tack routinely. Allowing dirt to build up can damage leather, because you'll have to scrub hard to remove it. Dry leather could break in the middle of a class, ruining your chance for a ribbon.

Before the show, examine all articles carefully to see if any repairs are necessary. Avoid the embarrassment and possible disqualification caused by a rein, halter, or stirrup leather breaking in the ring. In many shows, rules permit you no opportunity for a rerun due to broken equipment—you either continue the competition or withdraw.

You may have purchased a new bridle or saddle, which you should condition and darken well before the show. You can use the traditional oils to darken new leather, or speed up the process by dyeing strap goods yourself. Have a new saddle stained by a professional.

If your new Western saddle squeaks loudly, turn it upside down and shake talcum or baby powder into the areas between skirts and leathers. Squeaking won't count against you, but the distracting noise might make it difficult for you to understand the judge's instructions.

Leather tack usually looks better with a soft luster rather than a shine. After removing dirt or sweat with a damp sponge or coarse towel, rub with a dry lather of saddle soap, using a sponge or cloth. You can polish with a chamois for a sheen, and remove any soap from the holes in leather by poking a toothpick through them.

Apply an oil conditioner with care, avoiding a tacky or greasy substance that attracts dirt. Use only light applications so you don't over-oil your show tack. Treat a saddle only on areas that will be visible when you are mounted, so you don't stain your breeches or Ultrasuede chaps.

Try liquid glycerin saddle soap for cleaning braided reins or bridles. Apply it with a sponge, with no water. This will also clean a light-colored Western saddle without darkening it. A toothbrush can clean tooled leather.

Polish all metal, so your bit rings, shanks, and stirrups

shine. Silver on Western tack and clothing should sparkle. If you have allowed silver to tarnish, first clean it with Tarnex, then polish with Haggerty's Silver Spray or Duraglit metal polish. If the trim attaches with Chicago screws, you can remove the silver pieces for easier cleaning.

Clean suede on your saddle by using a stiff bristle brush or fine sandpaper. Wipe with a damp sponge after brushing the nap. You can also use a special liquid suede cleaner.

Proper storage of tack will keep it in show shape. Keep your show saddle protected in a saddle bag or tack trunk to avoid dust. Hang bridles and halters on rounded surfaces to avoid creasing the crownpieces, or take them apart to lessen the buckles' wear on the leather.

Don't forget to clean all saddle pads before the show. You can wash a fleece pad in liquid detergent (a powdered soap may not dissolve completely and could sore a horse's back). During the show, let the pad dry after use, then brush it with a steel-bristled dog brush.

Check association rules that govern schooling gear allowed at the show. Some rules prohibit certain tack anywhere on the show grounds. One questionable item would be the blinker hood. Morgan rules permit its use, with vertical half-cup blinders. Exhibitors showing in the Arabian, National Show Horse, and Saddlebred divisions also use this device in schooling, but AHSA rules prohibit all artificial appliances.

Packing Grooming Items

Tack and clothing requirements are the same for a one-day or a two-week show. The number of grooming items will vary according to the length of time you will be at the show grounds.

When you pack, collect all the grooming items you think you will need. Use a spacious tack trunk or grooming tote, and first gather the everyday tools and bathing products you will use on your horse. In addition, you might add the appropriate items:

Pre-class Grooming	Horse Care	Stall Furnishings
Braiding or banding kit	Bandages	Water buckets (bucket hooks attached)
Facial highlights	Sheet or cooler	Feed bucket
Hoof oil or polish	Rain sheet	Hay net or bag
Clippers	Show hood	Hoses (one long, one short)

Twitch	Mane tamer	
Mobile grooming cart, with two trays to carry supplies		stall cleaning tools
Extra buckets		Electric fan
Extension cords		Portable lights
Silver polish		Stall guard

Follow a checklist when you pack your grooming needs. Vendors often sell these items at the show, usually at inflated prices and not the specific brands or sizes you prefer.

At major shows, barns with several horses reserve extra stalls in the show barn. One serves as a tack room, for overnight storage of show tack and a dressing room for the rider. The other is the makeup or ready room, where you'll groom the horse and tack it up for its class. You'd most often need this room when grooming a breed that takes extensive preparation. With a large number of horses, a show stable might reserve two ready rooms.

Bring your own flooring, which will help keep a clean horse from becoming dirty. You'll also find it easier to apply hoof polish when the horse stands on a firm surface.

It helps if you know what type of stabling is available, so you can bring the right supplies. Use your tools to mount shelves, racks, and storage boxes, and secure temporary crossties in a grooming stall.

Planning Show Grooming

Tack/Feed Room	Ready Room	Tools for Setup
Bridle hooks	Shelf/racks for grooming supplies	Toolbox with hammer, nails, drill, screwdriver, screws, and screw eyes
Saddle rack	Portable lights	String
Blanket drying rack	Crossties	Masking tape
Bandage box, rack, or plastic shopping basket to store rolled bandages	Section of Astroturf, sheet of plywood, or rubber stall mats	Duct tape
Medicine cabinet	Hose	Wood frame and staple gun
Clothing rack/hangers		Stall drapes or upholstery fabric
Boot polishing box	Ribbon box	Bungee cords
Stall-size carpet as flooring	Electric fans	Wire cutters
Extension cords	Step stool	Ammunition box for tool storage
Broom or portable vaccum		Hasps and padlocks

Grooming a horse at the show is more difficult than at home, both physically and mentally. You'll work hard to present a perfectly clean and neat animal. With time a factor, the environment creates a competitive atmosphere and a pressure to perform.

If you're grooming and exhibiting, you'll endure even more stress. To cope with the tension of last-minute preparations, try to delegate tasks to support staff. At major stables, one groom prepares two or three horses at a show. For the animal's comfort, it's best if this is the same caretaker who handles it all the time. By being familiar with the horse, this person can recognize a minor problem before it affects the horse's ability to show at its best.

Even if you have only one or two horses, you'll still need at least one other person to assist you. Maybe you will groom the horse, while your instructor, parent, or friend concentrates on gathering your tack and show clothing. An ideal situation is to have an assistant groom and tack up, while you concentrate on perfecting your outfit.

Shipping

When it is time for you to ship your horse, remember that hauling can affect its appearance. Protect your animal from both injury and mental stress. Outfit it in shipping boots or thick wraps to shield its legs against minor scrapes. A tail wrap and fleece tubing on the halter will guard against rubbing.

If you're hauling a long distance to a major competition, plan to arrive maybe three days early to allow your

Be sure to school your horse in permissable training equipment. These side reins, acceptable aids in the warm-up ring for this horse showing in the Arabian division, are prohibited in the dressage division.

horse to rest. Prevent dehydration, which will result in the hair standing up, by being sure that the horse continues to drink. Adding electrolytes to the water will help.

Plan for the weather conditions anticipated at the show site, especially in the fall. If your horse has to endure a change of climate, such as chilling winter winds, you don't want the show coat to stand up from the chill. Plan extra clothing to keep the hair coat in show shape, and place lights in the show stall to help warm the environment. If you move to a location that's considerably hotter than home, pack electric fans so you can keep your horse cool and comfortable.

AT THE SHOW GROUNDS

Organize your tack room or grooming area for most efficient treatments. Before you become frazzled by last minute preparations, plan where you will groom and tack up your horse.

If you hauled your horse to the show for the day, you might not reserve a stall. Your van or trailer serves as a base of operations.

You will probably tie your horse to the side of the vehicle. Make sure it's accustomed to being tied, and use a secure halter and rope. Examine the side of the trailer to be sure it won't injure itself, before you tie it with a quick-release knot.

Try to keep all your grooming articles in a central location, such as a tack trunk or carryall placed inside the van. This will ease the stress of preparing your horse, since you or your helper will be able to locate items when you need them.

If you've reserved stalls, you can choose to groom the horse in the stall, in a ready room, or in the barn or shed row aisle. Storing your grooming products on the wall avoids having to bend over to search through a trunk or carryall. With a grooming cart on wheels, you deliver all supplies to each stall.

Store the tack trunk in the tack room, or leave it in front of the stall, locked for security. You can set it on the ground, or on blocks of wood.

At the show, you'll want to keep your horse as clean as possible. Make your job easier—outfit it in a sheet or blanket when it's in the stall or tied to the van. If you leave it loose in a stall, be sure the stall is immaculate and well bedded so the horse doesn't become dirty.

Sweep the floor of your ready room often so the horse doesn't pick up dust during your pre-class grooming.

You can keep white socks clean by wrapping them. Disposable diapers are useful substitutes for bandages.

At a show that lasts more than one day, you'll need to develop a schedule of preparations. You may prefer to bathe your horse the day before its class. Some horses need to be trimmed on the bridle path or muzzle right before they show, which could be two or three times during a seven- to ten-day show.

When you compete at a long show, you'll remain at the show grounds for one, two, or even three weeks. Besides compounding your grooming routine, the multi-day,

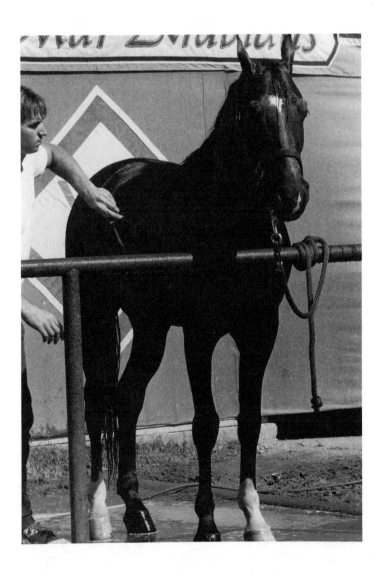

You may need to rinse or bathe your horse during a long show.

out-of-town show complicates your show wardrobe. If you expect to wear the same outfit over the span of the show, plan how you'll keep your turnout clean for every class. You could wash shirts overnight, in a coin laundry or at your hotel. Major shows will post names of local dry cleaners, who may pick up and deliver for convenient service. This alternative may cost less than relying on a hotel.

31. SHOW DAY

The day of the show usually means you arrive at the barn early. Some procedures take a certain length of time, and you want to allow yourself sufficient time to prepare, whether you have one or three horses to get ready to compete. If you must haul to the show that day, allow sufficient time for both at-home and at-the-show preparations, in addition to travel time.

SCHEDULING

The challenge of show day is that you must calculate your timing, usually without knowing exactly when you will need to be ready to enter the ring. (Only dressage shows and combined training events schedule competitors at posted times.) Aim to schedule yourself so that when you hear your class called, you wear the correct attire, have groomed your horse to perfection, and have verified that all your equipment fits in place.

Developing your sense of show timing takes experience. You will learn how to pace yourself at a show, where the pressures of a deadline can alter your normal behavior.

A vital component of show ring sportsmanship is being ready before you hear the announcer call your class or number. You never want to be responsible for holding up the class, with the judge and other exhibitors waiting for you while you apply hoof polish. The "two-minute gate" could mean that you miss the class entirely. (Some associations, like American Quarter Horse Association [AQHA], require all horses to assemble at the arena entrance and remain there until dismissed or directed by the judge.)

Sometimes your schedule will be off, due to incorrect planning, and you may have to alter your procedures in order to arrive at the gate in time. Cancelled earlier classes or classes with small entries can also affect your schedule, or officials who forego a planned break. Any of these events will shorten the time before you enter the ring.

It may help to post a timetable, especially if you plan to enter several classes or have more than one horse. Post the schedule from the show program, or use a marker board to list classes and expected times. With a string of show horses, you might also compose a card for each horse, with its name, class name, and class number. Attach this card to the horse's entry number.

With a clean, trimmed horse, allow yourself a good hour before your class to complete the last-minute preparations. This doesn't include the time you spend in the warm-up ring or holding area, before you actually enter the arena to be judged. You may decide to groom in phases. Plan to start the final touches about thirty minutes before you'd mount up.

The actual grooming may take only about ten minutes. Some grooms work on a horse for two or three hours, which shouldn't be necessary. Prolonged grooming will irritate the horse and possibly affect its showing in the ring.

GROOMING PROCEDURES

Even at a major show, your grooming procedures will vary little from your everyday routine. You will curry, brush, and towel the coat. Wipe out eyes, ears, nostrils, and underneath the tail.

If you see any new stains on white legs or coat, treat them as described in Chapter 2. You may need to perform a quick shampooing of the legs, if you have time to wash and dry them.

Brush or pick out all traces of bedding from mane or tail. On a horse showing in a halter class, wrap the tail to maintain a smooth look. For the flat mane desirable in Quarter Horse halter classes, apply a mane tamer about twenty minutes before the class (unless you've banded the mane). You may choose to leave this in place until the last minute. You could also place a dampened towel on the crest, which you can remove quickly.

Add highlights to the horse's face and body at this time. On a horse being shown in a halter class, you may wish to spray on a coat conditioner. Some grooms use Pledge furniture polish on a solid color horse for a fresh sheen. (This product will attract flies.) On mane and tail, spray a silicone-based dressing. Do not spray these products if you're outdoors and the wind is blowing, because the spray will not adhere to the hairs.

During fly season, you should apply fly spray, especially on the underside and legs of a halter horse, to avoid irritation. Be sure you use a brand you tested that won't cause an allergic reaction. Nothing is worse than to haul a thousand miles to a major show and have your horse develop bumps right before its class.

Before applying any hoof oil or polish, consider the show environment and the footing in the show ring. If the footing is deep, the feet will sink into the ground, hiding the polish. In this case, one coat will suffice, which demonstrates you cared enough to present the horse properly. If you're in a humid locale, apply polish early to allow it time to dry completely. Polish will dry immediately at a show in a dry climate.

Be sure to brush off the wall of the hoof. If your horse shows with its feet polished, you might want to do this earlier, before you start preparing for a class. Brush on hoof oil last, because it tends to collect dust.

If your horse happens to cut itself on the leg, some rules permit you to show it with a protective bandage. Before you scratch your entry, check with show officials about this option.

Braiding and Banding

When you braid or band a mane, or braid a tail, allow extra time for the procedure. Braid your horse the day of the show. Few horses will not rub a mane prepared the night before, so you may need to start braiding at 5 A.M. to present a perfectly braided hunter at 7:30 A.M. Don't leave a braided tail up overnight. If the horse rubs a few hairs from the top of the braid, you're faced with a time-consuming dilemma. "Fixing" those few loose hairs without redoing the entire tail poses a hairstyling challenge.

Some grooms prefer to schedule their preparations so they braid, groom, and tack the horse just before the class.

This prevents the animal from getting dirty or rubbing braids in the stall, since it remains on the crossties or in hand.

When you really need to prepare a mane quickly, two grooms can braid at the same time. One begins at the top, one at the withers, and they meet in the middle to complete the task in fifteen or twenty minutes. It's important that both braid in the same style.

Of course, you might have your horse ready exactly on time, and the management announces a lunch break. You can choose to leave the horse tied in the grooming area or ready room. Or, if you need the stall for another horse, you might cover the ready-to-show one with a sheet and put it in a clean stall. Hopefully it will remain clean during the delay.

ATTIRE

When you're ready to take your horse from stall or van to the show area, your helper can tack up while you change into your show clothes. Right before the class, you can warm up wearing a partial outfit—usually your show pants, boots, and shirt. You can put on your coat and hat at the last minute. If you're showing over fences, you should wear your protective headgear during the warm-up.

If you wear long jodhpurs or chaps, turn up the hems so you won't walk on them. Use jodhpur cuff straps to keep your jods off the ground. You may choose to lower the hems while in the saddle, or wait until you're ready to enter the ring.

At ringside, your helper should bring a tote or bucket that contains the last-minute grooming tools—usually towels, finishing brush, sweat scraper, and a sponge to clean the horse's mouth. He or she should also bring your hat and coat, ideally with your number already attached, along with a clean brush for final dusting of the hat. With a halter horse, also bring a hairbrush for mane and tail.

AT THE GATE

When preparing a performance horse, you need to allow time for a warm-up period before the horse is ready at the gate. This can vary from five to forty-five minutes, which may allow your groom time to prepare another horse or wait at ringside for last-minute polishing. Your trainer may coach you, then act as groom for the final touchups.

Your trainer can help during the last-minute grooming, while you concentrate on your performance.

During the warm-up, you might protect the horse's legs with polo wraps, especially over white markings. This keeps dirt off the wrapped areas, but the hair below the wraps will become dirty. These hairs appear even more discolored compared to those protected by the wrap, so plan to brush the legs.

At some show sites, with the warm-up area located near the show ring, realize that judges might observe you before you compete. Although you're not under official scrutiny, a sharp-eyed judge may notice you and remember you when you do enter the ring. Watch that your schooling tack conforms to accepted norms. Your practice gear might affect the judge's opinion.

With a halter horse, you will probably wait to show up at the in-gate until your class is imminent. At a large show, don't depend on hearing the gate call over the public address system. Your competitors may not help you to hear it, either, so enlist a runner who will check on the progress of preceding classes.

Rules may specify that you bring your horse to a holding area near the ring to wait for the class while under a steward's supervision. Be sure you schedule your preparations to allow for this requirement. A steward might examine every entry for legal tack and attire, so perform a last-minute check to confirm your gear. Ensure that you remove all items prohibited in the show ring. For example, AQHA equipment stewards examine ears for ear plugs, considered artificial appliances.

When you enter the ring, all preparations must be completed to present the ideal picture.

Before you leave for the ring with your halter horse, cover its coat with a sheet or cooler. A nylon show cooler, with an attached hood that covers partway up the neck, helps polish the horse's coat. (Choose the open front style, so you can quickly slip off the garment without mussing the mane.) Clean out the feet one last time, making sure you remove all manure and bedding. If you show with a light show halter, use a stable halter to lead the horse to the show area.

You can protect white legs with wraps or shipping boots. Place a stallion or gelding in a newly bedded stall to encourage urination, so it won't become fidgety while standing in the ring.

While you lead a young, unshod halter horse toward

the ring, watch that it does not inadvertently step on a rock. Without shoes, a foal can become sore from the minor injury. Going into the ring with a slight limp will ruin your foal's showing.

At the in-gate, perform your last-minute grooming. Wipe out the horse's nose and eyes. Knock off any dust from the feet, and remove the mane tamer and tail wrap. Oil the face last, because this tends to collect dust.

Brush hairs lightly to fluff the tail. With a long tail that drags the ground, unwrap it at the last minute. An assistant might follow you to hold the tail off the ground until you actually pass through the in-gate.

Do the same last-minute check on a performance horse. If you knotted the tail or it's still wrapped, shake the hairs free and brush to fluff the tail.

Your horse may have become sweaty during the warm-up. You or your assistant can soak a sponge in a mixture of water and Vetrolin, and wipe lather off the chest, neck, and between the hind legs.

With a towel, wipe off any foam from the horse's chest, shoulders, or legs. Dressage riders may leave foam around the horse's lips, which indicates a moist, soft mouth.

Although you shouldn't let your competition affect your preparations, you might scan the ring at this time. Here's your last opportunity to make any changes in your grooming, tack, or clothing, which may be necessary to contrast with another entry. For example, if another Western rider turns up wearing the same shirt you have, your helper can hold your horse while you dash to the tack

Waiting at the in-gate, a halter horse is ready except for the removal of its tail bandage.

room to swap your shirt or add a vest or sweater. Or, adding or reducing facial highlights can influence your horse's appearance, compared to a top competitor.

Check the horse's tack to be sure each piece is correctly adjusted and presentable. Look for your saddle pad to fit evenly on both sides. All keepers should be in place, and you should feel that the girth or cinch is adjusted snugly. If you outfit your reiner or cutter in boots for the class, check that they remain secure.

Lastly, as rider or handler, you need to be inspected for neatness. The helper looks you over to confirm that your hair's in place under your hat. If you're wearing a coat, button it, adjust the fit, and have your helper brush it clean. Check that your number is attached securely, right side up.

If you choose to put on your hat at the last minute, ask your assistant to give it one last brushing before handing it to you. With a Western hat, pin it securely so it doesn't blow off. You can use bobby pins to catch a lock of hair behind your ear and anchor the pin through the leather sweatband inside the hat.

In the saddle, complete your preparations. Your chaps might need adjusting, or you may need to attach the underpasses to the sides of your jodhpurs. Your helper should wipe off your boots with a towel, and also polish your bit or stirrups and brush dust from the skirts of a Western saddle.

WEATHER CONDITIONS

Often weather conditions at the show are not ideal. You must cope with the environment the best you can.

On a hot day, keep your horse comfortable. Stay out of the sun when possible. With a horse that has a white muzzle or pink skin that you've clipped close, take care to protect the sensitive skin from sunburn.

When you show in winter, protect a sweaty horse from drafts. A breeze can cause hair to stand up in addition to predisposing the horse to a chill. After you've warmed up and wait to enter the ring, toss a cooler or a dress sheet over your horse's body. The wool or wool-blend fabric will prevent the warm horse from becoming chilled.

In wet weather, many shows take place indoors. If you must wait outside, it will be difficult to present a perfectly clean horse in the arena. Preventive measures may serve as a stopgap, but the judge realizes that all exhibitors must cope with the same weather conditions.

After warming up, this pair of junior jumpers are protected from a chill breeze by wool coolers. The groom has placed a towel over the horse's back, ready to wipe off the rider's boots. For the horse's comfort, he has unbuckled the flash noseband.

When you have to warm-up in a muddy area, tie the horse's tail in a mud knot. Or, you can tie the tail by flipping up the end and tying a tail bandage twice around it. Before letting the tail down, two people with several buckets of water can douse all four legs from elbow to hoof, and between the hind legs. This will remove the gritty sand kicked up during the warm-up. Last, let down the tail.

No one looks good in the rain. You can wear a slicker or a vinyl rain cover while you warm-up, along with a clear vinyl hat cover. Protect your horse and tack when you dismount by throwing a water-repellent cooler over its body. The vinyl material can cause the horse to sweat if the temperature is warm. Plastic boots protect legs without absorbing sand or mud.

Another method for protecting your horse would be to cover it with two coolers, with a blanket on top. Wrap the legs in tall wraps.

It is extremely difficult to present a horse properly when the wind is blowing hard. Any oil-based grooming product will attract dust. A sheet, of light material in hot weather, may protect the body somewhat. Dampen a towel with alcohol and swipe the horse's sides and croup.

DURING AND AFTER THE CLASS

When you enter the show ring, your turnout should be complete. In a halter class, you may perform minor adjustments when the judge is not scrutinizing your horse. Be subtle when you smooth the horse's mane or forelock, or fix the position of the halter.

When the horse leaves the ring, your class is over, except in events with more than one phase. In these cases, your helper should meet you outside the gate for any additional grooming before you're called back.

After your hunter round over fences, you may remove the saddle while anticipating a callback to jog for soundness. If the horse wears a standing martingale, knot the chest strap loosely so it does not become entangled in the horse's legs. Don't remove the bridle, however, because a hunter must return to the ring wearing the same bridle in which it showed.

Cool out your horse if necessary. If this is your only class of the day, put the horse away after you have cleaned its coat thoroughly. Otherwise, the period between

Two assistants adjust equipment and wipe off any last-minute dust on this five-gaited Saddlebred. (The horse is not wearing boots because this class requires only walk, trot, and canter.)

classes determines if you need to prepare the horse right away, or allow it time to relax in the stall or van.

Saddlebred grooms sometimes wash the tail if classes are not too close together. With a braided or banded mane, brush the mane free after the last class of the day.

Finally, don't let disappointing results affect your enthusiasm for next time. Maybe you presented yourself and your horse as perfectly as you could and didn't place as well as you anticipated. If you prepared by performing everything you could to make yourself look immaculate, be content with your best efforts. Be satisfied that your turnout did not affect your placement. Today just wasn't your day to win, and look forward to the next class.

Waiting while the judge determines final placings, these riders will soon learn the outcome.

APPENDIX

POINTS OF A HORSE

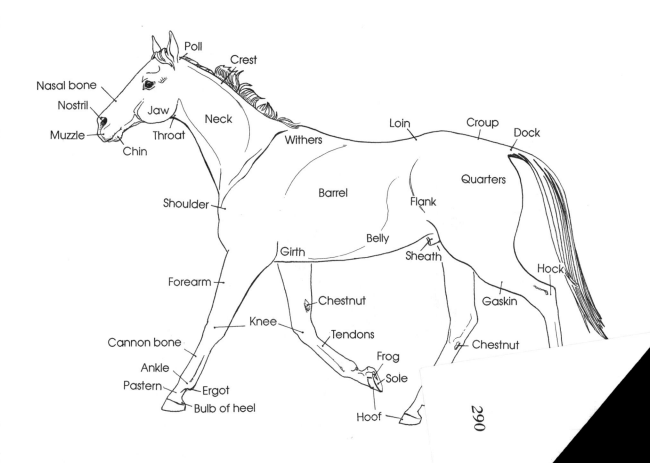

ENGLISH TACK

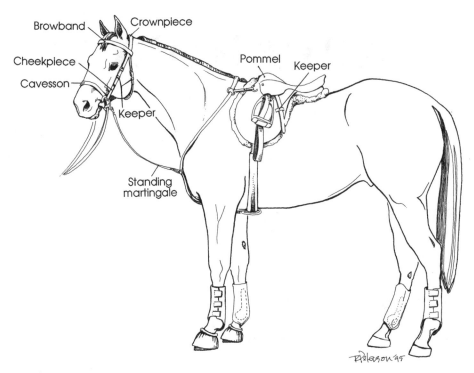

WESTERN TACK

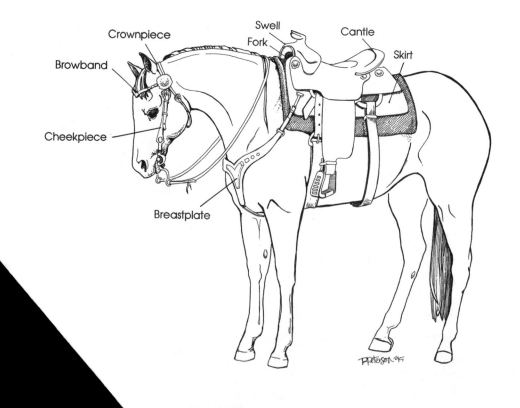

GLOSSARY

Bald	A very broad blaze.
Blaze	A broad vertical marking extending the length of the face.
Blinker hood	A head covering of lightweight fabric, with vinyl half-cups so the horse focuses forward.
Bosal	Noseband of plaited rawhide; a schooling device. (Spelled as bozal in Peru.)
Bowler	*See* Derby.
Brace	*See* Tail Brace.
Bridle path	A clipped section of the mane, starting behind the ears.
Brilliantine	An oily hair preparation that adds luster.
Cooler	A wool or acrylic garment that covers from ears to tail; absorbs sweat and prevents chills.
Cut-back	Notched at withers for a blanket, or at pommel for a saddle.
Derby	A stiff felt hat with a rounded crown and narrow brim. Also called a bowler
Ermine spots	Black spots on the coronet; contrast with white leg marking.
Ginger	A lotion, applied to cause the horse to carry its tail away from its body.
Glycerin	The substance glycerol.
Guard hairs	Stiff outer hairs that project from the hair coat.
Hobbles	Braided leather or rawhide loops that fasten the forelegs together; fastened to a Western saddle when riding with romal (closed) reins.
Homburg	A felt hat with a slightly rolled brim and a crown dented lengthwise.
Ichthammol	An emmollient.
Mecate	Braided horsehair reins; knotted to a bosal.
Melton	A heavy wool fabric, tightly constructed with a smooth face.
Near side	The horse's left side.
Neoprene	A synthetic rubber.
Notched collar	A separate collar, stitched to the lapels so a notch forms at the seam.
Off side	The horse's right side.
Pad	A leather or plastic cushion the farrier places between the shoe and the sole of the foot.
Periople	The protective outside layer of the hoof.
Polo wrap	A leg bandage of thick, fleecy synthetic fabric.
Pony	To lead a horse while riding another.
Pumice	Porous volcanic glass; used as an abrasive.

Reata	A braided leather rope; coiled and fastened to a Western saddle.
Romal	A leather quirt, attached to braided leather or rawhide reins, or "closed" reins.
Rowel	The extremity of the spur, a small wheel with points.
Scurf	Scaly portions of shed skin.
Shawl collar	A rolled collar and lapel in one piece; curves from the back of the neck down to the front closure of a riding coat.
Skirt	The portion of the tail below the tailbone.
Smegma	A secretion that collects inside the sheath or around the udder.
Snap brim	A fedora hat with a brim that you can "snap" up or down. Wear it with the brim up in back and down in front.
Steward	An official who assists the judge or reminds exhibitors of possible rule violations.
Switch	A wig for the tail.
Tail brace	A device that holds a set tail in place.
Tapadero	A leather hood on the front of a Western stirrup.
Track bandage	A knit leg bandage, made of stretchy polyester fabric.
Twitch	A control device, attached to horse's upper lip.
Vent	A slit in the skirt of a riding coat.
Windsor knot	A wide, triangular knot for tying a four-in-hand necktie.

REFERENCES

Rulebooks consulted:

The American Horse Shows Association Rule Book, 1994-1995

Official Handbook, American Quarter Horse Association, 1993

American Paint Horse Association, 1993 Official Rule Book

1993-1994 Official Handbook of the Appaloosa Horse Club

Official Handbook of the Pinto Horse Association of America, Inc., 1992

Official Handbook of the Palomino Horse Breeders of America, Inc., 1994

Official Handbook of the International Buckskin Horse Association, Inc., 1991-1992

Official Handbook, American Buckskin Registry Association, 1991

The National Horse Show Regulatory Committee, for the Tennessee Walking Horse, 1991

National Cutting Horse Association, 1993 Rule Book

National Reining Horse Association, 1993 Handbook

National Snaffle Bit Association, Official Handbook, 1993

INDEX

A

Alcohol, 15, 16, 25, 37, 56, 73, 88, 92, 94, 97, 99, 286

Almond oil, 57

American Association of Owners and Breeders of Peruvian Paso Horses, 201, 202

American Horse Shows Association, 111, 115, 123, 141, 142, 143, 147, 148, 154, 156, 158, 159-160, 161, 164, 165, 170, 173, 181, 182, 187, 191, 193, 194, 205, 209, 211, 212, 213, 221, 223, 231, 240, 241, 243, 246, 247, 249, 251, 252, 253, 257, 258, 261, 270, 272

American Paint Horse Association, 141, 244, 246

American Quarter Horse Association, 105, 110, 111, 115, 147, 221, 232, 244, 279, 282

Andalusians, 195-200, 254

Appaloosa Horse Club, 220, 232, 251

Appaloosas, 100, 117-118, 141, 160, 220, 233

Arabians, 58, 70, 92, 111, 114, 180-186, 187, 220, 231, 240, 253, 254, 265, 272

Artificial light, 13, 78-79, 100, 234-235

B

Baby oil, 30, 50, 51, 52, 58, 73, 84, 90, 97, 98, 99, 154, 205, 206

Baby powder, 15, 32, 168

Back protector, 251

Bandages, 116, 144, 150
  leg, (see Legs, wrapping)
  tail (see Tails, wrapping)
  track, 62-63, 96, 136

Bathing, 23-29, 30-32
  rinsing, 24, 36

Bays, 33, 75, 101, 184, 233, 234, 257

Belts, 224, 226, 231, 248

Bits
  dressage, 154, 159-160
  hunter, 141-142, 147, 182
  pony, 212
  saddle seat, 173, 178, 182, 189
  Western, 110-111, 182-183

Black hairs, 33, 44, 233

Blankets, 38-39, 49, 79, 84, 100-101, 275
  sheets, 20, 28, 79

Bleach, 56

Blemishes, 75

Bluing, 29, 37, 56

Boots
    care of, 246
    dressage, 249-250
    horse, 144, 149-150, 163, 174, 178-179, 184-185, 190, 194, 274
    hunt, 245-246
    saddle seat, 261, 265
    Western, 228
Bosals, 110, 111, 203, 206
Bot-egg knives, 7, 19
Braiding
    forelock, 132, 152, 166, 175, 198, 199
    mane, 42-43, 47-48, 123-131, 151-152, 166, 175, 180-181, 192, 195-200, 210-211, 280, 281
    tail, 58-59, 132-137, 181, 192, 280
Brass, 144, 155, 156
Breastcollars, 116
Breastplates, 144, 148, 163, 179, 184, 189
Breeches, 243-244, 249
Bridle paths. *See* Clipping, bridle path
Bridles
    dressage, 154-156
    hunter, 141-142, 147-148, 162
    pony, 212
    saddle seat, 173, 178, 182, 189, 194
    Western, 110
Brilliantine, 166-167
Brushes, 4-5
    body, 5, 16
    cleaning, 10, 16
    dandy, 5, 15
    finishing, 5, 18
    hairbrush, 7, 41
    mud, 5
    paint, 87, 89
    rice-root, 5
    rubber, 5, 7, 14, 15, 87
    shoe-buffing, 5
    vegetable, 7
Brushing, 15-16, 18
Buckets, 7, 24, 26-28
Buckskins. *See* Duns
Burlap, 4, 18, 22, 40

C

Cactus cloth, 4, 20, 22, 35, 40
Chalk, 119
Chaps, 225-228, 234-235, 260
Chestnut hairs, 33, 44, 75, 89, 101, 107, 233, 256, 257
Chestnuts, 99
Chokers, 242-243
Clippers
    blades, 8, 10, 69-76, 81-83
    body, 9, 80-85
    care of, 10, 69
    cleaning solutions for, 68
    medium, 8, 65-77, 83
    small, 8, 72
Clipping, 65-85
    body, 78-85, 118
    bridle path, 68-70, 109, 137, 154, 171, 176, 181, 192-193, 200, 202-203, 205, 276
    ears, 72-73, 171, 193
    face, 70-72, 154, 181, 206, 276
    foal, 101-102
    forelock, 69, 171, 192
    legs, 73-76, 120-121, 171, 176, 203, 206
    mane, 69-70, 109, 167, 191, 209
    scheduling, 73, 79-80, 84
    styles, 84-85, 171
    tail, 147, 153-154, 170
    training for, 65-67
Clothing (*see also* name of each item)
    Arabian costume, 186
    care of, 228, 230, 242, 246, 260-261, 270, 277
    for children, 223, 229, 244, 246, 247, 260
    horse (*see* Bandages; Blankets; Coolers; Hoods; Mane tamers; Sweating garments)
    sidesaddle, 231-232, 252-253, 264-265
Coat dressings. *See* Hair dressings
Coats, horse, 13-19, 33-40
    clipping (*see* Clipping, body)
    shedding, 40, 100
    stain removal, 15, 29
Coats, riding

dressage, 249, 250
   hunt seat, 237-242, 246, 248, 252
   for jumper riders, 241-242
   saddle seat, 254-259, 260, 263, 264, 265
Cold weather, 30-32, 79-80, 93, 275, 285
Color, horse. *See* individual colors
Combined training, 161-164, 251-252
Combs, 138-140. *See also* Currycombs; Mane
      combs; Pulling combs
Coolers, 20, 28, 30-31, 283, 285, 286
Cornstarch, 15, 119, 202
Cotton, 38, 95, 96, 156, 223, 242, 243
Currycombs, 3-4
   curry mitt, 4, 14, 15, 26
   metal, 4, 16
   plastic, 3, 4
   rubber, 3, 4, 13, 16, 26
   wash curry, 25
Currying, 13-15
Cutting, 111, 116, 227, 285

D

Dandruff, 27, 50
Dehydration, 94, 275
Diapers, 276
Dirt, 13-18
Disinfectants, 10, 36
Dressage, 151-160, 164, 249-250, 251
Duns, 33, 117, 121
Dust. *See* Dirt

E

Ear nets, 150
Ear plugs, 282
Ears, 16, 21, 25, 67, 99
   clipping (*see* Clipping, ears)
Eggs, 57
Electrolytes, 274
Entry numbers, 231, 279, 281, 285
Equitation

hunt seat, 144
   saddle seat, 255, 257, 258, 259, 261, 262, 263
   Western, 113, 221, 232, 236
Ergots, 74
Eyes, 16, 26, 71, 98

F

Fabrics. *See* Cotton; Flannel; Nylon; Polyester;
      Satin; Wool
Face, 15, 16, 25, 27, 98-99. *See also*. names of
      parts
   clipping (*see* Clipping, face)
   shine, 98-99
Federation Equestre Internationale, 145, 148,
      154, 158, 161, 241, 250, 270
Feet. *See* Hooves
Flannel, 58, 95, 96
Fly repellants, 37, 280
Fly spray mitts, 7
Foals, 21, 60, 100-102, 159, 284
Foregirths, 158
Forelocks, 19, 42
   braiding (*see* Braiding, forelock)
   clipping (*see* Clipping, forelock)
   shaping, 46, 109, 152
   tucking, 180, 191

G

Geldings, 14, 29, 79, 202, 283
Ginger, 169
Gloves
   English show, 248, 262
   grooming, 30, 45, 169
   Western show, 231
Glycerin, 92-93, 178
Gray hairs, 15, 33, 37, 89, 98, 101, 184,
      256-257
Grease, 162
Griddlestones, 40
Grooming kits, 3-9, 272, 273, 275

H

Hackamores. *See* Bosals
Hair
  horse (*see* Coats, horse)
  rider, 230-231, 247, 248, 253, 262
Hair coloring, 56, 121, 170, 175, 180, 205
Hair dressings, 17, 36-37, 42, 52, 57, 58,
    98, 280
Hair dryers, 30-31, 57, 151
Hair spray, 57, 180
Hairsetting gel, 47, 132, 141
Hairstyling mousse, 47
Halter classes, 89, 91, 98, 112, 142, 174, 178,
    183, 190, 194, 203, 206, 236, 249, 263-
    264, 266, 274, 282-284, 286
  Breed approvals, 158-160, 251
Halters
  grooming, 11, 67
  show, 112, 183-184, 190, 206-207
  stable, 11, 70, 142, 283
Hats
  dressage, 250
  hunt seat, 246-248
  saddle seat, 261-262
  Western, 228-230, 235, 285
Hemostats, 196
Hobbles, 12-13, 112
Hoods, 49, 79
Hoof dressing, 87-88, 90, 138
Hoof picks, 7, 20, 52, 196
Hoof polish, 87-89, 117
Hooves, 86-90
  oiling, 87-88, 154
  picking, 20, 87
  polishing, 87-89, 110, 171, 178, 181, 194,
    206, 280
  shoeing, 86, 162, 171, 177-178, 182, 187,
    189, 193-194, 203, 206, 211
  studs, 148, 161-162
  washing, 87
Hoses, 24
Hot weather, 93, 242, 275, 285
Hunter classes, 123, 240, 243, 247, 287

Hunter clip, 84
Hunters, 47, 123-144, 209

J

Jackets, 223-225 (*see also* Coats, riding)
Jeans. *See* Pants, Western
Jewelry, 231, 243, 249, 263
Jodhpurs
  hunt seat, 244-245

K

Kentucky, 256, 257, 258, 259-261, 263, 264,
    265, 266
Kerosene, 54, 68

L

Lanolin, 16, 56
Legs, 14, 25
  clipping (*see* Clipping, legs)
  wrapping, 94-98, 274, 282, 283, 286
Light. *See* Artificial light; Sunlight
Liniment, 25, 36, 89, 94, 97
Lipizzans, 15
Loofas, 22, 25

M

Makeup
  horse, 98-99, 193, 280
  rider, 263
Mane combs, 42, 44, 47, 108, 125-126, 152
Mane tamers, 49, 106-109, 279-280
Manes, 19, 41-51
  banding, 106-109, 118-119, 280
  braiding (*see* Braiding, mane)
  brushing, 41-42, 46
  clipping (*see* Clipping, bridle path; Clipping,
    mane)
  fluffing, 42

moisturizing, 50-51
shaping, 44-46, 105-106
training, 46-49, 102
washing, 27, 50
Mares, 60, 79
Martingales, 116, 143-144, 148, 164, 174, 179, 184, 189
Massage, 3, 4, 17, 36
Mayonnaise, 84
Mineral oil, 30, 36, 42, 58, 84, 178
Morgans, 58, 111, 191-194, 220, 240, 254, 265, 272
Mouthwash, 50, 92-93
Mud. *See* Dirt

N

Nail buffers, 88
National Cutting Horse Association, 111
National Horse Show Committee, 175, 178
National Reining Horse Association, 111
National Show Horses, 187-190, 240, 254, 266, 272
Neatsfoot oil, 42
Neckties
    dressage, 249, 250
    hunt seat, 242-243
    saddle seat, 263
    Western, 223
Needles
    carpet, 197
    tapestry, 130, 131, 132, 136
Nostrils, 15
Nylon, 38, 243
    stockings, 59

O

Olive oil, 28, 38, 98
Onion, 90
Overgirths, 148

P

Paints, 118-121, 220, 233

Palomino Horse Breeders of America, 141, 165
Palominos, 15, 78, 121, 233
Pants. *See* Breeches; Jodhpurs
    Western, 225
Parade Division, 121
Paso Finos, 205-208
Pasos. *See* Paso Finos; Peruvian Pasos
Peanut oil, 57
Peruvian Paso Horse Registry of North America, 201, 202
Peruvian Pasos, 201-204
Petroleum jelly, 47, 56, 73, 98, 99, 169
Pine oil, 36
Pine tar, 90
Pinto Horse Association of America, 165
Pintos, 118-121, 165, 233
Plastic wrap, 93
Pleasure classes
    English, 182, 194
    Saddle seat, 165, 167-168, 171, 175, 177, 178, 189, 257, 258, 265
    Western, 116, 206-207, 221, 236
Pliers, 45, 54, 146
Polyester, 223, 240, 256
Pommel pads, 6
Ponies, 209-213, 244
Pony of the Americas, 209, 211, 213
Pulling combs, 8, 56
Pull-throughs, 128, 137, 181
Pumice, 74, 99

Q

Quarter Horses, 47, 92, 105-116, 118, 220
Quarter marks, 138-140
Quartering, 31

R

Rags, 5, 18, 98
Rain, 285, 286
Rain rot, 38, 98
Reining, 111, 113, 116, 182-183, 285

Resin, 89

Restraints, 12, 21, 65-66

Ribbon, 43, 58, 166, 170, 175, 196-198, 223, 263

Roaching, mane. *See* Clipping, mane

Roans, 15, 33

Rubber
fabric, 92-93
stable, 5, 18, 28, 35

Rubber bands, 47, 106, 108-109, 127, 151, 191, 196, 198

Rubbing, 13-15, 40, 84

S

Saddlebreds, 92, 165-174, 254, 272

Saddle pads
cleaning of, 272
dressage, 156-158
hunt seat, 143, 148
saddle seat, 173, 182
Western, 114

Saddles
dressage, 156, 206
hunt seat, 142-143, 148
pony, 212
saddle seat, 172-173, 178, 182, 194
sidesaddles, 142, 182
Western, 113-115, 182, 206, 271

Safety, grooming, 12-13, 24, 31, 66, 275

Safety pins, 97

Safety razors, 9, 70

Sandpaper, 88

Satin, 22, 39

Scissors, 9, 55, 70, 146, 166
thinning shears, 8, 46, 55, 146

Scouring powder, 15, 88

Scratches, 16, 74

Seam rippers, 127, 132

Shampoo. *See* Soap

Sheaths, 29-30

Shedding. *See* Coats, shedding

Shetland ponies, 209, 210, 212

Shirts
hunt seat, 242-243
saddle seat, 259
Western, 221-223

Shoe polish, 89, 173, 174, 180

Shoeing. *See* Hooves, shoeing

Shows
assistants at, 274, 281, 287
officials at, 86, 88, 141, 175, 201, 206-207, 213, 217, 218, 219, 231, 232, 249, 263, 282, 285
planning, 269-277
rules (*see* names of associations)
scheduling at, 30, 98, 278-288
shipping to, 274-275
warmup at, 281-282

Silicone, 28, 36, 42

Silver, 110, 111, 112, 113, 114, 116, 182, 183
polishing, 271-272

Skin, 23, 34-39, 70, 71, 82, 83

Skin lotion, 37, 56

Soap
dishwashing detergent, 28, 56
saddle soap, 271
shampoo, 23, 26-27, 32, 38, 50, 56, 119

Socks, 58-59

Solarium, 13

Sponges, 5, 7, 15, 18, 19, 22, 28, 271

Sport horses. *See* Dressage; Hunters; Jumpers; Thoroughbreds; Warmbloods

Sprayers
fan garden, 25
pump, 7, 93
trigger nozzle, 25, 87

Spurs, 227, 248, 261

Stainless steel, 172

Stalls, 12, 39-40, 168, 273, 275, 281

Stallion tack, 212

Stallions, 14, 29, 79, 112, 160, 184, 212, 283

Static, 17, 54

Stenciling, 140-141

Stepstools, 9, 44, 69

Stomach guards, 149

Strip clip, 85

Stripping knives, 46
Suede, 228, 260, 272
Sunburn, 69, 99, 121-122, 285
Sunlight, 38, 78, 121
Sweat, 21, 36, 91-94, 284
Sweat scrapers, 7, 25
Sweaters, 223, 225
Sweating garments, 49, 91-94

T

Tabasco, 60
Tack. *See also* name of each item
   cleaning of, 271-272
   storage of, 273
   trunks, 272, 275
Tail bags, 58-59
Tails, 52-64
   banged, 55-56
   braiding (*see* Braiding, tail)
   brushing, 52-54
   clipping (*see* clipping, tail)
   crocheting, 57-58
   false, 109, 118, 169-170, 175, 187
   fluffing, 57-58, 109
   knotting, 63-64, 137, 284, 286
   moisturizing, 57, 58
   set, 103, 167-170, 175, 187, 210
   shaping, 54-55, 109, 145-147, 153, 202, 205
   washing, 26-27, 56-57
   wrapping, 58-64
Talcum powder, 20
Tanning oil, 16
Tape, 48, 58, 63, 97, 151-152, 198-200
Tennessee Walking Horses, 175-179, 254, 265
Ties. *See* Neckties
Thoroughbreds, 147, 156
Thread, 127, 136
Towels, 5, 18, 20, 22, 25, 28, 30-32, 73, 136
   hot towelling, 31-32
Trace clip, 85
Trail classes, 113, 116
Training, 21, 65-67

Trousers. *See* Breeches; Jodhpurs; Pants, Western
Turpentine, 90

U

Udders, 19, 29
U.S. Dressage Federation, 158, 159, 160, 251
U.S. Equestrian Team, 242

V

Vacuums, 6-7, 16-18
Vans, 275
Velvet, 240, 246, 248
Vests
   dressage, 250
   hunt seat, 243, 251
   saddle seat, 256, 257, 258, 263, 265
   Western,, 223-225
Vinegar, 25, 27-28, 36, 37, 38, 51, 56, 84, 97
Vinyl, 92

W

Warmbloods, 147, 156, 159-160, 251
Weight pads, 162
Welsh ponies, 209, 210, 211
Western horses. *See* Appaloosas; Duns; Paints; Palominos; Pintos; Quarter Horses
Whips, 160, 248, 250
White hairs, 15, 75, 76, 117-118, 120-121, 233, 276, 283
Wind, 30, 31, 280, 286
Wisps, 6, 34-36
Wool, 38, 156, 240, 242, 256, 259, 285

Y

Yarn, 9, 30, 31, 34, 36, 124-125, 126, 127, 128, 181